Editorial

In the economy and society, exactly how work and organisation are conducted is extremely important. The changes in gender relations are closely related to this. Gender is a key aspect of diversity. However, age, disability, ethnic or social background, sexual orientation, religion and world view, to mention only a few of the relevant aspects in this respect, can also contribute to discrimination and disparagement in the workplace. This series aims to provide a forum for theoretical and empirical works on the subject of work, organisation and diversity, and to allow findings from current research projects, conferences and academic theses from the fields of sociology, psychology, economics and their related disciplines to be discussed.

Arbeit, Organisation und Diversität in
Wirtschaft und Gesellschaft.
Schriftenreihe zur Geschlechter- und Diversitätsforschung

edited by

Prof. Dr. Maria Funder, Universität Marburg, Germany
Prof. Dr. Daniela Rastetter, Universität Hamburg, Germany
Prof. Dr. Sylvia M. Wilz, FernUniversität Hagen, Germany

Volume 12

Hannah Reiter

Women in Policing

Between Assimilation and Opposition

 Nomos

Diese Arbeit wurde durch das Uni:docs Förderprogramm für Doktorand*innen der Universität Wien gefördert.

© Coverpicture: Astrid Eisenprobst

The Deutsche Nationalbibliothek lists this publication in the Deutsche Nationalbibliografie; detailed bibliographic data are available on the Internet at http://dnb.d-nb.de

a.t.: Wien, Univ., Diss., 2021

ISBN   978-3-8487-8657-2 (Print)
           978-3-7489-3028-0 (ePDF)

British Library Cataloguing-in-Publication Data
A catalogue record for this book is available from the British Library.

ISBN   978-3-8487-8657-2 (Print)
           978-3-7489-3028-0 (ePDF)

Library of Congress Cataloging-in-Publication Data
Reiter, Hannah
Women in Policing
Between Assimilation and Opposition
Hannah Reiter
229 pp.
Includes bibliographic references.

ISBN   978-3-8487-8657-2 (Print)
           978-3-7489-3028-0 (ePDF)

Onlineversion
Nomos eLibrary

1st Edition 2022
© Nomos Verlagsgesellschaft, Baden-Baden, Germany 2022. Overall responsibility for manufacturing (printing and production) lies with Nomos Verlagsgesellschaft mbH & Co. KG.

Acknowledgements

I would like to thank my dissertation supervisor, Elisabeth Holzleithner, who not only supported me with aid when it was necessary, but also provided me with enough freedom to pursue my visions. Many thanks to Astrid, not just for proofreading but also for the emotional support throughout the process of the dissertation. Thank you also to all my wonderful friends, especially to the "post-postmodern" group for advice and support. I am also very thankful for the support of my family, who all assisted me in their own way – I am proud to have such an excellent support system.

Lastly, my thesis as well as this book could not have been written without the help of the many police officers and related officials who took the time to talk to me and allowed me a glimpse into their world. Many of them also supported me above and beyond this, put me in touch with other interview partners or passed on information. They all have my deepest thanks.

Inhaltsverzeichnis

1. Introduction

The following book is concerned with my study on the subjective lived experiences and attitudes of female police officers in two European countries, namely Austria and England and Wales.[1] It is the first to compare two European police forces in this manner, using qualitative methods to generate insight into the work-life of female police officers. With this approach and scope, it closes the research gap that presents itself in Austria concerning female police officers, as well as broadening the scope of international research into gender and the police.

The first chapter gives a short context and introduction to the topic of female police officers, their history and current status in both countries. The history of women in the police in the two countries is one of exclusion and institutional resistance (chapter 2.3). Historically, ideals of policing are closely linked to masculinity, and the masculinity of "cop culture" has received some recognition and discussion in an academic context (Silvestri 2017). Equality policies and regulations in both Austria and England and Wales have played a large part in the (legal) inclusion of women into the police.

The methodology that was followed in carrying out the research, as well as its methods are described in the two subsequent chapters. Following the particular epistemic interest of this research, a qualitative approach to answer the research questions is taken. Since the fundamental interest of this study lies in the self-experienced, subjective viewpoints of female police officers, semi-structured interviews with female officers in both countries were carried out. These lay the groundwork for the analysis and subsequent findings of this study. A brief participatory observation within the Austrian police as well as interviews with police professionals who deal with matters of gender, recruitment, and equality in the two countries undergird the conclusions drawn from the interview data. The

---

1 Law enforcement in the UK is organised separately in each of the jurisdictions: England and Wales, Northern Ireland and Scotland. The research focusses on the system in England and Wales. The comparison is therefore technically not between the police forces of two countries, but between the police forces of two legal systems. However, for the sake of simplicity, the comparison between countries is mentioned in the text.

information gained from this approach is analysed following the mindset and analytical toolset provided by Grounded Theory (Strauss 1991).

The discussion and analysis of the data is presented in the following chapter, which is divided by the themes which arose in the analysis of the interview as well as observational data. The points of interest which can be established from the data are: The factors that lead to women gaining an interest in working with the police; the experiences made during the recruitment phase as well as during initial and special training; the everyday experiences and perception of the job as a police officer; experiencing and dealing with sexism and exclusionary practices from within the police; gendered issues in interactions with the public; issues of gender within the police as a work environment (including the reception and impact of equality policies); intersectional issues regarding discussion around diversity within the police service. These issues are discussed and compared between the two countries, aiming to find similarities as well as discrepancies in the experiences of female police officers. The underlying conceptualisations of police, gender, and equality are of immense importance in understanding these experiences and their implications for future police research as well as policy development. As the topic of women in the police is a highly diverse and complex one, the individual chapters overlap due to their themes and findings. Each of these topics ends with a summary and analysis of the themes that have emerged so far, and attempts to link and support these with previous studies.

The last chapter then brings together and discusses these findings to answer the main research question: In which ways do experiences of female police officers in England and Wales and Austria differ/resemble each other, and how do gender and related equal opportunities policies influence these issues?

2. Context of the Study and Theoretical Approach

Against the background of a history of exclusion and discrimination, this research project examines and discusses female police officers' subjective views on their work and its social and legal context in two European countries, namely Austria and England and Wales, focusing on differences and similarities. This section highlights the relevant theoretical approaches and studies that concern themselves with gender and policing.

First, the role of the police in society as well as in (social) research is briefly discussed. Subsequently, the context of the police in both countries, specifically with reference to their recruitment is compared. Following, a short history of women in the police force in the two countries as well as the legal framework in which they operate is given. Of particular interest here are equality law(s) as well as equal opportunities policies effective in the police service in the respective countries. These are discussed in a separate chapter. Furthermore, the use of the word "gender" and the binary reference to "male" and "female" is reflected. In this respect, the research area of gender and policing is further elaborated upon, focusing on the specific hegemonic masculinity police culture embodies. Context is further provided by summarising any previous personal research that was carried out into both Austrian as well as English and Welsh police.

2.1 Police as Research Subject

The police constitute a (if not the main) way in which the state seeks to uphold its social order. They have a distinct position; they are sanctioned by governments to enforce laws and apprehend those who break them. Of course, they themselves can also be held accountable through law for their actions.[2] The role of the police as a means of law enforcement is highly diverse, and the gap that exists between the law 'in books' and the law 'in action' has been the topic of policing research (Dixon 1997).

---

2 However, the extent of said accountability is (quite rightly) criticised by various agents. See for example: Austrian Center for Law Enforcement Sciences 2018: 51; European Committee for the Prevention of Torture and Inhuman or Degrading Treatment or Punishment (CPT); Loick 2010.

Innes describes the police as "gatekeepers to the criminal justice process", deciding "when, why, how and against whom to enforce law" (Innes 2003: 64). The police's decisions are shaped by external factors, most significantly by what Reiner has famously described as police "occupational culture" (Reiner 2016:4).

In trying to describe what exactly it is that the police do, Innes (2003: 65f.) identifies three main roles of the police: crime management, order management, and security management. These three dimensions not only account for the majority of police work, but also relate to certain tensions that have recently risen within the police's role – perspectives that are discussed by policy makers, police leaders, and academics alike, debating on which aspect of policing to focus on, in what ways to best carry out the main tasks, and what these tasks consist of (examples of such perspectives and discussions are provided by approaches and concepts such as community policing, zero-tolerance policing, intelligence-led policing). Discussions about police and policing are therefore highly dynamic, and always influenced by circumstantial factors and new developments.

The responsibilities and powers of the police in Austria have been extended over the last years and decades, and they can roughly be divided legally as follows: The security police (Sicherheitspolizei) are responsible for "defence and suppression of general threats to life, health, safety, public order, and public security in the state" (Adensamer/Sagmeister 2016: 517, my translation), which is further defined as the prevention of and defence against crime, according to the governmental draft concerning the introduction of the Security Police Act (Sicherheitspolizeigesetz – SPG) in 1991. Officers of the criminal investigation division (Kriminalpolizei) have to prevent or intervene in criminal offences but are also involved in the investigation and prosecution of criminal offences according to the code of criminal procedure (Strafprozessordnung). The police may only act on the basis of the law, and always only to the extent that their actions are covered by the tasks that are legally assigned to them.

In England and Wales, the Police and Criminal Evidence Act 1984 (PACE) along with its amendment, the Serious Organised Crime and Police Act 2005, provide the legislative framework for the powers of police, while the Police Act 1996 serves to define the jurisdictions of the different police forces as well as their relationship with the Home Office. Specific police powers, such as the right to stop and search, are given to police constables – any police officer regardless of their rank is therefore considered a police constable by law. Police community support officers (PCSOs) are only granted limited access to these powers, as are other civilian employees of the police service.[3] These officers are uniformed members of police staff who have a variety of police powers but are non-warranted.[4]

The police in Austria as well as England and Wales have a state monopoly on the use of force within the country and are able to implement the law or prevent the breaking of laws by use of force and/or command. The law on the use of weapons (Waffengebrauchsgesetz 1969) allows police officers in Austria to carry and use firearms (Verhältnismäßiges Einschreiten, bmi.gv.at). In England and Wales, police officers are not routinely armed. There is a special armed force attached to each of the 43 police forces in the jurisdiction. Police's use of firearms seems to have increased over time in England and Wales – yet if this constitutes a trend or simply a short-time increase cannot be said from today's point of view. The frequency of police firearms operations as well as the number of incidents in which firearms were discharged at persons has seen an increase in the period from 2010 to 2019.[5] Police officers in England and Wales largely support the notion of reserving the use of firearms for special forces, and oppose the general arming of police forces throughout the jurisdiction.[6] An experimental study recently found that the public react negatively to encountering armed police officers in Great Britain, potentially because officers can no longer be considered "citizens in uniform", therefore restricting the perception of police officers as "one of them", in the manner of sharing a community which can in turn influence the trust in and the legitimacy of the police (Yesberg et al. 2020).

Research into the police nowadays often oscillates between being carried out by "insiders" and "outsiders" to the police and its culture (Davies 2016). In some countries, like England and Wales, researchers from outside the police have been given more and more access to studying police forces and working collaboratively with them. There is also research being carried out by "insiders", namely police officers themselves, who have become increasingly trained to work in an evidence-based manner (What is evidence-based policing?, whatworks.college.police.uk). This over-

---

3 Their powers are defined in the Police Reform Act 2002.
4 The numbers of PCSOs have fallen each year since 2010. There were 9,180 PCSOs (16.918 in 2010) in 2020 compared to 129,110 sworn police officers of all ranks, and out of 210,620 workers employed by the 43 territorial police forces in England and Wales (Police workforce, England and Wales, as of 31 March 2020).
5 Year ending March 2018: 8 incidents, Year ending March 2019: 13 incidents, with previous incidental rates ranging between 3 and 7 starting with the year ending March 2010 (Police use of firearms statistics England and Wales: 6).
6 See e.g., surveys by the Police Federation (Firearms).

lap between police and researcher can of course provide many benefits to police research, be it better access to data or a greater policy impact, yet it also produces challenges. One needs to keep one's independence as a researcher, and be able to critically assess police actions, be they on a macro (e.g., policies) or micro (e.g., individual misconduct) level. A smooth cooperation between outside researchers on the one and the police as an explored social field on the other hand is not always easy or completely achievable, especially due to the police's esprit de corps and a certain reticence towards scrutiny from the general public, and academic research in particular.[7] Similarly, the present research was heavily reliant on the collaboration with individual officers and police forces in gaining access to interview partners. The cyclic research process carried out in this study lent itself well to gain a comprehensive understanding of the research field, as well as to be able to reflect and create enough distance to adequately assess the gathered data (chapter 4.4). Going back and forth between data collection, data processing, and analysis stimulated reflection, while refining the collection of new data and clarifying ambiguities.

2.2 Police in England and Wales & Police in Austria

In analysing different European police forces, their respective diverging contexts have to be taken into account. In England and Wales and Austria, this difference is most obvious in their approach to recruiting police officers.

In the UK, there was no minimum educational entry qualification required to join the police at the time of data collection, and there were no externally recognised qualifications (College of Policing [4], college.police.uk). However, this recently changed, and police recruits now must have obtained two A levels, or an equivalent level 3 qualification as well as show competence in written and spoken English (College of Policing [5], beta.college.police.uk). There are currently three entry ways into the police as police constables: The most widespread is that of the apprenticeship, in which you "earn while you learn" (College of Policing [3], college.police.uk). The training is both theoretical and practical and lasts for three

---

7 As an example, see Fassin 2013. In his quest to carry out research with the police, Fassin encountered numerous obstacles, and authorisation of the project was not granted lightly, especially due to his request to shadow police patrols, carrying out observational research.

years, gaining the trainee a degree in professional policing practice. For degree-holders of any subject, there is a work-based programme to be completed in two years' time, which is underfed by further theoretical training. The third option is a so-called Pre-Join degree and aimed at those who obtain a degree in professional policing – graduates can then apply to a force and receive a shorter on-the-job training programme. Police recruits in the UK are likely to be highly qualified: a third have NVQ level 5[8] or above, another third are educated to NVQ level 3, and only 6% reportedly do not have any formal qualifications (Neyroud 2013). Additionally, police recruits are predominantly above the usual age of graduation (the majority being between age 22 and 30).

Currently, there are no educational prerequisites to start police training in Austria, although applicants have to undergo an entry test (similar to the UK). The basic training for police officers in Austria currently takes 24 months; 17 months' theoretical education plus 7 months of practical implementation of police work in an inspectorate. The theoretical education focusses on law, personal development, criminalistics, operational field training, and administrative work (Die Ausbildung zum Polizisten bzw. Polizistin, polizei.gv.at).

In both Austria and the UK restrictions on who is able to apply to undergo police training currently include personal characteristics such as age, nationality, criminal record, or tattoos and facial piercings (College of Policing [1], recruit.college.police.uk; Polizei – Einstellungsvoraussetzungen prüfen, polizeikarriere.gv.at).[9] A major difference to be found in eligibility criteria is the fact that England and Wales police accept applications from British citizens as well as EEA nationals or foreign nationals with no restrictions on their stay in the UK (College of Policing [1], recruit.college.police.uk). In order to apply to join the police in Austria, one

---

8 NVQ (National Vocational Qualification) was used as a work-based way of learning – which is carried out at a college, school, or workplace. Each NVQ level involved a range of on-the-job tasks and activities that were designed to test a person on their ability to do a job effectively. It is now replaced by the Regulated Qualifications Framework (RQF), which enables all qualifications (including vocational and academic) attained across England, Scotland, and Northern Ireland to hold the same common currency. NVQ level 5 is equivalent to any postgraduate degree or diploma (including doctorates), NVQ level 3 is equivalent to education at A levels (What qualification levels mean, gov.uk).

9 Tattoos are assessed on a case-by-case basis, and should not be considered offensive, prominent, or in direct opposition to the attitudes associated with the role of a police officer. Having visible subdermal and transdermal implants as well as the wearing of piercings and/or jewellery (with few exceptions) is forbidden.

needs to have an Austrian citizenship (Polizei – Einstellungsvoraussetzungen prüfen, polizeikarriere.gv.at). Current recruitment of police officers follows a set guideline of different assessments and exercises to be completed by the applicant, consisting of both physical and mental exercises and tests (UK Police Assessment Centre, how2become.com; Polizei – Ablauf des Auswahlverfahrens, polizeikarriere.gv.at).

(Pre-)Application processes, such as media portrayal and public debate, can play an important role as to whom the police attract or deflect, and therefore have to be taken into account when analysing gender in the police service. Explanations for women's (as well as ethnic minorities') under-representation in the police service are inherently linked to the recruitment process: Few women apply to become police officers (Walklate 2000). There have been mixed reports on whether gender influences the decision to join the police, and the motivational aspects behind the career decision, with some finding no difference in respective reasons for entering the police service (Meagher/Yentes 1986, Ridgeway et al. 2008), while others suggest distinctive (gender-related) influences on police recruits' intentions (Lester 1983).

2.3 Women in the Police

Traditionally deemed unfit for the challenging task of policing, women were only gradually granted access to the police force both in the UK and in Austria. In Austria, women have been fully integrated into the policing system since 1991. Prior to this (1971-1991), they worked as 'Politessen', not being allowed to carry a gun and working primarily with children and other vulnerable people (Frauen im Polizeidienst [1] 2011, bmi.gv.at). Not all areas of policing were willing to recruit women. The first recruitment of women to the police service in 1965 was due to a low number of male applicants, and women were only granted the power to police stationary traffic or to work with children and women until 1971. The first recruitment of a woman ever took place in 1909, but she was by no means a "police officer" but a so-called "police assistant" working in the field of youth welfare.[10]

In 2016, about 16% of police officers in Austria were female (BGBl. II Nr. 65/2017), while only 3.8% of management level employees at the

---

10 Franziska Wessely had a pedagogical education (Frauen im Polizeidienst [2] 2011, bmi.gv.at) See also Büchner 2019.

Ministry of the Interior were female (Bundesministerium für Inneres, docplayer.org). To further increase the number of female officers as well as improve the compatibility of family and career, the Ministry of the Interior has enacted a 'Frauenförderungsplan'. The obligation to do so stems from the women's advancement requirement and the mandatory introduction of a women's advancement plan according to section 11a of the Federal Equal Treatment Act (B-GlBG). As a potential result of the enactment, the aim of the Ministry of the Interior to increase the numbers of female officers by 0.5.% from 2016-2018[11] was met. The reported figures (31.12.2017 and 08.01.2018) show that almost 17% (16.6%) of police officers in Austria were female (Gleichbehandlungsbericht des Bundes 2018: 84). In an amendment from 2019 (BGBl. II Nr. 346/2019), the target of a 0.5 percentage point increase in female police officers was repeated, this time with a deadline of December 31, 2020. As of 2019, 18.7% of police officers in Austria are female (Gleichbehandlungsbericht des Bundes 2020: 113).

Starting in 1883, the Metropolitan Police Service had employed women to visit female convicts, acting as a sort of supervisor, leading to a group of women (mostly the wives of police officers) being formally employed as Police Matrons by 1889 (Women in Policing History, bawp.org). This seemed to have convinced the Metropolitan Police Service that women's needs could not be met by an all-male police force. In England and Wales, women started to vocationally access the police service in 1914, when the Women Police Service (originally named the Women Police Volunteers) was founded in London by Margaret Damer Dawson and Nina Boyle. The WPS was a voluntary organisation organised nationally across the UK. Dawson and Boyle, with the approval of the then-Commissioner of the Police of the Metropolis, trained women who would patrol London (on a voluntary basis) offering assistance to women and children (History of Met Women Police Officers, oldpolicecellsmuseum.org). The first female police officer with full powers of arrest was Edith Smith, employed by Grantham Police in 1915. In 1919, the Sex Disqualification (Removal) Act[12] was passed in the United Kingdom, ensuring women's entry into the professions. This made the establishment of a Women Police branch in London possible. However, the Women's Branch was separated from

---

11 From 16.06% in 2016. Frauenförderungsplan BMI StF BGBl. II Nr. 65/2017 § 3. (1) Abs 1.

12 An Act to amend the Law with respect to disqualifications on account of sex. Sex Disqualification (Removal) Act 1919, 9 & 10 Geo. 5 c. 71.

other sections of the service until 1973, when it became fully integrated into all police forces in England and Wales (History of Met Women Police Officers, oldpolicecellsmuseum.org).

Until the 1970s, female police officers were segregated from the men in that they had separate ranks, duties, and sometimes even facilities. During the 1970s, the Equal Pay Act (1970) and Sex Discrimination Act (1975) were introduced, changing the legal situation. As a consequence, women officers were pooled with the men on all shifts and departments from 1973. What is to be noted is that the changes in recruitment policy were due to pressure from 'outside' the police service, namely equality legislation in the UK. On March 31, 2017, 29.1% of police officers in England and Wales were female (Police Workforce, England and Wales, 31 March 2017, assets.publishing.service.gov.uk), with the numbers rising continuously: On March 31, 2019 the proportion of female officers was at 30% (Police Workforce, England and Wales, 31 March 2019 second edition, assets.publishing.service.gov.uk). In 2017, 26.8% of police chief officers (most senior police officers rank) were female, compared to 27,4% in 2019 (ibid.). The most recent equality legislation in the UK, the Equality Act 2010, protects female police officers from discrimination in the workplace, and a positive action provision enables employers to recruit or promote a candidate (who is of equal merit to another candidate) if the person has protected characteristics (e.g., female sex).

While the police, its culture, and even gender issues within the organisation are arguably well-researched in England and Wales (Cf. Spasić 2011), there is still an academic void concerning gender sensitive police research in German-speaking countries (Werdes 2003: 196), including Austria.[13]

2.4 A Short Remark on Gender

The study's research interest stems from a feminist curiosity in the realities of being a woman in a highly masculinised field. Of course, debates around gender cannot be accounted for fully in this thesis – it seems, however, necessary to establish the framework from which my deliberations and thoughts originate. A further discussion of masculinity within the specific framework of the police is provided in the next chapter. It

---

13 For an overview of the area of police research in Austria, which according to the authors reveals major research gaps, see Hanak/Hofinger 2005, Hanak/Hofinger 2008.

is assumed that gender is constructed around the principle of (mutual) recognition and acknowledgement (Holzleithner 2015: 138), and further that this recognition for individual gendered ways of existence can be either granted or denied (Holzleithner 2019: 459). The difference opened up by the gender binary, which will also play a role in the further course of the study, is recognised as socially constructed. However, as a researcher, I find myself in a dichotomy here, as I use this binary as a means of analysing the specific situation of women in the police – not only but also because of the narrative and explanatory structures that emerge from the interviews. Any mentions of gender and/or gendered practices stems from the information gained in the interviews. This means that respondents' ideas of what constitutes "female" or "male" behaviour, not synonymous with behaviour displayed by male and female colleagues, provides the basis for a gendered analysis of the data collected. Since the approach of the study lies in understanding the personal (dis)position of female police officers, it is obvious that constructions of gender and the understanding of gender relations presented in the interviews are also adopted – this does not happen automatically but is always critically reflected.

Police culture as well as debates around gender within the workplace in general are heavily defined by a presumed gender binary, e.g., the hegemonic masculinity prevalent in police culture. This theoretical dichotomy is adopted in most arguments as it brings out both the specifics of police masculine culture as well as an argued lack of regard for specifically "female" needs and issues (chapter 5.6.1). Furthermore, legal norms, which are considered from a personal standpoint, are prone to define gender roles and maintain a gender binary (Venditti 2018). While it is acknowledged that the assumption of a gender binarity limits the discourse, it cannot be denied that interactions between genders especially in a male-dominated (work) environment play a major role (Herrnkind 1999) – these are often inherently linked to the constructed male-female duality.

Framing the police service as a highly gendered, namely masculine, field, this research analyses women's experiences and their perspectives on their workplace environment as well as their perceptions of police and policing per se. Gender is hereby understood as "an emergent feature of social situations" (West/Zimmerman 1987: 126) that can legitimize existing gendered structures within the police as an encompassing social environment. The doing-gender approach lends itself to analysing the police as a justice occupation as "they involve more than a set of tasks or the source of a paycheck" (Martin/Jurik 2007:2). Working as a police officer can serve as a social identity and influences one's status outside of work; historically, police officers have viewed their job as a way of life (Fischer-Kowalski/Steinert 1982). This, along with the gendered division of labour that has been (and continues to be) prominent in police work, serves as a starting point for the analysis, which focusses on women's performances, choices, and perceptions within a masculine environment.

2.5 Police Culture and Masculinity

There is a substantial amount of theoretical and empirical work in the area of gender and policing. As Smart (1995) has observed in the 1990s, law enforcement is a male field, as it relies on traits stereotypically linked with masculinity, such as rationality, objectivity and emotional distance (although the latter has become less important in recent years, as acting empathically is attributed to "softer" forms of policing (McCarthy 2013). Despite Smart's work being written more than two decades ago, contemporary theoretical and empirical works also emphasize the relevance of gender in regard to everyday police work and the culture it encompasses (To name a few: Behr 2019, Brown 2000b, Brown/Heidensohn 2000, Heidensohn/Silvestri 2012, Loftus 2008, McCarthy 2013).

Gender has always been important in police and policing studies, as researchers attributed a distinctive masculinity to the nature of police work and its culture (Behr 2008, Reiner 2000, Skolnick 1966). Findings from early studies, especially in the 1980s and early 1990s, suggest that women in the police force either try to adapt to male roles and therefore appear as 'defeminised', or else take up subordinate or routine tasks, pushing them back into more stereotyped areas of work (Heidensohn/Silvestri 2012: 347). Even recent work still finds that aggressive or courageous behaviour is found to be constructed as a male attribute within policing, which may generate social consequences in leading to a gendered division of work (Fejes/Haake 2013). There is also evidence to suggest that the police culture and work surroundings as such are highly masculinised, and female officers are therefore seen as deviant and threatening to that system.

Police culture, as a type of organisational culture, can refer to several different aspects of policing, hereafter encompassing social rules and regulations, as well as group solidarity.[14] The term police culture has been

---

14 While the difference between police culture ("Polizeikultur", organisational culture) and cop culture ("Polizistenkultur", working culture) is of importance in understanding the logistics of police work (Cf. Behr 2008), the terms are used

subject to discussion, and mostly references the outline Skolnick (1966) describes in his book, based on a lengthy empirical study, in which he analyses the role of police and other law enforcement agencies in the administration of justice. The third chapter of the book focusses on the policeman's "working personality", meaning a set of cognitive tendencies which influence their work. According to Reiner (2016), however, there are widespread misinterpretations of Skolnick's work, which describes an ideal type rather than an actual embodiment of police culture. This ideal type as constructed by Skolnick consists of three shaping factors: the exercise of authority, the presence of danger, and the pressure to produce results (Reiner 2016: 5). As Reiner argues, these proposed "[c]ultural perspectives are mutually interdependent with practice, and structural pressures shape them both" (ibid.). These factors therefore vary across different environments (Wilson 1968), but the uniting factor in policing is the exercise of potential power over populations (Reiner 2016). Of course, each police officer brings their own traits and opinions to the trade, but "the structural weight of the problems they face [...] tends to shape some commonalities in response" (Reiner 2016: 6). Police culture as such is therefore "structurally rooted in the nature, stresses and strains of police work in different contexts, [...] interpreted variously by officers as they [seek] to navigate the pressures and mandates of their roles" (Reiner 2016: 7). A structural approach to understanding policing and police culture is vital in implementing and evaluating reform policies, such as gender equality policies, within the police service (Cf. Reiner 2016).

Historically, police culture is heavily influenced by and built upon different forms of masculinity. The defining form of masculinity found in police culture is reliant on the use of force, the assertion of authority as well as a high degree of loyalty within the members of this culture based on solidarity and protection. Behr (2017) argues that the unconditional loyalty found within police culture is fed by masculinity, namely a specific form of promise. This characteristic "is about loyalty, reliability, and the virtue of keeping one's word. These virtues presuppose the willingness to take risks (of one's own health, life, morality)".[15] Most gender-related research into the police service, therefore, puts the focus on these forms of masculinity and the experiences of male police officers. The realities

---

interchangeably in the following thesis which understands police culture as synonymic with cop culture.

15 Behr 2017: 543, my translation. Based on these and other observations, Behr creates his typology of police masculinities, which are discussed below.

of female police officers in academic discourse are thus constructed as outsider experiences within a male-dominated system.

The police force is still dominated by masculine themes; however, in recent years there have been developments that show a shift away from an idealisation of executing a 'hard' policing style and fighting crime. Consequently, forms of 'soft' policing have become more recognised and acknowledged in the everyday practices of police officers, at least in the UK (McCarthy 2013). These are methods and techniques which feature the police in a more communal way, including crime prevention practices and supporting or mentoring certain (groups of) people. These aspects of police work have historically had a female connotation, with women being ascribed to carry out these 'soft' forms of policing (Frauen im Polizeidienst [1] 2011, McCarthy 2013). Another notable gender difference is the use of force by police officers. Studies suggest that male and female officers respond differently to subject resistance, and that, overall, female officers are less likely to use a weapon (Bazley et al. 2007, Hoffman/Hickey 2005).

Gender relations in the police force are best understood as power relations, the authority (e.g., of a police officer) being associated with masculinity (Heidensohn 2005). Moreover, these gender relations stress the display of hegemonic masculinity in police culture as described by Raewyn Connell.

> "Hegemonic masculinity [is] understood as the pattern of practice (i.e., things done, not just a set of role expectations or an identity) that allow[s] men's dominance over women to continue." (Connell/Messerschmidt 2005: 832)

The concept of hegemonic masculinity has proven to be consequential in different areas of social research, including organisation studies and criminology. Applying the concept to an organisational setting, forms of gendered relations within certain organisations were described, most prominently in the military, where patterns of hegemonic masculinity proved difficult to manage (Connell/Messerschmidt 2005).

Behr (2008), in examining how male police officers create and adjust to different forms of masculinity, finds that aspects of gender, in particular hegemonic masculinity, are essential in understanding police culture. He describes the police as a highly masculinised field, both in the work they (are expected to) carry out, as well as collegial behaviour. What is to be noted is that "cop culture" in its pure form is only cultivated by a minority of officers, yet it does have a hegemonic effect as a means of identification. Behr furthermore refutes the notion of homogeneity within police culture and acknowledges the variety of masculinities he encountered in the police service, although pointing out that hegemonic masculinity still is the most widely accepted and encouraged form of gender performance. He calls this most influential model 'warrior masculinity' ("Krieger-Männlichkeit") (Behr 2008: 92ff., Behr 2017: 543). The warrior masculinity is a masculinity that is capable of and sometimes has an affinity for violence. Confrontation is at the centre of the identity, but it is not without preconditions, but framed in a construction of meaning that legitimises the power of the state. This type of masculinity combines law with power and uses both to assert its own interests. "Its dominance resides in the fact that – although it is not practised at all by most members of the police – it can shape the police at any time" (Behr 2017: 544). This form of masculinity is determined by binaries (good-evil, friend-foe) that make it efficient and effective.

Behr further empirically identifies a "protective masculinity" (Behr 2008: 123ff.) and an "inconspicuous aspirational masculinity" (Behr 2008: 134ff.) within the police, which appear to be attached to this hegemonic image of masculinity. In contrast to this, he develops potentially separating (but in parts quite integrable) masculinity models of "homosexuality" (Behr 2008: 147ff.) and "(false) idealism" (Behr 2008: 157ff.)[16]. While "protective masculinity" is not culturally hegemonic, quantitatively speaking it is the most widespread and common representation of masculinity within the police (Behr 2008: 123). Protective masculinity relates to and identifies with their local community and sees its mission primarily in peace-making in everyday situations, relying more on verbal conflict resolution strategies than physical violence. Nevertheless, this type also features a recurring narrative that identify these "protectors" as participants in risky operations. No different is the "achiever" ("inconspicuous aspirational masculinity") who tries early on to integrate himself unobtrusively into the organisation and who must largely share the warrior's patterns of action, at least verbally, in order not to be considered a novice or a theorist (Behr 2008: 146). For most male police officers, the fear- and aggression-ridden counterpart to "normal" masculinity is not feminine but unmanly, effeminate (being without honour, unable to keep one's place, unprofessional) (Behr 2008: 147). However, there are also forms of dealing with difference in the police that are not necessarily exclusionary. According to Behr, (male) homosexuality in the police is tolerated under certain circumstances (heterosexual masculinity, the boundary between masculine and unmasculine, as well

---

16 All archetype-translations by me.

as concepts of dominance of heterosexual men must not be questioned) (Behr 2008: 155f.). Idealist masculinity ("(false) idealism") is a source of danger for cop culture insofar as it is intensely concerned with the question of the ethically correct actions of the police. From a legal point of view, this may be supportable; however, it can lead to more serious problems in the respective unit if abuse of power is reported by colleagues. This kind of "betrayal" is in direct opposition to the lived loyalty of the cop culture (Behr 2008: 158).

According to Behr (2019), as of yet no female counterpart to these archetypes has been developed in police culture. Workman-Stark also argues that "policing remains a male-dominated and hyper-masculine occupation that is somewhat closed to the full integration of women" (Workman-Stark 2017: 31).[17] The resulting discrimination experienced by female police officers has been undergoing changes in intensity, but still, police culture and their practices can be seen as a highly masculinised field. A quantitative report on gender within the police force in Austria published in 2011 found that, despite gender equality law, women were still stigmatised and held to higher standards than their male colleagues (Kofler 2011). 9,680 police officers took part in this nation-wide study, that, while focusing on gender in the police, also included other issues such as the general work-experience of the officers.

This thesis acknowledges the distinct position of the individual officer within the institution and their relation towards the police as an organisation. The police as an organisation are considered through the lens of an actor within the organisation, i.e., an individual police officer. This means that the viewpoint will necessarily be influenced by the rules and expectations of the police as an organisation (Mensching 2008). Occupational practices such as shift work or long working hours, along with societal gender specific expectations (such as responsibility for the household) create a rather unfriendly work environment for female police officers. The Austrian 'Frauenförderungsplan' (BGBl. II 65/2017) makes reference to this in addressing family circumstances and different forms of part-time work.[18] Although equality legislation also aims to prevent indirect discrimination, such as an uneven division of labour (i.e., the division of care

---

17 As Behr argues, women in the police are not integrated so much as assimilated, as police culture as such does not willingly change to accept women in the service, but rather female officers simply have to adapt to the existing culture (Behr 2017).

18 § 8 - § 10 BGBl. II Nr. 65/2017, Also § 11 (2) and § 12 BGBl. II Nr. 65/2017.

work and household responsibilities vs. gainful employment), female police officers still struggle to negotiate these aspects. A significant factor
contributing to the perception of the police as a harsh work environment
is stress. Although police work is inherently stressful (Dowler/Arai 2008),
research suggests female officers experience this in a more intense way
than their male colleagues, even more so due to their presupposed domestic responsibilities (ibid.). The fact that female police officers experience
higher levels of stress than their male colleagues is also linked to the organisational culture of the police. Stress arises from goal negotiation (conflict
between personal and operational goals, among others), emotional exhaus-
tion and other job-related problems, as well as experience of gender- or
ethnicity-based bias (Dowler/Arai 2008, Houdmont 2013, Morash et al.
2006a, Morash et al. 2006b, Riggins 2015).

Research has suggested that male-dominated workspaces, in re-enforcing
cultural norms of male dominance, provide an adverse environment for
women because of an increased risk of sexual harassment, or discrimination because of gender (De Haas/Timmerman 2010, Sbraga/O'Donohue
2000). Women are at a greater risk of (sexual) harassment in a work
environment where women are outnumbered by men, than in other,
more equalised workplaces. Studies within the police force further show
that, while being at greater risk[19], women are also more distressed (mentally and physically) by sexual harassment than their male colleagues (De
Haas et al. 2009, Lonsway et al. 2013). This leads to women having to
develop coping-mechanisms, if they decide to stay in these workplaces.
Haarr and Morash (2013) found that rank and tenure affect these coping
strategies, high-ranking women being more equipped (because of their
power) and willing to respond to and report such incidents. Although
sexual harassment and "'unwanted conduct' related to a person's sex" (Sex
discrimination, acas.org.uk) is covered under the Equality Act (2010) in
the UK and under § 8 B-GlBG in Austria, few female police officers report
any such incidents (Lonsway et al. 2013). The most recent case (2014)
of sexual harassment in the Austrian police service which the Equal Treatment Commission dealt with involved four female police officers, who
turned to the equal treatment officer to report the incidents. The Equal
Treatment Commission found that repeated sexual harassment by the su-

---

19 Female officers experience sexual harassment more often and more frequently
    than their male colleagues – the most common form of sexual harassment for
    both male and female officers is offensive remarks on their body or appearance
    (De Haas et al. 2009: 395, see also Brown et al 2018: 369).

perior officer had taken place (138a-d. Gutachten: Sexuelle Belästigung, bmgf.gv.at). There are further incidents of gender-based harassment (142. Gutachten: Belästigung / Beruflicher Aufstieg, bmgf.gv.at) and violations of the 'Frauenförderungsgebot' (164. Gutachten: Beruflicher Aufstieg, 172. Gutachten: Beruflicher Aufstieg, bmgf.gv.at). In terms of acceptance, contemporary studies suggest subtler forms of discrimination being carried out by the white male majority of police officers in the UK (Loftus 2008).

2.6 Equality Law(s) & Equal Opportunity Policies

This chapter deals with the legal background and regulations that have to be considered when analysing female police officers in the considered countries. First, a brief theoretical background into the creation of equality laws and equal opportunities policies is given. Following, the countries respective equality legislations that are applicable and relevant to the respective police forces are described. Furthermore, any previous research that addresses equality policies' impact or their reception within the police service is discussed, as well as possible implications of these policies.

As equal opportunities policies play a vital role in this work's research interest, it is important to note their theoretical background as well as any developments in the field of equality laws. Any previous findings of studies on equality laws and equal opportunities policies make a further exploration of the topic necessary in order to ensure a positive working environment for female police officers.

2.6.1 Why Equality Policies

Discrimination against women occurs in various forms (Cordes 2010: 924): Two legal concepts are direct discrimination, in which individual legal norms immediately and directly discriminate against women (previously wage reductions for women), and indirect discrimination, i.e., norms which are actually formulated in a gender-neutral manner but which have a particular negative impact on women (e.g., discriminatory regulations for part-time work, which subsequently affect 90 % of women). Additionally, equality policies have to consider the theoretical concept of structural discrimination, i.e., the fact that the practical use of rule systems results in social inequality or discrimination against women (e.g., opportunities for women in professional/career leadership positions). The aim of gender equality law and policies is to eliminate these inequalities. The focus is on two elements: equal rights and the creation of equal opportunities. The first is aimed at eliminating direct and indirect discrimination. The creation of equal opportunities turns to the elimination of structural discrimination. For (legal) measures to take full effect, structural changes must be made. This in part also justifies the application of unequal law (compensatory law) (Cf. Holzleithner 2002: 63ff.). These laws contain regulations that are intended to help cushion the effects of discrimination against women, such as quota regulations.

Equality policy as a policy furthering the advancement of women makes use of various strategies. These include reconciling work and family life, supporting women in accessing male-dominated areas, and increasing the percentage of women in management positions (Cordes 2010: 927). However, these strategies can appear problematic in many respects: They have only a low social and operational acceptance – above all because positive incentives for men are lacking, support measures to reconcile family and career are primarily designed for women[20]; and the idea of promoting women can seem to be based on a deficit model (women have individual qualification or motivational deficits) (Cordes 2010: 928).

It should be noted that gender disparities in the working environment are based on socially constructed gender binarity and repeatedly affirmed differences in the behaviour and abilities of women and men.

2.6.2 Equality Policies in the Police

The legal framework of the police does include equality opportunities, in context of EU-legislation as well as national policies in both Austria and the UK. The concept of equal opportunities policies is multidimensional, therefore making it difficult to study these issues cross-nationally.

Equality laws in Austria (starting with the 1979 Equal Treatment Act, which enacted the right to equal pay for men and women in the private sector) have been extended further following EU law, to farther extend the set of grounds for discrimination.[21] Since 1993, there has been a separate Equal Treatment Act for employees of regional authorities (public service), the Federal Equal Treatment Act (B-GlBG), which also applies

---

20 Which leads to a reinforcement of women's traditional role as family care takers.
21 Gender, sexual orientation, ethnicity, religion and/or philosophical belief system, and age, see: Bundes-Gleichbehandlungsgesetz. B-GlBG StF: BGBl. Nr. 100/1993.

to the police. Equality in the workplace is dealt with in the first section of the B-GlBG, banning any vocational discrimination based on gender differences. The Federal Equal Treatment Commission (B-GBK) which is, amongst others, responsible for the police, is established in the Federal Chancellery and consists of two senates (§§ 22-25 B-GlBG). It is a special federal administrative institution that can be called upon in the event of discrimination in connection with state employment or training. This institution does not deliver enforceable judgments, but it still plays a vital role in exercising control and monitoring compliance to equality policies.

Employees, employers, members of the works councils, persons affected by discrimination, or an interest group can file an application for a review of the violation of the equal treatment requirement at the Equal Treatment Commission if they suspect such a violation. The procedure serves, among other things, to mediate between employers and employees, aiming at an extrajudicial settlement (Gleichbehandlungskommission, bundeskanzlerlamt.gv.at). Counselling and support regarding legal measures concerning (un)equal treatment can be obtained at the GAW, who further provide information dissemination (Gleichbehandlungsanwaltschaft, gleichbehandlungsanwaltschaft.gv.at). With similar duties and functions as the Equal Treatment Commission, the Federal Equal Treatment Commission is a special administrative body of the Federation which can be appealed to on grounds of discrimination in connection with employment with the Federation.[22]

Recent key legal acts regarding gender equality passed by the UK government include the UK Equality Act 2010, the UK Equality Strategy (Building a Fairer Britain) 2006 – 2016, and the UK Strategy 'Think, Act, Report' (for private and voluntary sector organisations). While the UK Equality Act 2010 harmonises all previous legislation on equality and focusses on essential issues like the gender pay gap, the UK Equality Strategy further features the notion of changing cultures and attitudes in Section 4, which includes cultural attitudes in the labour market (The Equality Strategy, assets.publishingservice.gov.uk). The Equality and Human Rights Commission in the UK can provide advice and guidance, while also having a range of enforcement powers set out in the Equality Act 2006. It is the regulatory body responsible for enforcing the Equality Act 2010 (Equality and Human Rights Commission [1], equalityhumanrights.com).

---

22 While the first two institutions are responsible for issues in the private sector, the FETC is responsible for discrimination in the context of state employment (Bundes-Gleichbehandlungskommission, bundeskanzleramt.gv.at).

While aiming pre-dominantly at extrajudicial settlements in cases of unequal or discriminatory treatment, formal enforcement actions the EHRC may take are: inquiries, investigations, unlawful act notices, agreements, assessments, and compliance notices (Equality and Human Rights Commission [2], equalityhumanrights.com).

Research has shown that legal changes in themselves are insufficient in causing social shifts, if they are not supported by broader policy reforms and political action to bring about change (Dedeoglu 2012: 286). In Austria, quota rules apply in the federal service, and therefore the police. According to § 11b B-GlBG, female applicants who are equally suitable for the position as the best-suited male competitor must be given priority in accordance with the provisions of the plan for the advancement of women. This is to be done until the proportion of women in the total number of permanent employees (in the relevant sector/group) is at least 50%, and provided that there are no predominant reasons in the person of a competitor. Furthermore, according to § 11c B-GlBG ("priority in professional advancement"), female applicants who are as suitable for the intended higher position (function) as the best-suited male competitor are to be given priority, unless the reasons for the preference lie in the person of a competitor. This is in effect until the proportion of women permanently employed in the relevant function group in the field of the respective service authority is 50%. This provision includes the employer's obligation to check the professional and personal competence of each candidate on the basis of uniform criteria and, after comparing the qualifications of the candidates, to determine the degree of suitability.[23]

While equality policies have the potential to increase actual numbers of women in the police service, they further influence internal dynamics and conditions within the police service, as well as relationships with the public:

> "[I]f a male police officer can relate in a non-sexist manner to his female colleague, then the possibility that he might also relate to a female member of the public in that same way is greatly enhanced." (Walklate 2000: 244)

---

23 Dworkin describes and justifies these kinds of policies with the 'right to be treated as an equal', which discriminated or disadvantaged persons and groups should be able to make use of (Dworkin 1977: 273). For reasons of lack of space, the debate on justice and equality cannot be further explored at this point.

In this way, equality policies are framed as providing a mechanism for significant organisational change; they raise awareness for equal opportunities issues, challenge the occupational culture, and incidentally raise the question of what constitutes 'good' or 'proper' policing (as seen above, e.g., 'soft' policing). Because the effective implementation of these policies can greatly influence the future of policing, evaluating them through the viewpoint of those affected plays a vital role in the planned research.

The already mentioned 2011 study by Kofler (2011) asked about the participants' reception of positive-action policies within the police: Men's acceptance of women's promotion measures was found to be significantly lower than women's (71% of women, but only 37% of men, were in favour) (Kofler 2011: 57). This must be preceded by the fact that knowledge about gender-policies is very scattered within the police. Most respondents knew about the commissioner for equal treatment ("Gleichbehandlungsbeauftragte(r)"), and "contact-women"[24]. Other measures, such as flexible timing of education and work courses were fairly unknown. The advancement for women in senior positions was well-known and also very negatively received among male participants, while female participants did know little about these measures (Kofler 2011: 58). While these findings raise an important issue in police work-culture, namely the overall negative reception of equal opportunities policies, as well as a certain lack of information, the following research looks at the reasoning behind these perceptions.

Similarly, Brown notes that police forces in England and Wales, along with Northern Ireland, Scotland and the Republic of Ireland, were "slow to see the full implications of equality legislations" (Brown 2000b: 107). It is further observed that, although female officers in England and Wales were more likely to report incidents of sexual harassment than in the other three jurisdictions, this may be due to higher levels of feminist awareness of female officers serving in England and Wales police forces.[25]

---

24 So-called "contact women" act as a connecting link regarding issues of gender equality between police officers and the Ministry of the Interior, similar to equality commissioners. In every state, there are a number of contact women, and one equality commissioner.

25 Brown explains this cultural difference by referring to the influence of the Catholic church on values and traditions in Northern Ireland, and the patchy and slow-progressing recruitment and integration of female officers in Scotland. Nowadays, awareness around gender issues and the maturity of equality policies is described as greater in England and Wales and Scotland than Northern Ireland (Brown 2000b: 107f.).

Furthermore, the evidence presented in the article further reinforces the argument that the relationship between gender ratio within the police and levels of discrimination or harassment are not linear – a higher rate of female officers does not necessarily lead to a diminishing of discriminatory practices – but rather consistent, varying with levels of awareness (Cf. Brown 2000b: 108). Still, the state of gender equality policies at the start of the century in England and Wales seemed most promising compared to other British Isles.

The findings of these studies make further exploration of gender issues seem appropriate and necessary, to ensure a positive work environment for women in the police service. Examining their viewpoints and experiences provides an aid to better understand gender relations within the police. How these issues are addressed as well as the aim of the following work are the focus of the following chapter.

2.7 Background of the Study

In my previous research for my bachelor's thesis in 2014/15, I carried out a qualitative study of women in the police force in Austria. My findings stem from three interviews with female police officers and suggest a very limited knowledge of gender related benefits in addition to highly conservative attitudes displayed by male and female police officers as well as citizens. Furthermore, I carried out research on potential differences in South-East England's male and female police officers' motivations and their respective attitudes toward the job for my masters thesis (2016), with a focus on any possible gender-related differences. The findings do not support any vital differences in respect to officers' motivation pre-joining but suggest that gender influences officers' approaches and attitudes towards issues of equality within the police service. Further exploration of the specific topic of equality and the meaning of gender in the police service therefore seemed to hold a lot of promise.

This chapter has dealt with the theoretical as well as the practical background of this study, which includes gender theoretical and legal aspects, as well as aspects of police research. A research gap arises in two points: First, the qualitative study of the working realities of female police officers in Austria, which as such has not (yet) been carried out and seems particularly fruitful, especially in the light of a general lack of police research in the country. Second, a comparative perspective in the gender-themed research of the police across two European countries that are similar in the police's fundamental positioning in society, but slightly different in their context with regards to police culture and history.

The following chapter looks at the research question, and the subsequent aspects that have to be considered. Following, the research design of the present study is described. The theoretical embedding of the research methods (semi-structured interviews, participatory observation) is presented consecutively. Furthermore, the methodological stance of the Grounded Theory approach is explained and put into context. Lastly, any ethical issues the research touches on are discussed.

3. Methodology

In this chapter, the methodology of the present research is given due consideration. In the first part of the chapter, the research question along with its implications and further aspects that need to be considered are presented. The second part then focusses on the methods that were used to answer the research question. In this part, not only are semi-structured interview and participatory observation as methods described and put into context, but the methodological stance of the approach that was taken during the carrying out of the research, namely Grounded Theory, is depicted. Lastly, the chapter also deals with the ethical implications of the carried-out research.

3.1 Research Question

I now turn to the research question, the subsequent aspects that need to be considered, and further implications of the study's focus. The research question is: What are the experiences of female police officers in the UK and Austria, in which ways do experiences differ/resemble each other, and how do gender and related equal opportunities policies influence these issues? The focus of the study is on personal experiences and vocational attitudes of female police officers in Austria and the UK, and their perspective on (perceived) governmental gender-related policies. This includes examining motivation and background of the individual, with respect to their countries' specific training, duties, and policies of the police service. Furthermore, female police officers' personal experiences are taken into consideration. This includes perceptions and behaviour of male and female colleagues as well as citizens, and possible different standards female police officers have to adhere to both in contact with citizens as well as colleagues and superiors. An important feature of the research focus is the participants' position on (perceived) equal opportunities policies and their perception of the current state of (gender) diversity in the police service. These opinions and positions are inevitably influenced by and linked to their countries' respective social and cultural environment. Relating these opinions and experiences to actual legal frameworks and interpretations is a vital part of the research.

I have explored the research question by conducting personal interviews with female police officers, thus evaluating their subjective viewpoint of their everyday work-life, and the approval and/or struggles they experience due to them inhabiting a male-dominated workspace. As such, the objective viewpoints of participants are of importance; however, the interests and objectives of the study mainly lie in the underlying (social) phenomena that are to be made visible.

With my study, I hope to contribute to the field of gender research in policing by putting the focus on female police officers' personal experiences and perceptions of their workplace and surroundings. Furthermore, through the international comparison, any cultural and social differences that may influence their respective viewpoints are explored. The study further broadens the knowledge of international policing research as well as provides an understanding of gender issues in the police force of today. In better understanding the experiences and needs of women in the police force, governments will be able to provide better-tailored enhancements and benefits regarding the work experience of female police officers in the respective countries. Furthermore, the impact and reception of already existing gender-related assets, such as actively inviting female police officers to apply for promotions, can be analysed and evaluated. This will further broaden the insight into female police officers' work life and environment. By comparing and contrasting these issues in two different countries, I am able to gain a broad understanding of positive and/or negative aspects female police officers encounter in their daily life. The study fills a research gap, in that it explores police culture through a female perspective, focussing on individuals' perception and experience in an international context. While earlier studies focussed on quantitative assessment (Kofler 2011) or male experiences within a male-dominated culture (e.g., Behr 2008), this research contributes to police studies in adding female experiences and their subjective viewpoints of gender-relations in the police service. While there is substantial work concerning gender within a policing context and/or female police officers in the UK (e.g., Brown/Silvestri 2020), the same cannot be said about Austria. This thesis therefore addresses this research gap, while furthering and expanding upon earlier findings from UK studies.

As the study aims at subjective viewpoints, rather than generalisations, a qualitative approach is taken. This means leaving behind pre-conceived ideas and theories about equality and gender and trying to evaluate the participants' subjective point of view clearly. In personal one-on-one interviews, female police officers were asked about their experiences and opinions on their work in the police service. The following section gives further insight into the research design which is catered to serve the research aims.

3.2 Research Design

A case study approach (small-N) is particularly helpful in examining the reception and impact of certain policies; an in-depth analysis provides a solid basis for inductive theory building (Ertan 2016). As the study tries to deepen the understanding of individual perception of everyday work life as a woman in the police force, as well as trying to understand the background of these women, a qualitative approach, generating hypotheses, is feasible. To undertake my research, I proposed to conduct around 40 semi-structured interviews with female police officers (approximately 20 in the UK and 20 in Austria).[26] In doing so, I generated new data, rather than relying on data from my previous research into the police service, because the research question necessitates further data collection. In developing a semi-structured interview guideline, I can address aspects that the research is interested in and target certain areas, while remaining open to adapting to any possible topics arising from the conversation. This further allows for comparisons between the interviews and the responses interviewees give. A pilot project, testing the feasibility of the developed interview guideline with Austrian female police officers, was also carried out at the beginning of the research.

Participants were asked about their motivations, experiences, and opinions about their occupation (their work as well as contact with colleagues). The questions also included references to gender-related issues such as diversity and equality strategies, and the officers' personal opinion on the police as a male-dominated area of work. The research relied on one-on-one interviews as well as group interviews, while these findings are further broadened and deepened by observational data. The interviews were analysed and coded with the qualitative coding software MAXQDA, interpreting and analysing generated interview data. Examining these findings, I built a framework of the personal experiences of the interviewees' work-environment in each country. These were then compared to each other and any possible differences were analysed. Following a Grounded

---

26 47 interviews were carried out in total, 23 in Austria and 24 in England and Wales. For further information see chapter 4.1.

Theory approach, thematic bundles that arise out of the coded material were analysed and accumulated to provide a basis for developing hypotheses.

Grounded Theory, following Strauss (1991), is better understood as a style to interpretatively analyse qualitative data, following a set of characteristics. First and foremost, I focussed on two key characteristics: theoretical sampling, and coding and comparing. The process of data collection and interpretation in theoretical sampling was done unanimously, whereby the goal was to form a theory arising from the collected data (Lueger 2010). By constantly going back to already collected and analysed data while at the same time collecting new data, theoretical sampling helped in finding new ways to access participants or work as a signpost as to where to go next for new data. The constant comparison of 'old' and 'new' data further helped in generating codes and arranging them into concepts. Because of a rather long fieldwork period, which was due to the research being carried out in two different countries, it was very helpful to revise theories when new data arose.

I further interviewed the head of the "Zentrum für Organisationskultur und Gleichbehandlung" (Centre for Organisational Culture and Equality, ZOG) in Austria, as well as leaders of equality (support) groups in different police forces in the UK[27] and a leadership development officer for Police Now.[28] Through this, I was able to gain a different angle on issues of diversity and gender in the police service and familiarised myself with common practice and standards in both countries. It further provided a helpful organisational and legal background to issues that may be raised in other interviews and the course of the research.

3.3 Method – Semi-structured Interviews

There are many possibilities and variations in carrying out a qualitative interview, depending on the research focus, objectives, and the characteristics of participants. Most literature refers to interviews as a sort of continuum, ranging from structured through semi-structured to unstructured interviews (Brinkmann 2013), with the structured interview being

---

27 E.g., the chair of the women's support network "STAR" in Durham Police Constabulary (Durham Constabulary – Who are we?, durham.police.uk).

28 Police Now are a national graduate programme that provides a faster entry route into the police force.

on the quantitative end of the spectrum (e.g., surveys) and semi- and unstructured interviews being predominantly carried out by qualitative researchers. Semi-structured and unstructured interviews offer a vital flexibility and versatility, which further increase the diversity of usage and interpretations of the method. Some examples of these types of interviews are narrative, biographical, ethnographic, or in-depth interviews. Although types of qualitative interviews are varied, there are some points that all of them have in common (Edwards/Holland 2013):an interactional exchange of dialogue; a fluid and flexible structure, while covering a certain topic or theme; context-related research – meanings are created in a certain context, co-produced by participant(s) and researcher in an interaction.

As Brinkmann (2013) argues, it is not possible to be completely void of preconceptions, and there are no entirely non-leading questions. The function of a semi-structured interview, the most wide-spread type of interview in social sciences, is to lead participants to talk about certain topics or themes, rather than evoking certain opinions on these themes. The structure of the interview should provide enough flexibility for interviewers to raise questions or probe certain issues, as well as seek confirmation or clarification from interviewees; interviewees should also be given room to express their concerns and perspectives on issues in their own words. Therefore, a semi-structured interview guide provides the researcher with a set of questions or topics they want to cover, but still offers flexibility as to when and how to elicit responses from the interviewee(s). In this way, interviews provide a space for participants to give answers on their own terms and in their own words, but still offer a certain structure (in covering particular topics) for comparison across different interviews. The interviewer in semi-structured interviews is, in being a participant in the knowledge-generating process, more involved in the interview practice as they would be in a structured interview approach; at the same time the interviewer has considerable influence on the focus of the conversation as opposed to an unstructured interview and can therefore aim attention at themes relevant to the research project. Brinkmann defines the semi-structured interview through four key elements: 1. Purpose 2. Descriptions 3. Life world 4. Interpretation of meaning. The emphasis therefore is on 1) the interviewer's purpose (producing and obtaining knowledge), 2) the descriptions provided by the interviewee(s), which are commonly about 3) life world experiences, and 4) the interpretation of these provided descriptions, a process of trying to understand the meaning behind them. Interpretation of meaning can be assisted during the interview process, giving the interviewee a chance to clarify or object to certain interpretations of their descriptions (e.g. in directly asking to clarify/confirm statements). It is universally acknowledged in qualitative research that there is never one correct way in carrying out a technique or method, and that much of the particulars of a research process depend on the research purpose and distinct circumstances. The definition and approach to qualitative interviewing must therefore be adapted to fit the research purposes.

As personal face-to-face interviews offer the richest source of knowledge and information to an interviewer (Brinkmann 2013), I have opted to use this approach in my research. When carrying out face-to-face interviews, researchers not only have conversational data and information, but also body language, surroundings, and expressions to protocol and analyse. To do so effectively, one has to make sure the interviews are transcribed as soon as possible, preferably by the interviewer themselves, to make sure every detail is sufficiently recollected (Brinkmann 2013). Interview sites are important, as the specific context of each might offer an insight into the participants' person – for example, interviewing participants in their workplace (as was done more than half of the interviews during this research) enables the researcher to gain a glance at their professional as well as personal life.

3.4 Method – Participatory Observation

Observations can be a valuable tool to supplement data from other sources such as interviews or published statistical evidence. In particular, methods that require an intervention in the field, such as interviews, make accompanying material gathered from (planned and unplanned) observations valuable, because it can make certain structures visible (e.g. how the field reacts to a researcher) (Lueger 2010). For example, the social and physical context of an interview, the social setting of the interview[29], and even the environment the interview takes place in (building, furnishings) can be of value.

In a planned participatory observation, the researcher inevitably has to integrate themselves into social activities of the field. This requires a particular analysis strategy, as observations can only be recorded to a limited extent. Often, what we record is also pre-interpreted.

---

29 In Austria this was prevalent through the varied use of the formal "Sie" or informal "du".

"Protocols in this case are reduced, supplemented and altered records of events or processes (usually in the form of written observation protocols, photographs, videos or sounds) that observers have recorded and processed within the framework of their observation schemes, the recording technique they may have used and the horizons of meaning relevant to them." (Lueger 2010: 41f. my translation)

The simple accumulation of data can therefore never be the goal of an observation. Less material but more and intense processing and interpretation of said material seems more appropriate.

In a systematic approach to observation, it is advisable to concentrate on various aspects of a phenomena and treat them as variants to an approximation to the totality of the phenomena (Burgess 1982). For this study, I centred my focus on actors, i.e., the police officers and their social interactions. In this approach, the actions of a certain person or group of persons are followed. Furthermore, the actors themselves can also play the role of an informant, being encouraged to explain their actions, and the motives and context associated with them. As Bratich (2018) remarks, observation nowadays is not merely a type of data collection, but needs to be seen in a collaborative context, with the researcher not being at a distance from the observed field. This enables research "subjects" to interact with the process and the researcher themselves. The effects of this more collaborative approach can include a possibility to empower certain communities or groups of people in giving them a chance to participate in a public forum (Lueger 2010). Furthermore, the access to the field is of importance, as the relationships built between researcher and research field are crucial to a study's outcomings but also further exploration of a certain subject (Lueger 2010).

Observations further need to be timed, if only for practical reasons. As a rule of thumb, it is wise to at least observe and analyse one secluded cycle of activity. These cycles can differ in length, from a few hours to weeks or even years. Sticking to this rule, I observed two full cycles of activity with my chosen field.[30]

Interpreting the recorded findings needs to take into account the social context in which certain actions are set (Lueger 2010: 66). First, the data is recorded and analysed from the point of the observer, with a high sensitivity for the unfamiliar. Second, one turns to the context of the action and the potential structures of meaning behind them, to get a better

---

30   A cycle of activity is a full 12-hour shift, see chapter 4.2.

understanding of the field. Next, in an interpretative process, the material is analysed trying to both separate and integrate the general from the particular and the entirety from the details. In a last step, the preliminary findings are re-examined and compared to previous findings.

The continuous analysis and handling of material in a cyclic process can lead to a systematic expansion of knowledge in the research process. Having already collected data available for future research can be helpful, in that it can widen the scope of the study. A permanent exchange between short observational periods and longer analytical workups is one of the key components of observational data gathering (Lueger 2010: 91). This approach also lends itself perfectly to the general methodological frameworks of a Grounded Theory approach.

3.5 Method – Grounded Theory

Methods and methodology in social research should always be consistent with the philosophical stance of the researcher as well as fit the research questions and aims. As I was aiming to find out about personal views and experiences and trying to build a framework around the gathered knowledge, the theory-building approach of Grounded Theory appeared feasible. Grounded Theory offers flexible methodological guidelines rather than rigid instructions and allows the researcher a certain flexibility. As such, being reflexive about personal preconceptions and impressions is seen as an obligation in the approach (Charmaz 2014). The coding technique – or rather the concepts emerging from it – was used to form a theory around my research questions. One of the vital things to consider in using Grounded Theory as a theory-building design is the issue of theoretical sampling (Urquhart 2013). This means taking already gathered data and analyses into account when deciding where to sample from next. Theoretical sampling helps to densify particular concepts but also widens the scope of the research by sampling more diverse data. This implies an overlapping of the collection of data and the analysis process, which creates a circular procedure of analysis/comparison and sampling/data collection. The emergent categories of data are 'saturated' when sampling new data no longer leads to new insights nor reveals any new characteristics of said categories (Charmaz 2014). In practice, researchers have to decide themselves to cease their activity at a point where they think no important fresh data will emerge, or they have generated enough data to satisfy their research questions – it therefore remains a quite subjective approach. Nevertheless, theoretical sampling offers a logic for organising data and creating or refining links between categories that allow to explore the subject matter in depth.

Methods of data collection fit to a Grounded Theory approach are primarily interviews, participant observation, and/or fieldwork (along with field notes) (Urquhart 2013). The first step in analysing collected data is the process of open coding. Coding means categorising segments of text or data, assigning it with a name that tries to summarise or interpret the data. The initial coding process is very open, led by the data and either analytical or simply descriptive (Charmaz 2014, Urquhart 2013). It moves beyond the collected data in trying to interpret and compare different sequences. These codes are then analysed themselves, trying to make sense of them in a broad matter and categorising them accordingly. These categories are then densified, related to subcategories and specified ('Axial Coding'. Charmaz 2014). The final step in building a theory is theoretical coding – the process of relating categories (Charmaz, Urquhart 2013). It conceptualises how the emergent concepts and categories (the substantive codes) relate to each other (theoretical codes). Theoretical Coding can be inspired by existing theories or generated solely from the codes the researcher develops. Again, the theories and frameworks built from the process are not fixed, and can be adapted to new data or interpretations, which implies a constant and recurring preoccupation with the codes and data.

Grounded Theory is used to produce low-level theories around certain phenomena on a micro-level (Urquhart 2013). It exists at different levels of abstraction – theoretical sampling, as well as relating findings to relevant literature can be helpful in widening the scope of the research and the degree of conceptualisation. The research examines a particular 'case' (female police officers in two different countries) to provide an extensive exploration and analysis of a certain setting. Carrying out a case study further implies that the research aims to draw out unique features of the case in question – an idiographic approach (Bryman 2008). The study therefore does not aim to be generalisable but rather to serve as an exemplifying case, capturing the particulars of a common setting. The starting point of the analysis are the self-evident assumptions and unspoken preconditions in the perception and thinking of female police officers. Certain systems of knowledge and standards of the respective subject area can be derived from the everyday interpretations of social actors within the microcosmos that is formed by the police (Cf. Behr 2003). With this research, I aim to build a theory around the understanding of a micro-phenomenon in a certain context, which may be used to initiate further research on the subject area. With the help of this study, researchers and policy makers will be able to better understand the issues female police officers face, while the participants' perception of equality and equality policies will help in tackling any issues there are with the current state of equality in the police service in both countries.

3.6 Ethical Issues

In my research ethics approach, I refer to ethical codes of the British Society for Criminology (BSC Code of Ethics, britsoccrim.org). The research was carried out in cooperation with adult female police officers (who have finished their training and been sworn in) of the Austrian and English and Welsh police forces. Participation in the face-to-face interviews was voluntary, and people were able to decide to withdraw from the study at any time. This includes the ability to withdraw statements or the whole interview. Furthermore, participants were asked for permission to record the interview – no interviews were recorded without the authorisation of the interviewees. In cases where interviewees did not consent to being recorded, transcripts were taken on the spot. If participants wished to review their answers and/or transcripts after the interview, I provided them with the notes and interview data used in my analysis to get participants' approval.

The interview might be touching on subjects the respondents could find sensitive. If that had been the case, suitable arrangements, such as referral to a counselling service, would have been made in case respondents felt upset or concerned after or during the interviews. The participants remain anonymous to everyone but the researcher, and the storing of the data produced is secured. This will be achieved by keeping anonymised transcripts on a personal device and deleting audio recordings as soon as possible. Even in cases where interviewees reported being comfortable with being identified as participants in the study, it was still important to anonymise data and input as much as possible.[31] Every effort was made to ensure that the social, psychological, and physical wellbeing of participants was not at risk at any time.

My previous experience with conducting research into the police service shows that police officers, especially in England and Wales, were generally

---

31 This is especially true for those participants who had high exposure e.g., due to the uniqueness of their position.

happy and willing to talk to me, and participants have deemed the interest in their work life and experiences as something positive. In Austria, although gaining access to interview partners is associated with an additional effort, female officers were likewise very welcoming of my research and the interviews themselves proved highly informative.

This chapter dealt with the methodology of the present study, first and foremost the research question and subsequent aspects to be considered in answering it. The design of the research was presented, and with it the methods that are used within its context. The methods described are that of the semi-structured interview (for both countries), as well as the participatory observation (for Austria). Furthermore, the Grounded Theory approach that is taken was described and put into context. This last section furthermore dealt with ethical issues that had to be considered in carrying out the research.

The next chapter will further explain the method and actual field research that was carried out in the course of this study. The access to the field, as well as the sample drawn from it, will be thoroughly described. Further, the specific research process is presented, and the means of data analysis discussed. Lastly, a reflection on the research process will be undertaken.

4. Method and Field Research

This chapter will highlight the specific approach I took to gain, record, and analyse data. Due consideration is given to the sampling method and access to participants, as well as to the different settings in which the interviews were carried out and any implications this has for the data analysis. I will further explain my analysis process in detail and regard potential ethical challenges of the research. This is done through a reflection on the research process, while the role of the female researcher within a male-dominated research field is also given due consideration.

In the first subsection, the sample that was drawn from the researched field is described in detail. The next subsection then deals with the research process as such and gives an insight into the way in which the research was carried out and data was generated. Subsequently, the analysis of the generated data is described. In the final subsection of this chapter a reflection on the research process as a whole is undertaken, as well as any difficulties encountered in the course of the study described.

4.1 Access and Sample

On the one hand, the selection of the two countries was made for pragmatic reasons; the language and the accessibility of interview contacts in both countries. On the other hand, a comparison is also to be considered particularly profitable, as both European countries share a similar socio-cultural context, although they show differences in the cultural understanding of their respective police service (as mentioned above).

As the focus of the research lies on the experiences and attitudes of female police officers, the study relies on sworn female police officers for the collection of data. The aim was to interview around 20 police officers from each country, totalling in 40 interviews. Due consideration was to be given to the diversity of the interview candidates – this refers to their rank, grade, and police force, as well as their age, sexual orientation, and ethnical background.

Access to the participants was gained through personal contacts, as well as approaching police officers and forces directly. My approach differed slightly in the two countries. In the UK, I primarily contacted forces and related organisations (such as Police Now) via e-mail and asked for their help in forwarding my request to their officers. In some cases, I contacted individual officers, either because they were referred to me by their colleagues or, in one case, because of the officer's appearance in the media. In Austria, I primarily approached individual officers and related professionals after receiving their contact details from colleagues or associates, with exception of the leader of the ZOG whom I contacted through an official request. This was due to the rather cautious attitude of the Austrian police to scientific research endeavours. As I was conducting my interviews anonymously, there was no need to go through the Austrian police's official channels and have my research be approved by management.

Sometimes it could prove a challenge to arrange interviews with the study's target group due to busy but also changeable work patterns of the officers. Nevertheless, in Austria I managed to interview 17 police officers face-to-face while another 5 filled out a short questionnaire resembling the interview guideline used for the interviews.[32] Additionally, I interviewed the head of the ZOG to get an idea of the managerial view (Ministry of the Interior) of the situation of women in the police. In England and Wales, I managed to interview 23 police officers, 17 of them face-to-face, a further 6 via phone[33]. In getting a managerial view, similar to my approach in Austria, I interviewed a leadership development officer for Police Now[34]. I managed to achieve the set goal of 40 interviews and even exceed it by completing interviews with 45 female police officers and a further two interviews with related officials.

Regarding the aforementioned diversity of my interview candidates, I mostly succeeded in providing a well-balanced and diverse sample of female police officers. I will not include either the head of the ZOG in Austria nor the leadership development officer for Police Now in the UK in the following sample description, as their interviews were not treated in the same way as the other participants due to their specific experience and professional position.

Considering the rank of my interview partners, I managed to talk to at the least 2 of each rank, except the uppermost rank in each country. The

---

32 These interviews were carried out in spring and summer of 2018.
    The data obtained purely in writing by officers who filled in the questionnaires was mainly used to confirm and further saturate the codes generated by the interview data.
33 These interviews were carried out in November and December 2018.
34 She is also a co-founder and director of the first women-only police leadership programme in the UK.

rank structure of police in the UK and Austria differs slightly. In Austria, following a completed training and final exam, aspirants are appointed "Inspektor", similar to the UK's rank of constable. In ascending order, the list of ranks in the UK then goes on to sergeant, inspector, chief inspector, superintendent, and at the highest level chief constable (including assistant chief constable and deputy chief constable).[35] In Austria, the rank of "Inspektor" is part of the lowest rank group "Eingeteilte Beamte". The other ranks in this group are distinct only by years of service. The next highest-ranking group is that of "Dienstführende Beamte". These range from clerks or group commanders at police stations to detectives or head of a police station. The highest-ranking group is that of "Leitende Beamte". For legally trained officers, the rank structure differs slightly, but is still based on the basic rank structure of Austrian police. In the UK, the prefix "detective" signifies the ability to conduct criminal investigations, being a member of the CID (Criminal Investigation Department) or other special branches but is not a rank in and of itself.

Table 1: Rank of UK Participants

Rank (England and Wales)	Interviewees
Constable	9
Sergeant	2
Inspector	7
Chief Inspector	2 (1 of which temporary)
Superintendent	3

Table 2: Rank of Austrian Participants

Rank (Austria)	Interviewees
Eingeteilte Beamtin	10
Dienstführende Beamtin	7
Leitende Beamtin	4 (1 of which in training)

In terms of departments or units, I managed to speak to a variety of different police officers. In fact, the following tables can only give an idea

---

35 In the City of London and Metropolitan Police, the highest rank is Commander or Commissioner.

which departments most interviewees belonged to. Even in these broadly generalised and approximated categories, there is a lot of variety between the different interviewees – for example, "standard duty" can include standard patrol duty in a certain area as well as frontier policing.[36]

Table 3: Department of UK Participants

Department (**England and Wales**)	*Interviewees*
Detective	11 (6 of which CID, 3 of which professional standards department)
Police Now (neighbourhood policing, project-related work)	4
Commander/Managerial Position	5
Other (e.g., HQ, custody)	3

Table 4: Department of Austrian Participants

Department (**Austria**)	*Interviewees*
"Standard" Duty	10
Criminal Duty	2
Crime Prevention	3
Other (e.g., legally trained officers, Cobra)	7

Another distinct category is the interviewees age at the time of the interview. My youngest interviewee was only 22, while the oldest was in her 50ies.[37] This wide range of life and work[38] experiences was indeed very helpful to achieving the aims of the study.

---

36 The category stems from the idea of being appointed to a certain regular police station rather than working in specialist departments.
37 The regular pension age for police officers in both UK and Austria is 60.
38 Not only referring to police work.

Table 5: Age of UK Participants

Participants' Age (England and Wales)	*Interviewees*
25 or under	5
26-34	3
35-44	9
45 or over	6

Table 6: Age of Austrian Participants

Participants' Age (Austria)	*Interviewees*
25 or under	3
26-34	7
35-44	6
45 or over	3
No information	3

Connected to the participants' age, yet categorically different, is the work experience participants had with the police. To create this unit of measurement, I excluded the training period of the officers interviewed.[39] However, I included years served in a quasi-police environment – examples of this are being police staff or PCSOs before becoming a sworn officer or being a customs official.[40] Some, because of their young age, only had about 18 months experience, while others served for 25 years and more.

---

39 These training periods varied in their length not only in the different countries but also with the year in which people started their training, i.e., previous training periods being shorter.
40 The Austrian "Zollwache" was integrated into the police system in 2005.

Table 7: Police Experience of UK Participants

Police Experience (**England and Wales**)	*Interviewees*
Up to 2 years	5
2.1 – 10 years	2
10.1 – 20 years	9
More than 20 years	7

Table 8: Police Experience of Austrian Participants

Police Experience (**Austria**)	*Interviewees*
Up to 2 years	1
2.1 – 10 years	8
10.1 – 20 years	5
More than 20 years	5
No information	3

I further talked to two current and one former "Gleichbehandlungsbeauftragte" (equality commissioners) in Austria, and two leaders of local women's networks in England and Wales. Although this study focusses on the situation of female police officers, an intersectional approach is very important to this work. Considering the lack of diversity in the police itself, it was still of importance to include women of all social and personal backgrounds. I managed to talk to members of the LGBTIQ+ community within the police service in both countries. Three of these were the respective leaders of the national (Austria) or a local (England and Wales) LGBTIQ+ network. In these interviews I included a question specifically addressing these networks and the community's relationship to the police service. In the UK, I further managed to interview two women of colour. Unfortunately, this could not be realised in Austria.[41] As mentioned above, these shortcomings are to be accepted given the quite uniform makeup of the police, especially in Austria.

Arranging the availability of my participants with the methodological needs of my study remained a challenge throughout the research process.

---

41 I tried contacting a woman of Turkish descent yet was unsuccessful.

Theoretical sampling in qualitative research is described as being flexible and adaptable.

> "[The] selection is made on the basis of relevance for your theory, in order to produce a sample that will enable you to develop the theoretical ideas that will be emerging in an iterative process between your theory and your data, and to enable you to test these emerging ideas." (Edwards/Holland 2013: 6)

This means that, after getting first access, the sample can still be modified, and particular cases can be selected to aid the needs of the study. I have developed my sample through the method of snowballing, as Edwards and Holland suggest for this approach. Accordingly, the first participants are accessed through "whatever access route you can find" (Edwards/Holland 2013: 6) and these participants then grant the researcher access to other potential interviewees or contacts. As this approach is useful in contacting and gaining access to hard-to-reach groups or individuals, I found this method to be the most feasible for my sampling aims. Brown et al. also specifically suggest a non-probability sample for hard to reach groups, in their case senior women in policing (Brown et al. 2019). This approach is also consistent with the objective of theoretical sampling, as there is a constant interchange of analysis and further data collection, and the researcher is able to specifically select (in asking participants for contacts) where to sample from next and which cases are still needed to provide a satisfactory description of the phenomena.

4.2 Research Process

I carried out three pilot interviews during April and May 2018 to test the feasibility of the designed interview guideline and validate the research method. Access to the participants was granted through personal contacts and acquaintances. All of the participants in the pilot study worked for the Austrian police force. The questions and probes were mostly suitable in generating rich and insightful responses. Following this pilot study, I slightly adapted the interview guideline and deleted one question entire-ly[42] as it disturbed the flow of the interview and did not yield any added

---

42 The question was asked right after the issue of career development was raised and was phrased "Gibt es etwas, das Sie aus heutiger Sicht anders machen würden?" - "From today's point of view, would you do anything differently?".

value. On the whole, I found the method used quite feasible, and my questions generated rich and interesting responses. As the changes to the interview guideline were only minimal, excluding a very small part of the proposed road map, I kept the pilot interviews and treated their analysis in the same way as the other interviews. Using the insights from my pilot project, I further enhanced my research aims to not only focus on motivation, training, work-life, and equality policies, but also interviewees' personal stance and view of equality in general and the context of the police in particular.

After reviewing my findings, I tried to access more potential interview partners via personal contacts, participants themselves, and through official channels. The fieldwork then lasted almost a year, from May 2018 to the end of December 2018. During the time I was constantly processing and analysing data as well as engaging with possible participants and collecting new data. The gathering of interview data in Austria was finished in September 2018, while the interviews in England and Wales took place in November and December of the same year. Additionally, I managed to partake in participatory observations in Austria in October 2019, shortly before finishing my analysis of the collected interview data. Unfortunately, I was not able to carry out participatory observations with the police in England and Wales, as one needs to be a resident of a given area to participate in and apply for a ride along. The interview guideline includes questions on preconceptions as well as career development and current experiences and attitudes towards the occupation of a police officer. Due regard was given to the issue of gender in participants' working life, and their reception within the police service. Additionally, issues of gender equality policies and their possible implications were discussed. The first two questions take a retrospective approach in asking the participant to recall their position as an applicant to the police service and the time thereafter. It can be likened to stimulated recall methods (Gass/Mackey 2000), which elicit data about particular internal processes involved in activities such as decision making. Following, the daily work routine is thematised, at first without any particular regard to gender of the interviewee and others. Afterwards, a closer look is being taken at the daily dealings of interviewees taking gender into account. This includes the participants' reception within the police force (colleagues, bosses) as well as within the broader context of society and the public as a female police officer. Furthermore, I asked interviewees about their personal opinion on any possible changes the issue and perception of women in the police service has faced over the last years, depending of course on the length of experience participants have had within the service. Finally, gender equality policies are brought into perspective, and participants own knowledge about policies but also their viewpoint on gender equality and the implementation of different equality provisions are brought up in the interviews.

The interviews were mainly carried out face-to-face (34 police officers and two additional interviewees in managerial positions). Some were carried out via phone – 7 in the UK, due to scheduling issues and manageability. A further 5 participants filled out an interview survey similar to the interview guideline used in the personal interviews, due to scheduling issues and practicability. In total, 47 interviews were carried out in the course of this research, 24 in England and Wales and 23 in Austria. Most of the face-to-face interviews were carried out in the participants' workplace, e.g., their own office or a common area. Another notable group of interviews was carried out in public cafes – the protection of privacy of the interviewee being kept during the interview. These different locations allowed for a contrasting interpretation of the data I gathered – some offering me more insight into their professional space and the social context they arrange themselves with every day, while some granted me personal insights such as small talk or exchanges with third persons such as waiters etc. I used the interview guide to direct the conversations to research-relevant topics – whilst always encouraging interview participants to talk about issues that came to mind – and issued probing questions when appropriate or necessary to clarify details. This allowed for a certain standardisation in the interviews in covering the same topics, but still the phrasing of the question and the resulting narratives were varied.

4.3 Data Analysis

Most interviews were recorded with the permission of the participants using my personal mobile phone[43] and the recordings were then transferred to an external hard drive. The gathered interview material was transcribed and visualised in textual form with the help of a transcription software and afterwards analysed with the qualitative assessment software MaxQDA. As the process of data analysis and data gathering overlapped, I was constantly engaging with the new as well as the old interview data and adapting or changing codes and themes that arose.

---

43 Two Austrian interviewees did not give consent to being recorded. During the interviews, notes were taken.

The gathered material was coded and later bundled into thematic fragments that cumulated from the coded data. To illustrate: An example of an emergent code is "family connection to police (father)". The codes were then aggregated into themes, such as "police officers in family/friends", some of them richer than others which brought me to develop my core themes (e.g., motivational factors in joining the police). To connect and relate these themes to each other, I referred back to my transcripts as well as the codes themselves to gain a deep understanding of the data. Visualising my data with the help of MaxQDA, I mapped the connections between my main themes.[44] This further allowed me to find illustrative quotes from the transcript to include in the presentation of my data and findings. Additionally, I used the material gathered from the participatory observation with the Austrian police to undergird my findings from the interview analysis. This led to a deeper understanding of the produced data and its reasoning.

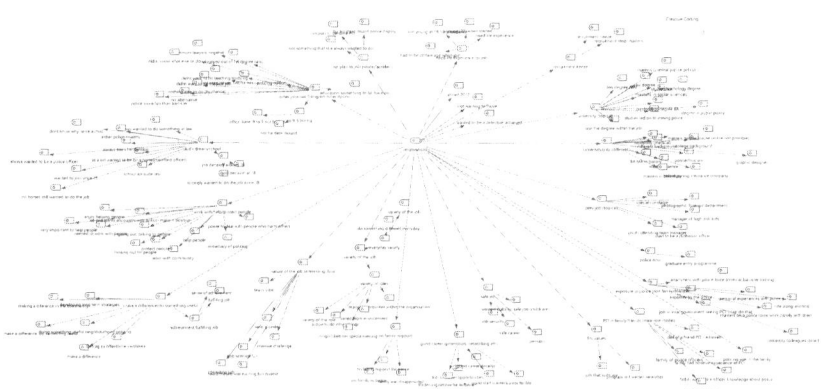

Figure 1: Creative Coding Cloud "Motivation"

4.4 Reflection on the Research Process

While positivist quantitative research tries to eliminate, reduce, and control the influence of any "outside" variables, such as the researcher(s) themselves, the postmodern qualitative paradigm is a different one (Holliday 2016). Here, the influence of the researcher(s) themselves is seen as, quite naturally, unavoidable and furthermore considered a resource of itself.

---

44 For an example of this see figure 1: Creative Coding Cloud "Motivation" (p.55).

Crucial to this approach is the reflexivity of the researcher. Each researcher therefore has to come to terms with the potential influence on the field and their role in the research process. Furthermore, the interaction with the research field can also lead to revelations about the particular culture that is being investigated. Especially in a male-dominated environment such as the police, being a female researcher can have many (undesired) effects on the research process as well as the interactions between participants and researcher (Horn 1997).

In my research process, I found it rather difficult to get in touch with and create an open setting with my interviewees in Austria. Interestingly, when mentioning this in front of some of the participants, they agreed with my perception and stated that this was due to the mistrusting nature of police officers in general. Without any remote personal contacts of my own to get in contact with officers and ask for interview permission, reaching my desired 20 interview partners (and more) would have been a lot harder, if not impossible. Contrarily, in the UK I did not rely on any personal contacts (save the ones made during interviews) to reach my interviewees. I simply wrote to singular police forces as well as related organisations such as Police Now, asking them to forward my information and request to their officers or responsible authorities. Most of them complied with my request and I got many responses from willing participants in a rather short time – the fieldwork only lasted about one month. It can be said then that, on the whole, police officers in England and Wales appeared more open to the proposed research than those in Austria.

Laying open any probability for a bias in or influence on my research findings, I further have to state that police officers in the UK more often conveyed ideas and attitudes that I, as a private person, could relate to more than those of their counterparts in Austria. Needless to say, my appearance and conduct were not influenced by my personal opinions about any matters that were discussed – I rather tried to give each interviewee room to voice their opinion which helped me in trying to reconstruct their ideas and understand what place their arguments were coming from.

Still, my contacts into the police in Austria later made it possible for me to participate in a ride along with the local police, as this is a rather rare occasion for the Austrian police. In addition to being really helpful in achieving my research goals, these observations further strengthened the collaborative aspect of my research, as I had to provide the respective authorities with feedback to my experience (Cf. Bratich 2018). The constant back and forth of information, requests, and feedback between myself as a researcher and individual officers and related authorities in the research field worked quite well with my general cyclic research process of gathering and analysing data. In this sense, the data discussed in this work can truly be seen as "the result of a sensitive set of relationships between all parties concerned" (Holliday 2016: 170).

This chapter discussed the details of the research process such as the access to the field along with a description of the sample. Furthermore, the generating of interview and observational data was discussed as well as the data analysis. A reflection on the research process as a whole completes this chapter.

In the next, very extensive, chapter, the results of the study are presented. These are divided into seven topics. Firstly, motivational factors that led interviewees to join the police are analysed and described. Secondly, the process of recruitment and application, as well as general training processes are examined. Next, aspects of daily police work are discussed, along with notions and ideal types of policing. The subsequent two subsections then deal with police internal as well as external dynamics that female police officers experience and navigate in their work. This is followed by an analysis of gender dynamics in the context of police culture, that do not necessarily derive from officers' everyday work. Finally, intersectional aspects that have to be considered when dealing with gender and police culture are given due consideration.

5. Findings

The focus of this study is on the subjective views of female police officers on their job, its milieu and implications, as well as any (perceived) (legal) measures to enhance gender equality in the workplace. These issues are discussed in the following subchapters; some of these subchapters are guided by the questions posed to interviewees, while sub-subchapters are mostly derived from themes that arose in the analysis of the interviews. Each subchapter first presents the context of the data, its implications and limitations; afterwards, differing issues that present themselves when analysing the data are discussed and finally outlined at the end. The data is divided into seven overarching topics, while bearing in mind that all issues presented are of course inextricably interlaced with each other. The following subjects are discussed.

First, the reasons interviewees give for wanting to join the police service are presented, be they of an intrinsic or extrinsic nature, by design or by accident. Following, the recruitment phase, including the application as well as subsequent training is thematised, including further training received when applying for special units or positions of ranks. Afterwards, police work in general is discussed. This includes participants' view on their daily work but also policing as a way of life, and its positive and negative implications. The subsequent two subchapters deal with the reactions and circumstances officers have to deal with specifically because of their gender. The first of these subchapters speaks about issues that arise within the police, emanating from colleagues or superiors; the second chapter thematises discerning behaviours from the public, as well as perceived gendered differences in dealing with them. The most substantial subchapter deals with some of the aforementioned problems more in-depth, widening their implications as well as introducing further issues that female officers have noted in their perception of the police service. This subchapter also includes respondents' take on equal opportunities policies and other (legal) measures in their respective countries and police forces. Additionally, the last subchapter in the findings section deals with other issues of diversity and intersectionality as introduced and discussed by the interviewees. Each subchapter's findings are summarised at their respective end as well as put together and discussed in the following chapter 6. Discussion and Conclusion.

5.1 Motivational Factors for Joining the Police

What motivates people to join the police has been the subject of studies for many decades – in fact, the research into this began at a time when marginalised groups, such as women and ethnic minorities had no, or close to no, representation in the police force (Colvin 2017). In trying to figure out what it is that attracts people to the police, officials can target their recruitment strategies in the desired direction. The first part of the study's findings reports on motivational factors in joining the police in the two countries. Here, the participants' intrinsic and extrinsic motivations are described and analysed, comparing data from Austria and England and Wales. Often, participants in the two countries gave comparable or even similar answers and statements. Some factors, however, were only mentioned in one of the two countries. This section reports on both of these occurrences and links them with existing international literature and data while keeping the comparison of the two countries as a central theme.

The responses this section predominantly refers to and uses in the analysis were given to the question "What were the main reasons for you to become a police officer/join the police?".[45]

5.1.1 Doing Something Meaningful

The reasons participants gave for wanting to join the police service are, of course, manifold, yet there is a thread that runs through all of their accounts: the want for an active, result-yielding job. Other, often previous, jobs were described as either boring or seen as pointless, such as working an office job. These positions were defined through a lot of passive elements such as sitting at a desk, working with a computer, and having the same work routine each day, while working a standard 9-to-5 shift. Although participants recognised these options as valid job opportunities, some even described them as easier and more accessible, they were constructed as mundane jobs, and the desire for acquiring a more significant role in their career outweighed these potential benefits. This is linked to a need for constant change or excitement, which the job of a police officer seems to promise.

---

45 The German wording is "Welche Gründe waren für Sie ausschlaggebend Polizistin zu werden/zur Polizei zu gehen?".

Most interviewees chose their job out of a need to make a difference and do something useful for their communities.

"Yeah, and I suppose, it sounds a bit corny but, you know, to kind of make a difference, to feel that you're doing something worthwhile." – Interview 19, England and Wales.[46]

The aspect of having a sensible and meaningful occupation, rather than doing mundane office work, was quite common among interview participants from both countries.

This is connected to two further aspects: The social aspects of the job, including helping people and communities, which was raised by participants across the countries; and the possibility of personal development and the personal gain to be had by carrying out a demanding job, which was brought up by interviewees in Austria.

The possibility of personal growth was seen in connection to the professional and personal challenge the job poses.

"That there will be a challenge every day, something you have to face, where you can grow personally; for your life and where you can certainly gain something for yourself; in experience." – Interview 4, Austria.[47]

The job itself is therefore seen as not only providing opportunities for professional development but also promising to enrichen officers' personal life. The police are therefore pre-perceived as an organisation that furthers not only professional but also personal development and advancing officers' life experience.

A factor influencing both Austrian and UK[48] participants to join the police is what I dubbed "social potential". In the same sense as participants tried to find meaning in their work, they praised the possibility of working with people in general. Here, making an impact on people's lives was seen as something positive, finding many different reasons for and outcomes of this impact. First of all, the impetus to help people was brought up quite

---

46 Quotes have for the most part been "cleaned up", i.e. cleared of extraneous sounds/fillers for better readability.

47 All Austrian interviews were carried out in German. Each extract used is translated by me.

48 Here as well as in the continuing findings chapters, "UK" will be used when referring to England and Wales specifically, as a means of simplifying statements.

often from participants in both countries.[49] Some described aiding people as something that they already did in their free time, even before joining the police. Being able to carry out this inherent feature of their personality in their work-life is, of course, seen as attractive.

> "And then one of the girls said you can get paid to do this [providing aid and assistance to a drunk acquaintance, AN][50] for a living and I was like alright, that's weird." – Interview 5, England and Wales.

In a unique way, policing fulfils the "helping people" category better than other jobs. Firstly, there's an immediacy to it. Secondly, officers have the state-officiated power to deal with people who have harmed others. Finally, the protection of vulnerable people can be seen as a core element of ideal police work. Furthermore, the rather negative connection the public is presumed to have to the very nature of police work can be turned into something positive for involved individuals.

> "[W]hen people have to have contact with the police it's never for a good thing is it, you're either a victim or you're an offender. So, no one ever wants to use a police service, I guess, cause it's never for a good reason. And I just wanted to try and make that experience as positive as it could be [...] under the circumstances it was." – Interview 11, England and Wales.

Bayley (2001) states, in a somewhat related context – namely that of including ethnically marginalised people – that one of the most crucial roles of the police is to be able to lessen distrust towards the police by members of the public and raise their level of comfort in the community. In this way, perception of not only single police officers, but the police organisation as a whole can be influenced. Similarly, for interviewees, to help people in need was connected to a certain want to improve people's experiences with the police, respectively their view of the police, while at the same time ensuring justice for vulnerable people by either protecting or supporting them. Foley et al. (2008) report the opportunity to help people as a rather gender-neutral factor over time when it comes to mo-

---

49 In Austria, participants used a specific term for someone who is prone to helping people – "Helferlein-Syndrom" (helper's syndrome) – although the term does tend to have a negative ring to it, interviewees carried the trait with a sort of loving nonchalance.

50 Notes in square brackets are used to provide additional information (marked as AN – author's note), represent redacted statements (see footnote 51), or anonymise names of persons or places.

tivational aspects for joining the police – incidentally, it is the topmost noted reason given by officers in their study. A similar report comes from Colvin (2017) in South America, while Pagon and Lobnikar (2000) find the social dimensions of the occupation to be of more importance to female police applicants than male applicants in Slovenia. However, the fact that female applicants often describe the possibility to help and support their community as a vital aspect in their motivation to join the police is widely regarded as a given by police authorities, and even features in advertisement. When targeting women (and minorities), US police stressed, among others, helping tasks as a key element of police work, while focusing on the aspect of "crime fighting" for their male target group (Jordan et al. 2009). Indeed, enforcing laws and wearing a uniform or carrying a gun – i.e., a certain power and status – is found to be of more importance to male police applicants than female in some studies (e.g., Pagon/Lobnikar 2000, Lester 1983).

Even so, respondents in Austria mentioned that there is a significant disparity between their underlying motivation to pursue justice and the actuality of the everyday job.

> "[A]nd the main reason was actually already then the ideology that I can help people and see to justice. So that's how it was in the beginning, you soon realize that it's not primarily about that. But that was the motivation. To help, yeah." – Interview 17, Austria.

The main difference however was not the absence of possibilities to help people and provide justice, but rather the black-and-white image of crime and "crimefighters". This image stems from the fact that these respondents did not have any contact with police officers themselves, but rather saw their responsibilities through various media. In this way, the job helped participants in broadening their sense of right and wrong and elevate their understanding of the job of a police officer from one who is relentlessly pursuing criminals to one who is understanding and helpful to members of the public.

5.1.2 Career Plan vs. Spontaneous Application

Many interviewees were following a lifelong dream in applying to the police service, and subsequently followed a more or less rigorous plan in their career decisions. This does not differ much in the respective countries. The police were described as a "childhood dream", even though some admitted not even knowing what the job would entail as a kid, or knowing exactly how this dream came to be.

> "I always wanted to be a police officer. From as young as I can remember I wanted to be a police officer. I don't know what the motivation was. I've no idea." – Interview 9, England and Wales.

Others have a clear sense of how this idea of their juvenile dream job came to be. This has almost always to do with the sense of security and helpfulness the police provids.

> "And for me that was really, it was the epitome of help as a child [...][51]. And that was a big selling point for this profession." – Interview 2, Austria.

The idea of the police officer's job as a childhood dream is as universal as it is diverse: Some mentioned a childly love for horses[52], playing cops and robbers, or a more sober approach in seeing that they could provide aid to people, as mentioned above.

While many reported fulfilling a (lifelong) dream in joining the police service, some state that their application and subsequent career in policing was mostly down to coincidence – some called them "accidents". While it may not have been their career of choice, respondents reported having a certain affinity towards the job, paired with a want to try out the job and see if it would fit them. Triggers for these coincidental applications were manifold, ranging from suggestions from family members to simply seeing police displays in the park. However, still a certain affinity towards different aspects of the job cannot be denied.

In Austria, some participants mentioned a late interest in the job, incidentally, joined with a certain nudge in the direction by family or friends.[53] Some even state that they had never thought about the police as a possible career option for themselves, and had different plans, whilst

---

51 Dots in square brackets are used to signify a redacted statement.
52 It is to be noted that most police forces in England and Wales do not make use of horses anymore. One counterexample is the Mounted Branch of the Metropolitan Police Service, which was founded in 1760 (prior to the establishment of the Metropolitan Police as such). In Austria, a special mounted police unit was introduced around the time of the interviews in 2018 and has since been abandoned again.
53 On the importance of family and friends as well as the exposure to police pre-joining in general see chapter 5.1.6.

sharing ideals with those respondents who had seen the job as a police officer as their aspired career.

> "I always wanted to do something social. I always wanted to work with people. But I never thought I would go to the police." – Interview 13, Austria.

Different career aspirations, however, did not turn out the right way, either because of internal (training/job not fitting) or external (financial issues) troubles. Nevertheless, all of these respondents stated that they, perchance, had made the right choice after all in joining the police service.

5.1.3 The Importance of Previous Experiences

All participants from both countries brought something to the job, whether it was their life experience, previous training and school/further education experiences or previous job experiences. A certain amount of life experience was explained to be necessary when joining the police, if one were to take it seriously. Being ready for applying to the police started, quite simply, with taking the application process seriously.

> "And I applied a few times before but never went to interviews, right; and then you get older (..)[54] And then I not only applied but also went there [to the interview, AN]." – Interview 12, Austria

Due to the age limit when applying to the police[55], some used this "spare" time to dabble in other jobs or finish their current training or school. Others felt like they needed even more time to make sure to gather experiences and be ready for police training.

> "I came to [place] University, erm, did a criminology degree, 'cause I felt I was too inexperienced at 18 years old, to join. I didn't have enough life experience." – Interview 3, England and Wales.

Some also lament the fact that they were too young at their time of entry and therefore had too little life experience to deal with issues arising in

---

54 Pauses are represented by dots in round brackets, each dot representing one second.

55 The minimum age to be able to apply to the police is 18 in both countries (College of Policing [1], recruit.college.police.uk; Einstellungsvoraussetzungen prüfen, polizeikarriere.gv.at).

police training. Of course, some also mention that they grew with the job and its respective training (see chapter 5.2.2).

As mentioned before, previous occupations, especially office jobs, were often seen as negative compared to the job as a police officer. From this negative experience, two conclusions can be drawn: First, making sure what it is you definitely do not want in your career, to then secondly, being able to positively realise the opposite aspects of these unwanted occupational qualities. Negative experiences in previous occupations could bring out the positive sides of the police as a workplace even more. Similarly, while working in police-related fields, or even as police staff, one might get a clear picture of what it is the police do, and whether that work environment would suit a person. Diverse career aspirations are also seen to be able to be fulfilled by joining the police due to its diverse career opportunities.[56] In the end, the police often seemed the most suitable option, combining positive work-life elements with the absence of any negative repellents experienced previously.

> "[W]hen previously I'd worked in courts and in prisons and I loved being out and about, so the police then seemed a natural move where I wouldn't be desk-bound and I'd still get to work in that field. So, I suppose, yeah, that was really the reason why." – Interview 6, England and Wales.
>
> "I found out [...] with the police one could also become a teacher. Because police officers also have to be trained. And there are also police magazines. Where you can write articles. And that's what I did. And that's how it all worked out somehow. These three[57] things." – Interview 7, Austria.

Still, some erred on the side of caution, in case the job did not turn out to be what they expected – most did this in the previously mentioned way of finishing a certain education or training, to have something to fall back on.

In terms of previous educational and occupational experiences, or even career aspirations, a wide variety of topics and interests is noticeable. What is to be noted is that in England and Wales, police aspirants had often already finished their university degrees, some even to a master's level, at the point of application. Sometimes these degrees were seen as merely providing an option to pass time and gain life experience before applying

---

56   On the topic of career diversity as a pull-factor see chapter 5.1.5.
57   Her three career aspirations were teacher, journalist, and police officer.

to the police, more so if respondents were not sure of their job choice beforehand. Organisational issues were also mentioned in relation to interviewees taking on alternative jobs or undergoing further education.[58] Other times these degrees fit well with the respondents' interest in a law-related, people-centred field, and were found to be at least of some use in the application and training process.

> "My master's was research-based, so it was social sciences by research but because it was funded I did it on decision making in [area] police. So, it led on quite naturally, 'cause I got to work quite closely with the officers." – Interview 3, England and Wales.

Interviewees completing non-topical university education were most likely to join the police via their quite novel Police Now programme. For this graduate entry programme, the field of study is not relevant, but rather the academic success achieved in the respective field of research.

On the contrary, in Austria respondents often mentioned not being able to study, be it due to a lack of funding or lack of confidence in personal abilities. Some even started their studies but had to discontinue due to various similar reasons. On rare occasions, interviewees did finish university degrees after joining the police, often on topical subjects. This class disparity is discussed in police research as a clash of idealism: viewing policing as an artisanal trade in contrast to employing highly qualified and trained officers (Cf. Neyroud 2013). Currently, in England and Wales, police recruits are highly qualified, ranging from various social backgrounds – historically, this has not always been the case.[59] Unfortunately, no comparable statistics could be obtained for Austria.

Regarding previous occupational experiences, respondents from Austria were most likely to work in a field that would later be taken over as a police responsibility – for example customs official.[60] Interviewees from England and Wales, on the other hand, worked in different areas of the criminal justice system, from working as police staff to being a probation

---

58 On the issue of recruitment freeze on application processes see chapter 5.2.1.

59 Despite the fact that most of the UK police in the 19th century were drawn from the working class, a generous minority were drawn from the lower middle class, and this pattern turned out to be progressively widened in the period from the late 19th century to the mid 20th century (Cf. Weinberger 1995).

60 The customs guard was abolished based on a political decision by the Federal Government in 2003. Since July 1[st,] 2005 there have been no customs guards. This happened at the same time the Federal Gendarmerie, Federal Security Guard, and Criminal Investigation Corps merged to form one Federal Police.

officer. Both groups had the opportunity to not only see the work of a police officer through different lenses, but also explore the realm of law-related occupational fields before settling on their current career.

5.1.4 Nature of the Job

While finding out what type of job personally fits them, participants described the nature of the job as a police officer as fitting in many ways. The everyday work life of a police officer was and is still seen as varied and providing many opportunities for excitement and interesting activities. The need for a diverse and constantly changing workplace was expressed in the positively connoted phrase that "no two days are the same". This is provided for by the fact that one does not simply carry out the same task for a whole work shift, as well as the fact that even in these varying tasks there is an element of unexpectedness.

> "[S]o, really, the main aspect was basically that I wanted to have a job that was varied and exciting, that was really the main point, because I used to sit in an office where you do the same job every day and, at some point, it was just too boring for me to be honest, I wanted a little variety, to experience something, really" – Interview 6, Austria.

In this regard, participants viewed a job with the police as the anti-thesis to the aforementioned and very negatively received "desk-job". The fact that one could not always plan ahead, the diversity of the job, and the difference in experiences it promised was of course seen as a main attracting feature for participants in both countries, but more so for interviewees in Austria. This supports Ermer's (1978) reports about diversity of job assignments being a large factor in applicants' motivations to join the US police service.[61] In Europe, namely Slovenia, the variety of the job as a police officer was also seen as very influential on their decision by female police officers (Pagon/Lobnikar 2000).

Next to excitement, the job also seemed to hold a possibility for personal development, a certain opportunity to grow with the job. In this respect, the job as a police officer was also seen as a personal and professional challenge.

---

61 One should, however, note the limited generalisability of the data.

"That every day there will be a challenge, something you have to face, where you can grow personally. For your life and where you can certainly gain something for yourself. In experience." – Interview 4, Austria.

"[A]nd I used to listen to their [group of police officers, AN] stories, and it was exciting, and it was fun, and no two days were the same. [A] massive challenge" – Interview 17, England and Wales.

In this respect, the job as a police officer differed from other job opportunities participants had, in that it offered not only an element of excitement, but also provided a potential for personal growth and development. In this respect, the job was seen as a challenge that one could take up and needed to master – not only in the application process, but every single consecutive day.

A further aspect that was mentioned by participants in both countries, is one that commonly might not immediately be associated with police work: fun. This has less to do with the topical aspects police work deals with, but rather the nature of police work itself. To interviewees, the job seemed promising and interesting, while in particular the challenges and variety associated with it – the everyday work life – were seen as fun. Of course, personal interest in the themes of the job itself was seen as a contributing factor.

Furthermore, interviewees in Austria sometimes mentioned their personal affinity for sports, and how that fit into their perception of a career in policing. Sport was not merely seen as a hurdle one has to overcome during application or regular (yearly) check-ups, but rather a relevant factor in a police officer's daily life, as well as providing direction for a possible career development.

A facet of the appeal of the police that mostly participants in Austria mentioned, is the feeling of solidarity and team spirit within the organisation. The social cohesion police show externally, as well as the feeling of solidarity within your own police station was regarded as very positive – also in contrast to the private sector.

"Then the core idea, too. Of the police, that really complied with me, and the [internal] cohesion, which is always represented to the outside, and I have always really experienced that through the years." – Interview 4, Austria.

This motivational aspect for some was validated through their experiences throughout their career. Some compared the police, and their present police station respectively, to a sort of family, due to the social and emotional closeness of team colleagues. This further included the inter-reliability of police members, as one could always count on one's colleagues for help or support in any sense.

In that respect, the job of a police officer also corresponded with the personal values of participants in both countries. Crank (1998: 81), in the context of US policing, refers to morality as being a key factor in the occupational culture – the recruits' personal worldview aligns with that of the police culture. Be it a sense of justice, team spirit, a readiness to help, or a drive to make a difference, the core values of the police were favourably perceived and seen to match personal ideals of interviewees in both countries.

> "From the way the program [Police Now, AN] was structured and from the values and what they wanted to achieve with it, I say it was very well compatible with what I actually wanted." – Interview 2, England and Wales.

Consequently, as one is able to combine active work (being outdoor, helping people) that appears as interesting and worthwhile, with a positive work environment and supportive colleagues, the very nature of the job as a police officer was deemed appealing by participants.

5.1.5 Career Opportunities

A different, but connected, aspect of how police work that was perceived pre-joining, is the quality and diversity of possible career paths within the police itself. Interviewees praised the variety of roles within the police service, a diversity that was often described as unique to the police.

> "Probably career opportunities, in that you are able to work for one organisation but do a lot of different roles within that organisation, so, variety of the job, without having to have a kind of huge upheaval of going to work for another organisation." – Interview 19, England and Wales.

Within the police, not only promotion and advancement can lead to a novel role, but also lateral movement is possible and seen as beneficial for police officers. In this sense, some stated that almost anyone can find themselves something fitting and worthwhile to do within the organisation. Some even had a preconceived idea of which specialisation they were aiming for when joining, whilst others developed their interests over time, or even found a constant change of roles as most fitting. The fact that Foley et al. (2008) note that the possibility of advancement as a reason for joining is more prevalent among female police officers, affirms the present data.

Additionally, the police service was seen to provide good career opportunities in three ways. First of all, the career opportunities themselves were seen as good. This includes the quantity and quality of career opportunities, as well as the possibility for advancement and building networks. This is connected to the possibility to not only move through the ranks but also perform different functions within the police, as mentioned above.

Secondly, the police seemed to provide a secure and safe job possibility. One was sure to stay in the job for a long time and remain with one organisation for a whole work life, again, as opposed to most jobs in the private sector.

> "And I suppose incorporated into that is job security. In that, I joined the job 15 years ago, and I think it was a more secure job then than it is now, because I've seen so many changes and I think when I joined the police it was definitely viewed as a career for life." – Interview 19, England and Wales.
>
> "[A]nd for me it was important to have a permanent job, that is, a job where I know I won't end up on the street tomorrow or the company will close down. I'll say, you'll always need a police officer, right." – Interview 8, Austria.

In that way, joining the police was seen as a safe career choice compared to other opportunities. There is evidence to suggest that job security as a reason for choosing a career in policing has gained in importance over the last decades, gaining the status as one of the top five reasons given by current police officers on their career choice (Foley et al. 2008). Incidentally, job security is widely regarded as a gender-neutral attractive feature of police work (Colvin 2017, Foley et al. 2008, Ridgeway et al. 2008).

The last aspect related to the quality of a career within the police was the issue of wages and wage security. Interestingly, the possibility to earn as much money as their male counterparts was a contributing factor in Austrian participants' decision to join the police. This was, again, seen as a contrast to employment in the private sector, where gender wage gaps are much more common. Similar findings are reported for the US by Ermer (1978), who states that police hiring methods should focus on this aspect in an attempt to draw more women to the job. In line with this, Jordan et al. report that, in the US, an increase in starting pay of a police officer did result in more female applicants – however, not in more hires of women (Jordan et al. 2009: 338). More commonly though, the issue of wage security was raised by interviewees. For them, this was strongly connected to their private needs and feeling of stability a regular income can provide.

> "I was a new mum. [..] And I needed a regular income, to support me and my child, my ex-partner, [...] he was self-employed, so he's, his salary was up and down, so it was stability, really." – Interview 14, England and Wales.

For all interviewees who raised this issue, it was not merely a fact of personal desire for a good and stable income, but rather a matter of financing their family's[62] lifestyle and ensuring their job's dependability. Indeed, as working mothers often fail to develop a stable job situation (Cf. Huang/Sverke 2007), the possibility of a secure and well-paid job that one can easily re-join after maternity leave is an important aspect to female applicants.

5.1.6 Exposure to Police

Participants in both countries sometimes mentioned the fact that they had had friends or family in the police as a contributing factor to their application. Usually, it was the father, father of a good friend, or another male relative that interviewees mentioned as a sort of role model, or at least source of information on the job. This male contact and connection to the police was experienced as very positive, which often fuelled participants' young interest in the career. Rarely, police officers in the UK would mention female family members (sisters) being connected to the police service – if so, these, in contrast to male "role models", came from the same generation as the interviewees. Sometimes, there was a strong personal admiration for these people, that may have projected onto their job and create a sort of ideal type of the police officer – an aspiration interviewees then wanted to pursue. Yet, there were also those who stated that the fact that they had family connections to the police did not have that much of an influence on their decision, and that it rather provided them with knowledge about the daily job of a police officer and the experiences the career entails – they found the familiarity of the job to be appealing.

---

62 Including relationships with or without (young) children.

"[O]ne of my good friends growing up, her dad was a police officer
and I always looked up to him and it was always a vocation I kind of
admired." – Interview 3, England and Wales.

"And I have to say, my father is a police officer, too. But it didn't
primarily influence me in that I say that's why I have to take up the
profession, but of course I got to know what it means to be a police
officer or what's going on there, what can happen there." – Interview
4, Austria.

In this way, familiarity with the police service cannot simply be seen as
a push-factor per se, but rather an accompanying positively connotated
closeness to the police (Cf. Foley et al. 2008).

A family connection was, of course, not the only exposure to the police
participants had pre-joining. Less often, primarily with interviewees in the
UK, friends or acquaintances, such as colleagues from university, played
their part in respondents' interest in the police.

Furthermore, as mentioned above, some had experiences with the police
themselves, primarily in working for them as staff, in similar institutions,
volunteering, or even simply going on a ride along with their local police
station. These circumstances were more prevalent with interviewees in
the UK, as participants educational or career path led them to an entan-
glement with the police service. Getting to know the job of a police
officer from an outside view either created a new interest in the career or
endorsed interviewees pre-conceived ideal of the job.

"[I]nitially I wanted to go to local government [...] I applied for a
job, a civilian role, within the police, in the fixed penalty office. [A]nd
I was there for a good three or four years and was watching police
officers coming and go and I thought, I can do that, you know, I'd like
that job." – Interview 18, England and Wales.

"And she was working in [police station], so she organised what we
call a ride along, so I went in the back of a police car for a day,
which at the time I thought was terribly exciting, I look back nothing
happened, it was the quietest day in [police station] and through the
world ever. [A]nd that was it, I was just like, yeah, I wanna do this." –
Interview 5, England and Wales.

Having friends or family in the police is not seen as a highly influencing
factor in related studies (Foley et al. 2008, Pagon/Lobnikar 2000). It can,
however, contribute to people's knowledge about policing and the everyday work it entails. In that way, it can serve as a way to gain insight
into the job via others, and in this way work out the adequacy of the

occupation for oneself. Of course, pre-existing ideas about the police both as a social component and as an employer are highly influenced by the personal familiarity towards the organisation as well.

That an early connection to or contact with police can, indeed, have quite a drastic impact can be seen when comparing two examples interviewees give: one of a police officer in England and Wales, who talks about how her experience with the local police in Austria has resulted in a personal negative bias and disfavour of the Austrian police, the other, quite contrarily, talking about how her early personal experiences with the Austrian police has led her to regard the police highly and created a positive association with the organisation as a whole.

> "[T]hey [the police, AN] were more or less omnipresent for me, […] unfortunately they were also at our home again and again. And for me that was really, that was the epitome of help, as a child virtually, really, I really called them so that they could just end any disputes in the family. And that was a big plus for this profession." – Interview 2, Austria.

> "Well, I mean I experienced it on my own skin, so to speak, so my dad is from Nigeria. And just in the small town in [state], he was one of three maybe, and they knew exactly who he is, and if he forgot his passport at home then he was imprisoned […] every time although they knew exactly who he is. Every time they see him, they push stupid reports, so really this harassment (..) that's where I think, no, that's not possible. So much for the question whether I could ever join the police service in Austria: no. I can't imagine it, I just can't imagine it at all." – Interview 2, England and Wales.

Here, the distinction is clear, and the intersectionality of the quality of experiences regarding the police is broken down: Both interviewees had regular, more or less indirect – through parents – contact with the police as a child. A crucial factor in their perceived experience, however, is not only their gender, but also their ethnic background – this is where their otherwise concurrent accounts differ. While one, as a white person, remained "unmarked" (Frankenberg 1995: 1) and was able to encounter the police service as an aiding institution one can rely on in emergencies, the other, as a black person, witnessed quite a different sort of police behaviour – that of racial discrimination.[63] In both instances, these early

---

63 On issues of police racial discrimination and its implementations for recruiting and serving BAME groups see chapter 4.7.

interactions and associations had a self-reported massive impact on their decision for or against joining the police in Austria. Conversely, as the latter interviewee did not associate any negative experiences with police in England and Wales and reported noticing a different approach in regard to issues of race and ethnicity, she was not opposed to the country's police service. This subjective view might contrast the general academic and public opinion of police in the UK – one might only think about the evaluation of police incident response as "institutionally racist" in the MacPherson report (MacPherson 1999). However, it might also show that the readiness of an institution to talk about and work through such issues, however (un)successful these attempts might be[64], paints a different picture than that of an institution which readily denies their issues, or keeps them under wraps (Second European Union Minorities and Discrimination Survey 2018, fra.europa.eu).

Of course, some mentioned no (family) connection to the police at all, and a few, mostly UK, interviewees further mentioned the fact that they received little or no family support when deciding to join the police. Some talked about the fact that their family was not sure what to expect of their role as a police officer, not least because of their gender. A lot of preconceived ideas of the police as a male-dominated field, where a female officer would not feel at home, as well as knowledge gaps (from older generations) on whether or not they would carry out the same duties as a male police officer were substantiating these concerns.

The differing reactions and support from family or friends did little to prevent interviewees from joining, while positive reinforcement had an important role in female police officers' career decision. One interviewee described observing these very mixed reactions, based largely upon societal standards, gender roles, as well as an underlying generation issue, within her own family.

> "I told it to my family, [...] my mom was a bit worried, my grandpa was super enthusiastic, he was totally proud, he was really happy, and my grandma said 'Well good I'm happy for you' [...] my grandparents had a discussion about whether or not I would wear a uniform and my grandpa was like, 'Of course she's going to [...]', and my grandma was like, 'No why should she [...]', and then I said to [her], 'Why shouldn't

---

64 Circumstances are adamant to change (Police chiefs admit failures on diversity 21 years after pledge, theguardian.com).

I wear a uniform?' - 'Well, you'll just be sitting in an office' and I was like [stressed] No." – Interview 2, England and Wales.[65]

Expectations and the image of the police and policing in the respective countries was, interestingly, less a factor in participants decision to join the police, but rather something they had to deal with after their career choice had been set.

However, in Austria, interviewees particularly mentioned the fact that policing was seen as a male domain as a contributing factor to their interest in joining the police. That this was not mentioned by participants in the UK could of course be due to the fact that some of the Austrian interviewees were indeed among the first women to become fully-fledged police officers in Austria, whilst the pioneering role for female officers in England and Wales could have been a potential issue about two decades earlier. Some even stated that they did not know about the possibility of joining the police as a female applicant for a long time, a fact that often media brought to their attention. Yet, the thrill of joining the police at a time when such a thing as a female officer was rarely or not at all heard of, was something early applicants described as quite unique and exciting.

> "And, I was one of the first women, that is, when I was in the last [stage of] HAK [commercial high school, AN], in the state in which I lived at that time [...] the first woman joined the Gendarmerie, of course that entailed a huge media interest, and from that time on it was clear to me, I also want [to join the] police. That was simply the reason, there was nothing more than that, I just thought it was insanely exciting [to see] what was going to happen with women in the police force." – Interview 3, Austria.

Being part of this cultural and organisational "movement" then became quite a relevant factor not only in interviewees interest in the police pre-joining, but also in their further career development and the vocational focus and mindset they cultivated (Cf. chapter 4.6.3.4).

---

65 What is to be noted about this interviewee, and therefore the particular dynamic she describes, is that her family lives in Austria, while she has lived in the UK for some years, and also joined the police service there.

5.1.7 Interim Findings

There were many overlapping themes in Austrian and UK female applicants' reasoning behind wanting to take up the occupation of police officer. Predominantly, the desire to help people, contribute to the community – the social aspects of the job – were mentioned by participants across almost all interviews. This comes as no surprise, as literature is divided on just how much gender influences this particular motivational factor, yet it is generally agreed that the factor in question plays one of the most important roles for police applicants across the globe (Colvin 2017, Pagon/Lobnikar 2000).

Two interesting issues that were seldom raised by previous literature is the role that previous work or educational experiences play in officers' decision to join the police, as well as the divergence between a planned and a spontaneous or "accidental" application. The difference between those participants who "had always known" that they wanted to join the police and those who, through varied triggers, made their decision later in life, was not represented in a different attitude towards the job. Connected to this is the significance of former educational and/or vocational experiences that applicants had. While organisational issues within the police[66] made an interim occupation or education necessary for some, others stated that they found further training or vocational experience themselves as necessary prerequisites for joining the police. A difference between the two countries could be seen with regards to the quality of the received qualifications pre-joining. In England and Wales, a study has found that police entrants are usually quite qualified, a third having academic experience of graduate level or above, while another third are educated to A level (Neyroud 2013). There are no similar numbers for Austria available, but respondents do not mention receiving a university degree before joining the police, in contrast to participants in England and Wales, who are quite often educated to graduate level or even master's degrees. This difference in educational level pre-joining is quite striking, considering that there currently are no educational limits to be met when joining the police in both countries. As previous research suggests, there can be no definitive conclusion in the effects of higher education on police recruits, it is of yet unsure what the outcome of this disparity might be (Brown 2018). Interestingly, Jordan et al. (2009: 335) mention that higher education requirements can deter women from applying to a certain job.

---

66 On the topic of recruitment freeze see chapter 4.2.1.

Nonetheless, interviewees in England and Wales, most of all recent joiners, were highly skilled (i.e., graduate level or above), while participants in Austria most commonly reported being educated to A level[67], with some subsequently studying for a degree in relation to their occupation.[68]

Another similarity to be found in interviewee's accounts is the appreciation of the variety of job opportunities, as well as everyday diversity in the job routine in the police. First of all, interviewees in both countries appreciated the fact that every workday is possibly different to the last, creating a work environment that is rich in variety. This diversity creates an atmosphere that makes the job seem fun and exciting. According to Behr, there are two specific ways of breaking through everyday routines found in police culture: 1. Something "big" can happen at any time and 2. When something really big happens, you're usually overwhelmed (Behr 2017: 542). Leaving aside the latter factor[69], this cornerstone of police work seems to be very positively received among potential police recruits, as well as it is found a positive aspect of their daily work (See chapter 5.3.1). Additionally, some respondents in Austria mentioned the importance of sportiness, and, more often, a feeling of team solidarity as further aspects that drew them to the job. While research has shown the importance of team spirit and companionship with co-workers to lessen in importance over the decades (Foley et al. 2008), there still remain some remnants of it within female applicants with the Austrian police. Whether or not this speaks to a certain lack of development in the motives and themes the police represent and produce in Austria can of course not be stated, due to the small size of the sample. Furthermore, this aspect of police work, despite the recent drop, remains one of fairly high importance for police aspirants. The variety in career opportunities combined with the safety of the job, however, was something that participants in both countries could agree on – a fact that is also supported by international literature (Colvin 2017, Foley et al. 2008, Ridgeway et al. 2008).

Previous experiences and exposure to police at an early age, often associated with a (male) role model in policing, was mentioned by some interviewees from both countries. Even though it did not come up in every

---

67 The school leaving examination is called "Matura" in Austria, and, similar to A levels, establishes eligibility for university admission.

68 It has to be noted here that the highest rank of "Offizier" in the Austrian police is connected to a Bachelor's degree, "Polizeiliche Führung" ("police leadership"), which candidates have to complete since 2006.

69 This issue is discussed further in chapter 5.3.3.

interview, those respondents who did mention an influence from previous contact with the police often found it to be a profound one, with some mentioning it as the main factor in their approval (or rejection) of the respective police force. Although these issues do not play a highly significant role in international research on police officers' motivation to join the service (Foley et al. 2008, Pagon/Lobnikar 2000), their influence on a case-by-case basis should not be underestimated – previous contact with police can be a make-or-break factor. Family support and pre-conceived ideas about and images of the police in the respective countries also play a part in interviewees' decision-making process. Interestingly, negative images of policing and a lack of family support did little to deter people from joining, as most stated valuing the importance of personal experiences (almost like a trial-and-error situation) over external opinions. Furthermore, police officers in Austria sometimes even described the fact that the police are seen as a male-dominated field as an attractive asset to the job. While some studies report that the low numbers in female police applicants is associated with the lack of recruitment specifically geared towards women (Cordner/Cordner 2011), respondents in Austria saw the absence of female officers as an incentive for the job. Associated with this is a sense of excitement and the prospect of a challenge, as some of my interviewees were indeed among the first women to become fully-fledged police officers in Austria. While some may argue that because policing is seen as a male job, its reputation and status in society is generally higher than that of "female jobs" (Teubner 2010), which in turn makes it attractive to applicants of all genders, many respondents discounted this notion[70] by stating that in fact the reputation of the job had fallen over the past years and decades.

Drawing on this study alone, one can hardly discuss discrepancies in motivational aspects with regard to officer gender, however, previous research might provide an interesting base of analysis. While some studies found motivations for entering police work were consistent regardless of officer gender (or race) (Raganella/White 2004), others found gendered differences in the weighting of important aspects attracting respondents to police work. Regarding gender relations, three issues are worth mentioning: It is notable that almost all policing role models mentioned in the interviews (friends or family) were male. This is paralleled by the perceived masculinity of the job being a strengthening factor in female officers' deci-

---

70 Without the interviewer explicitly mentioning the possible reputation of police work, the issue came up of its own accord, sometimes related to interactions with and perception of the public.

sion to join the police. Finally, job security and equal pay are relevant factors especially in women's career decisions[71], rendering the police service a suitable work environment. In this way, the particular environment of the police as a male-dominated field serves as an incentive, while at the same time promising equal treatment and fair working conditions regardless of gender.

5.2 Recruitment, Application and (Further) Training

Police training and recruitment plays a crucial part in an officer's career – it is often in training experiences that applicants find their passion for the job, and it is recruitment issues that regulate who is able to apply to the police in the first place. It is also possible that police training perpetuates certain ideals of policing which are inherently linked to portrayals of masculinity (Prokos/Padavic 2002). Furthermore, the nature of the police allows for a continuous training experience, insofar as lateral career development as well as promotion is possible and carried out by most respondents.

Distinctive issues, such as the Police Now graduate entry scheme in England and Wales, and the recruitment and training for the Austrian special unit Cobra, are also discussed. The qualitative evidence featured in this section was predominantly generated by the prompt "How did you come to pursue this path? OR What did the training/application process look like?".[72]

5.2.1 Recruitment and Application

The recruitment of police officers in both Austria and England and Wales is tightly connected to political budget and resource decisions. Therefore, it is not surprising that interviewees have different experiences to relate concerning their application and enrolment in the police. In both coun-

---

71 Many women do still work in precarious working conditions (see e.g., Notz 2010). Women's employment stability is considered relatively low, not least because of unemployment due to care work (Frederiksen 2008).
72 German wording: "Wie kam es dazu, dass sie diesen Weg eingeschlagen haben? BZW Wie sah ihr Ausbildungsweg aus?".

tries, some applicants had to wait long time periods after their application and before getting enrolled in a police training course.

> "So, in 1992 there was a freeze on police recruitment, cause financially the country was, pretty much where it is now, in recession, relative difficult in terms of finances of policing. So, they said, yes, you passed, yes, we will accept you as a police officer, but unfortunately, you're gonna have to wait. So, then I had like 18 months of waiting to become, to be employed [...]." – Interview 9, England and Wales.

This intermission between was handled in different ways by the interviewees. Some were using the time to work (full-time) at a different job and continue earning money and job experience, while others opted to enrol in a (funded) master's programme at university, some just for something to do, others on a topical note. It is to be noted that the second option was chosen exclusively by interviewees from the UK. Others reported that the transition from application to actual training was quite swift. The standard time it took from application to the start of the training was measured to on average be about a few months, and to be anywhere between 6 weeks and 18 months.

The application itself is fairly similar in the two countries and also remained somewhat consistent over the decades. In both countries applicants first fill out an application form, some with letters of motivation. This process nowadays takes place online. After a successful first application there are personal interviews, written tests, psychological testing, medical and fitness tests, and various assessments based on the application programme and time of appliance. These tests (mostly) take place over the course of two assessment days, sometimes carried out in a special assessment centre. It is to be noted that, for Austria, the fitness test was not always included in the application process, and in both countries the respective limits are naturally changing over the course of time, so the individual limits that had to be met differed slightly for most of my interviewees. The psychological testing also varied in its form and was either carried out via a one-on-one interview with a psychologist, a group interview, or a computer test. Some criticised the psychological testing as being very see-through, while its relevance was questioned as well.

> "[...] and this psychological test, which is...really weird, I think it's like 200 computer questions like "do you feel persecuted" and stuff like that [...] I still don't understand the test. What that has to do with the "right" psychology, [laughs] but apparently it worked" – Interview 5, Austria.

The personal and/or group interviews were given more leeway, as their relevance was plain to see for all interviewees. These mostly included asking about personal motivations, but also determining how applicants behave in stressful situations, either by one-on-one interviews or in a group discussion.

> "[You were asked] how you can imagine mastering certain situations in your job, with case examples like, I don't know, the group inspector makes a bump in the car and you are sitting next to him as an inspector and don't really know how to handle it. Whether you then stand by your colleague or whether you report it [...] stories like that." – Interview 11, Austria.

The application topic that was most discussed, however, was that of the fitness test. As mentioned earlier, some interviewees did not even have to fulfil certain fitness criteria when applying and were simply assessed by a medical doctor on their physical measurements such as weight requirements (which are still in force). Additionally, pregnant applicants were (and still are) rejected, due to the fact that pregnancies exclude applicants from taking part in an ergometry, which is a prerequisite for a police application.[73] Lately, applicants have to complete a fitness test with differing limits as well as different types of exercise such as running or swimming, and different areas such as strength and coordination. It was further noted that, in all cases in Austria and few in the UK, the fitness test limits were different for male and female applicants. In Austria, the limits are lower for female applicants than for male applicants: for example, to complete a certain run ("Achterlauf") the time limit given to male applicants is 77 seconds, while for female applicants the limit is 88 seconds (Polizei – Ablauf des Auswahlverfahrens, polizeikarriere.gv.at). In England and Wales, there currently are no gendered differences in the set limits for the application fitness tests. However, some interviewees applied to the police at times when there was still a gendered difference – albeit a slightly different one: female applicants (indirectly) had to fulfil higher standards than male ones.

> "[...] when I first joined (.) the fitness test was different for women than it was for men. And I could never get my head around why; why have I gotta do 15 press ups and he's only gonna do 6. [I]t's all

---

73 The medical reasoning for this being additional strain on both the foetus and the pregnant person.

about physical strength, but we are built differently to men, so; but that has changed now. [I: so it was a lower threshold then for female] no, higher. Higher threshold. We had this, it's like a bar, and you had to do, like, push ups on the bar, (.) your weight and your height would determine how many you'd have to do. [...] that was back in 2000, and [...] it's the same now, across the board, so it has changed." – Interview 18, England and Wales.

Female applicants did not have to fulfil higher limits than male applicants per se, but the set limits were rather defined by a person's physical measurements. In contrast to Austria's direct form of gendered differential treatment, this approach takes seemingly objective measurements to determine its varied limits. It has to be noted that all of these named approaches, differential treatment on the basis of gender/physicality as well as equal treatment, have received negative comments by the interviewees.[74] All but one approach, namely the one where female applicants, due to their physicality, had to reach higher thresholds, received a mixed overall reception. Having lower fitness standards for female applicants was mostly received positive, while some mentioned that the limits are unjustly asking too little of women, compared to male limits.[75] Equal limits for applicants regardless of gender were, however, critiqued more – mostly due to the fact that police officers do have to retake their fitness tests periodically.[76] A yearly compulsory fitness test was introduced in 2014 in the UK, and 2015 in Austria (Fitness Standards, college.police.uk). It is to be noted, though, that in Austria regular fitness checks are only carried out for officers who joined the service in or after the year 2013, while in England and Wales these tests are carried out for all officers regardless of their date of joining ("Polizisten müssen zum Fitness-Check", wien.orf.at). Keeping a certain level of fitness can, of course, be a problem for anyone regardless of gender, but creates a particular obstacle for those officers who have recently given birth or are of a certain age. Internal screenings also show that female officers struggle more with the regular fitness test that features the same standards as the application test than their male colleagues ("Police fitness tests failed 1,863 times in 12 months", bbc.co.uk).

---

74 I only briefly mention the problems that arose in discussion here, for a more in-depth analysis of the issue of gender and sports/strength see chapter 5.4.2.
75 Again, further discussion of this issue proceeds in chapter 5.4.2, where relevant quotes are provided.
76 The intervals and also limits differ due to the officer's respective role and rank.

5.2.2 Training

The content and length of police training of course differs in both countries according to interviewee's date of application, and, in England and
Wales, according to police force. I focus on the standard training received
by most police applicants.[77] The training consists of a mix of theory
and practice in both countries – there are variations on the length and
quantity of each training "unit", as well as the order in the theory and
practice rota. In both Austria and England and Wales, the time it takes
to finish training and probation as a fully-fledged officer is two years.
Theoretical knowledge is delivered in residential training centres or police
training colleges. This includes classroom-based learning such as law-based
training, but also mock scenarios and skill exercises such as officer-safety
training. Practical training is delivered at police stations – these can be
pre-selected by trainees or assigned due to demand and availability. After a
certain amount of time, trainees are allowed to make arrests and perform
other official acts, while still being supervised. In England and Wales, this
is called probation period, where trainees have to perform certain tasks in
order to fulfil all requirements needed to be signed off as a fully-fledged
officer. Trainees are assigned a so-called tutor constable, which was widely
received positively by the interviewees. These tutor constables are then
responsible for signing off trainees to work independently until the end
of their probation period. In Austria, there is no assigned tutor constable
per se, but rather the head of the individual police station is responsible
for trainees during their training period. Many interviewees describe their
training period as a make-or-break point during which not only the feasibility of the job for oneself is tested, but also first acquaintances in the
workspace are made and personal bonds established. Often, after being
signed off as a police officer, respondents found themselves applying for a
permanent position at the police stations they were trained at. Almost all
interviewees stated that they got placed in their desired area or borough
after completing their training. These experiences were fairly similar across
the two countries and the varying application dates.

A part of the training that is only found in Austria, naturally, is the
handling of firearms. As the standard police officer in Austria is armed,
trainees need to learn how to correctly operate handguns. Here, gendered
differences can play a role, in that as a male trainee, it is possible to

---

77 Distinctive issues such as the Police Now programme or special units are discussed in chapter 5.2.4.

have already undergone firearms training during one's respective military service.[78]

> "Yes, partly I noticed, during shooting, you know, of course a lot of people were in the army, and with us (.) they just took extra time or explained it to us again because we just never did that before, but not like 'you're stupid', but just really nice [...] also with colleagues who had done civilian service [instead of military service]." – Interview 9, Austria.

In this way, female applicants and those male applicants who did not choose to fulfil their compulsory service in the military have equal prerequisites for firearms training.[79] This was not described as being a negative experience per se, yet it still creates a small divide between groups of trainees – associated with the disposability of a certain expertise.

Some interviewees emphasised the fact that there were no discrepancies between male and female applicants in training. This was seen as a highly positive point in the received training for respondents in Austria, as most of them value equality and equal treatment – not being treated differently than their male colleagues – greatly.

> "[A]lso during training the three years I was with nine men in the class, I have been just as much a member as all the others, we were with the Federal Army some weeks, and with the Cobra we also had some training, and I was with them and in it just the same and have done everything just like the men – that was also a concern for me, I also never wanted to be treated differently, I do not think that is right." – Interview 13, Austria.

The importance of not being treated differently – in any regard – as a female police officer than a male officer came through in most of the interviews conducted in Austria.[80] Many regarded this commonality as

---

78 In Austria, compulsory military service exists for male Austrian citizens. Civilian service is a substitute for military service.

79 In Austria, upon submission of a valid declaration of civilian service, the possession of firearms requiring a permit and the carrying of firearms is prohibited for a period of 15 years (§ 5 Abs 5 ZDG). Through an amendment to the ZDG in 2010, people who have undergone community service could revoke their statement renouncing firearms and where thus allowed to join the police service.

80 There are, of course, some issues with this standpoint that make certain tasks and ways of action, e.g., supporting female police officers by enforcing quota rules, difficult to justify and be accepted by those affected.

a condition that is not to be tempered with and being more than just of symbolic value. By going through the same experiences as their male colleagues, many feel validated and more deserving of their status within the police organisation.

Whilst UK interviewees seldomly discussed the value of their training for their respective work life, officers in Austria often debated the merit and usefulness of their received training. Interviewees from England and Wales deemed the training process as a whole to be quite formidable and fitting. Furthermore, the possibility for personal development was mentioned. This coincided with the probationary period, where aspirants have to complete a personal development profile, evidencing their experiences and growth in the job. The learning-by-doing approach might prove challenging at the start, but most thought it beneficial for their personal approach to the job.

> "So, you're attached to a tutor constable, [...] and that person will be intensely attached to you for ten weeks. So, you'll never be alone as a bobby, and then you'd learn the know-hows, the practical know-hows, so essentially you be, I guess shadowing them initially and then you would gradually take over jobs and they would observe you and make sure you got the skills." – Interview 3, England and Wales.

This approach is praised as providing an environment in which participants felt they acquired a range of different skills in a timely manner. Although the training is described as being 'easier' than doing 'actual' police work, it is still seen as a challenge that applicants have to overcome in order to start their career in the police service. The relevance of practically applicable police training, both in and outside of the classroom, was highlighted by many interviewees.

Similarly, in Austria, some respondents praised their practical training and respective police station they completed their education at. Again, it was of great importance to the trainees to learn how to deal with as many different situations as possible, to be able to undergird their skills and know-how as a police officer. Although there is no detailed formal requirement to undergo these diverse situational difficulties, many were able to draw on a range of varied experiences in their training periods and, apart from raising people's interest and enthusiasm for the job, found these circumstances to be helpful in their career development.

> "But the practical phase was very interesting, [...] I think it's always good to be thrown in at the deep end and, I think the first few months there, what you actually learn and get to know there is very

formative. For me it was simply normal what was going on there, it was a department where there was really a lot going on, from small things to robbery, thank God everything was there. [...] I think it is very important for a young person to get to know the whole range of topics, [...] and then you are not so overwhelmed in later life or professional life, it is quite good if you have already seen and experienced everything somewhere." – Interview 2, Austria.

Some interviewees described the training as quite challenging, which was seen as a positive aspect, as police work itself was often described to be demanding as well. Interviewees did negate the fact that their previous further education had any bearing in their experience of police training.[81]

Although the relevance of police training is sometimes belittled in casual talk, especially the applicability of theoretical training to the actual professional practice, respondents overall saw the use and value of their training. This has changed over the course of time, and interviewees who finished their training some decades ago do report a noticeable shift in the setup and purpose of police training. This, in turn, immensely helps the respective officers not only in better dealing with a situation at hand, but also personally coming to terms with aspects of their work.

"You have to deal with situations, because that's what people expect, that's what your colleagues expect, that's what your employer expects, you have to be able to deal professionally with such things, no matter what you see, whether there's a dead child in front of you or a raped woman, no matter what, you have to play down your part professionally and be able to deal with it. [...] in the past, they said, you can do that simply because you have police training. But when I started, the topics were only subject matter, only learning topics. Only the laws were important and nothing else. We didn't have any psychological training at all, it wasn't an issue at all. And it's only now, little by little over the last few years, that psychology has become a topic at all in the police force." - Interview 7, Austria.[82]

This development can be seen in the context of an international stride to professionalise federal police forces (Baylis/Matczak 2019). In this way,

---

81 However, some chose a particular entry scheme due to their having completed a university education, see chapter 5.2.4.
82 The topic of psychological influence of the job as a police officer and its implications, along with the reception of supervisory concepts and other assistance is discussed in chapter 5.3.3.

respondents also supported the current system of first having to complete a certain amount of theoretical training before being allowed and required to perform duties as a police officer. In line with earlier international findings (Brand/Matranga 1993), the interviewees overwhelmingly found the current training system to adequately prepare them for the work as an entry-level officer.

5.2.3 Policing as a Career

Completing police training, as all educational and vocational education, takes a certain amount of dedication and commitment. In a policing context, this aspect is spoken of quite often, not least because of the career possibilities and stable opportunities that are provided within the police service (chapter 5.1.5). As mentioned above, some interviewees had preconceived ideas about their career in the police, while others only built up their interest over their training period, and some are still exploring different pathways in the police, skipping between whatever role suits them best at a certain time. Those applicants who were at first unsure about their decision to join the police or described their interest and subsequent application as somewhat of a coincidence or try out, went on to recount their training phase as quite formative, positively reinforcing their decision.

"No never, I must say, I never had that. [doubts about their decision, AN] At the police school it turned out that this is exactly how I want to work and live, or what I want to do in the future." – Interview 10, Austria.

Furthermore, those that went into the job without a clearly formed plan described their current status in the service as satisfactory.

"So, yeah, it's nothing like a plan, I didn't have that plan, but I'm really happy to be exactly where I am. This is the job I want. Definitely." – Interview 12, England and Wales.

Interestingly, both those applicants without a plan and the ones that had a clear career path in mind often described lacking in job or educational alternatives that they could pursue in case of their police application failing or alternatively not being happy with the job. Although some of the more assured candidates had alternatives up their sleeves, most mentioned that you need a certain amount of will and ambition for the job to work out.

"Yeah, so I was kind of like that, I thought I really wanted to do it, and, if it doesn't work out, [laughs] I have to look around anyway, but I wouldn't have had anything where I'd say, yeah, [if it doesn't work out] that's what I'm doing." – Interview 9, Austria.

Whether the job as a police officer was something participants always wanted to do, or the drive towards the occupation came as late as the first practical training sessions, almost all interviewees stated that they saw their current job as a predominantly positive and fulfilling occupation.

Turning to career paths and professional developments, many interviewees had a highly diverse career background, both in and outside of the police service. Those that previously worked outside the service either did so in order to fill the waiting time until their admission went through, or because they had trained in that particular job and only developed their interest for the police after some time – some through direct professional contact with the police. Internally, participants showed differing approaches to their personal career in policing. Some were trying out a lot of different roles, while having little to no aspiration for promotion. Those that settled on lateral development praised the diversity of options they were presented with in the police. They mentioned no or only little drive to pursue promotion.

"I've not gone up the ranks, I'm a sideways crab. I don't fancy promotion, not my thing, no." – Interview 13, England and Wales.

Others, however, have gone up the ranks and went for promotion, either early on or after they felt ready. Some progressed very quickly through the ranks and mentioned the particularity of going through promotion processes early on in their career, while often still being of a young age as well.

"So, I was relatively young getting promoted to inspector, 30 maybe, which in the force it meant, it was historically the end of your career" – Interview 17, England and Wales.

Still, those interviewees did find their fit in their respective roles and gradually developed their own fields of interest. Of course, there were also those candidates who followed a more standard advancement through the roles and ranks over time.

The promotion process itself differs slightly in the two countries. In the UK, promotion processes differ slightly between the different forces – generally speaking, one first needs to demonstrate competence at one's current rank, complete an examination (law and procedure based), and afterwards pass a board hearing. Applicants are then temporarily promoted and can be assigned to vacant positions, where they undergo a work-based assessment. In Austria, to become a commanding officer one has to complete a course and pass a test, while attaining the highest rank of Offizier is connected to completing a bachelor's course in police leadership ("Polizeiliche Führung").[83] The process of promotion in both countries is by its nature (lots of work hours, locality) more arduous for female officers. Often, decentralised training schemes could aid these circumstances to become more inviting for applicants.[84]

Generally speaking, interviewees who completed their promotion process had a positive outlook on the course and their respective performance. It goes without saying that achievements come with a certain sense of pride, and some respondents displayed this quite openly – especially those who had completed their ascension through the ranks quite early on.

In this way, the subject matter of policing as a career protrudes in all interviewee's accounts. From police-internal advanced training to previous career expertise and other further education in related (e.g., law) or unrelated (e.g., energetics) fields, respondents remarked that they are able to use their expertise to advance their career or assist in their daily work life. This concurs with the narrative that the police provide a diverse and ever-changing workplace. Often, if interviewees were not overly fond of their field of work, they proceeded to a different department or strand of police work, rather than changing employers altogether – which is seen as a benefit by female officers. Furthermore, the possibility to undergo further education or specific vocational training during their time with the police was not only taken advantage of quite often but also brought up as beneficial by interviewees.

5.2.4 Special Issues

There are country-specific issues concerning police training and application that arose during the interviews. The two distinct issues that are discussed in the following paragraphs are the Police Now scheme in Eng-

---

83 The bachelor's course is mandatory since 2006. It is held in cooperation with the FH Wiener Neustadt and can therefore only be obtained at this one location.
84 On the nature of promotion itself and the experiences female police officers of rank have see chapter 5.4.3.

land and Wales and the specialised training for Cobra, a special force in Austrian police.

"Police Now attract, recruit and train outstanding graduates with leadership potential to be inspirational police officers and detectives who transform communities" (Police:Now, What we do, policenow.org.uk). Since its inception in 2015, it is a graduate entry scheme for police that has grown quite quickly and currently operates in over 30 police forces in England and Wales. The application process differs slightly from the standard entry route: As it is a graduate entry scheme, an academic degree at a certain standard is required (2.2. or above or non-UK equivalent), and, as it is an independent national enterprise, the application process is streamlined and equal throughout the whole of England and Wales regardless of the requested police force applicants choose. The programme has the potential to positively influence the historically rather flawed relationship between academia and the police, by having research outcomes be connected to police practice (Fenn et al. 2019).

Currently, there is no restriction on which type of university courses are accepted into the programme, which one the one hand, is positive in that it opens up the police to applicants of many different backgrounds, but on the other hand, it can be seen as a waste of specialised expertise (Paterson 2011). At present, graduates of all disciplines are treated in the same way – which, incidentally, slightly differs from the idea of a standard recruit. A respondent who has undergone Police Now training mentions that the programme seeks a different kind of aspirant than the standard police recruitment does:

> "So, I would say it was because it was simply, to a certain extent, a different [...] picture of applicants they were looking for than in the normal procedure, so it was organised differently." – Interview 2, England and Wales.

The Police Now training is shortened and more condensed than the standard police training and takes place in London. The training is not provided by the police themselves but by the Police Now organisation, who work with former police officers and related professionals. Interviewees who have undergone Police Now training appreciated the differing focus of the programme.

> "Normal training school they teach via PowerPoint, and write down PowerPoint, write down PowerPoint [..] we learn to much more of a, go and learn it yourself, and then we'll discuss it in groups. And

with scenarios, so Police Now is a bit different. Yeah. Very different." – Interview 8, England and Wales.

The methods used in Police Now training, such as roleplaying scenarios, were also praised, and the practical approach of the programme appeals to respondents. It was further mentioned that the training experience is made to resemble the everyday work-life of a police officer, challenging recruits right from the beginning. After the initial training phase, Police Now recruits focus on neighbourhood policing and related areas for a certain period, after which they can either decide to continue on those paths or are placed in other related posts such as immediate response teams. Interviewees particularly stressed the importance of neighbourhood policing[85] in the concept of the Police Now scheme.

> "[O]ur training is specifically directed towards problem-solving, and long-term issues, and neighbourhood policing. So, they're trying to instil in us future leaders, effectively. So, they teach a much wider range of skills than just the legislation or the law that you would learn at normal training school, it's a very different kind of learning." – Interview 8, England and Wales.

After the first two years, applicants are free to choose the nature of their further involvement with the police. In this sense, Police Now is seen as a more open programme, allowing aspirants to have a go at policing, while simultaneously keeping other career branches, e.g., ministerial work, open. One of the respondents had, at the time of the interview, decided to take up such a post and leave the police.

> "[B]ut thank God there's a rule that, if you stop [...] you have four years to come back, without me having to start all over again." – Interview 2, England and Wales.

The possibility to continue working for the police after a certain time of absence was received positively, not only by Police Now graduates – some interviewees from both Austria and England and Wales did mention the fact that they worked in partner organisations or related ministerial positions for a certain amount of time before going back into the police.

---

85 Neighbourhood policing focusses on community engagement and collaborative long-term problem-solving with communities – working with organisations and agents from different sectors (public, private, and voluntary) is an important part of the approach. The reception of neighbourhood policing by interviewees and colleagues is discussed i.e., in chapter 5.3.2.

However, the Police Now programme seems to present a slightly different outlook on policing than the standard training, where outside knowledge is seen as an asset and policing is presented as more open and flexible in terms of career planning – which differs somewhat to the previously mentioned idea of policing as a life-long career.

Additionally, the Police Now programme offers certain bonuses to applicants.

> "[I]n the second year of the program we also have the possibility to do a four week internship or secondment, either in a special unit or with partner organizations, so, for example, a friend of mine has been with a consulting firm, so PWC, Accenture, PA consulting, KPMG, for example. Or Home Office, national crime agency, those were a few possibilities, I did it very differently [laughs] […] I spent time in [place in USA], in the [place in USA] police department […] so those were the (..) icings on the cake [laughs] which of course you don't get as a normal rookie, so at least not, I'd say, in the first few years." – Interview 2, England and Wales.

Apart from the deviation from the standard police application and training process these added bonuses are supposed to work as an incentive for graduates to make their decision for this specific police entry programme. The questions that remain are, how effective these incentives are – respondents saw it as an added plus, but not a definite pull-factor – and how this approach will change in light of the ongoing process of professionalisation that should "create formal links between initial training, career progression and academic qualifications" (Paterson 2011: 286).

The following paragraphs focus on a different kind of special police training, that of the largest and most relevant Austrian special unit "Cobra". The unit has its headquarters and training facilities in Wiener Neustadt (near Vienna), while other stations are also located in some larger cities around Austria. One of the main tasks of the Cobra is to support police officers by intervening in situations of increased or high risk, e.g., in conflicts where weapons are involved. The application requirements are a completed standard police training and two years of experience in the field service of the police. The entrance test consists of both a psychological and a fitness test. Especially the sports test is a large obstacle for female applicants: Out of the approximately 450 officers, 3 female officers are currently in service.[86] Having less women in a certain special unit of course makes it harder for recruitment practices to actively engage with female would-be applicants (Cf. Rogers 2004). An applicant recalls that, although her superiors and trainers were encouraging her to join the special unit, it took some time – and a little push from colleagues – for her to finally apply. Although not everyone was content with her decision.

"I wanted to withdraw [the application] [...] and then [...] [colleagues said] they will stand there with banners and I should do the application procedure, and (...) and then something else motivated me because three days earlier I went there [Cobra headquarters, AN] and there were some colleagues and they said [imitates suppressed laughter] [mockingly] women and Cobra, well [/] (..) [laughs] that was, I thought to myself, the motivation, and if I only sit there for one day, so I did it and then I was in the upper third at that time and [...] I joined the Cobra training" – Interview 2, Austria.

As the first woman to ever enter this special force, the interviewee remembers the sometimes very tedious times she has had at the Cobra. Concerning recruitment and training, a particular incident was difficult to handle for her. After some years in the special unit, a commission was sent to determine the fitness standards for applicants and take a particular look at possibly altering the set standards for female applicants. After a few days, the responsible officials asked for her opinion on the matter, since she was the only female officer serving in the Cobra.

"[They said] what about the selection procedure and just that the selection procedure is not manageable for women, [...] and then I thought, well, funny, now I've been there for 5 years, I did the selection procedure. And then they said, well, but there's this Irish table at the selection procedure and women can't make it, because it's not possible due to, I don't know which prerequisite, it's not possible. Then I said, well, first of all it was also in my selection procedure, but I can show it to them with pleasure, and then 20 people with clipboard and ballpoint pen genuinely followed me over there, and then I showed it to them and then [they went] 'aha, okay' and then, that was that" - Interview 2, Austria.

---

86 Unfortunately, there are no official statistics, these numbers were given by two interviewees who are currently employed by the Cobra unit. The latest official numbers are from 2012, where two out of approximately 450 officers were female (Scherschneva-Koller 2012).

For one, there is a clear display by the committee of underestimating women's ability to master the fitness test, which implies and corresponds with an underestimation of the respondent's abilities. At the same time that these expectations create a dividing line between the respondent and her male colleagues at the special unit, it also creates a disconnect between her and her female peers. By stating that "women" are not able to achieve something, while acknowledging the fact that a particular woman can and did achieve it, a feeling of alienation is constructed. This experience, described by the interviewee as "quite bizarre", therefore creates separation not only between the respondent and her male colleagues, but also her gender peers. This dilemma of finding oneself between different groups is in fact a recurring theme also displayed in everyday police work (see e.g., chapter 5.4.1).

5.2.5 Interim Findings

Overall, different admission times and incidents of recruitment freezes did not deter respondents from joining the police. Though recruitment freezes due to budget cuts can have a lasting impact on police service as well as its hiring techniques (Wilson 2012), they did little to influence female officers' perception of and motivation for their aspired career path. Interviewees made use of the time they had on their hands due to recruitment scheduling issues in different ways in the two countries: respondents from Austria often turned to some other kind of work, while respondents in England and Wales frequently enrolled in university courses, either at entry or graduate level.

An issue that was brought up by female officers in both countries was that of the (entrance) fitness exam. According to Holzleithner (2017), physical requirements' gendered effects, namely the strain they can put on female applicants, stand in an apparent opposition to legal gender equality. Consequently, the discussion of these (differing) standards unravels in the tense field between exclusionary practices and unjust gendered preferences. There seems to be no gendered version of this test that does not receive critique from the respondents, although the response to the two different systems in the UK and Austria seem to complement each other. When Austrian respondents critique the current system in their home country, they refer to the system being skewed towards favouring female applicants, which, in their perception, does not side with the notion of equality that the respondents held. Contrarily, officers in the UK voice their concerns about the ability of female police officers to be able to adhere to the same standards as their male colleagues, especially after giving birth or being of older age. However, none of the respondents mentioned having had problems with the fitness standards themselves. Indeed, police applicants who fail the assessment hardly ever have the fitness test to blame, most applicants in Austria, for example, fail because of their lack of German language skills ("Neue Polizisten: Das Niveau sinkt ab", kurier.at). Some, especially UK respondents, even mentioned that the common hurdle that is the regular (sometimes annual) fitness test binds together colleagues that train together and encourage each other. In this way, the esprit de corps of the police that is often criticised by activists and scholars alike, serves as a mechanism to deal with certain internal obstacles.

Prokos and Padavic's (2002) notion that police training teaches and encourages masculinity seems to offer an explanation as to why female officers, in their depiction of the training process, speak of a steep learning curve and are aware of the number of skills they learned. In fact, interviewees talk about their own personal and professional advancement through the job quite frequently, as opposed to deriving their expertise from personal predispositions.

Furthermore, there is a certain discrepancy to be noted between the experience in police training and actual day-to-day police work (Cf. Fielding 1988). In this way, alternative entry routes such as the Police Now programme can help create an atmosphere similar to the everyday practice, such as shift work and dealing with high stressors. However, the theoretical background provided by the training school is found to be necessary in order to navigate the experiences made "out in the field".

The practical applicability of police training is something police officers value greatly (Oliva/Compton 2010), an aspect that came up in the analysis of my data as well. The importance of a suitable training experience not only contributes to the appeal of the police training itself, but also assists respondents in their transition from training to fully-fledged police officers.

The idea that policing is seen as a life-long career was carried by almost all respondents in both countries. Officers who have been with the police for a long time either decide to opt for promotion, some more rapidly than others, or focus on lateral development. As diversity of the work life has a major appeal to police applicants, it is not surprising that, although the selection process was not filtered in any way, respondents all had differing careers and opportunities to talk about.

The fact that the Police Now scheme in England and Wales seeks a particular, and somewhat different, type of police applicant was seen as a positive influence factor for officers who had undergone Police Now training. This differing approach, focusing on community engagement, also necessitates a specialised training schedule, and leads to certain particularities of the programme, such as benefits in the form of work placements. In this way, Police Now might appeal to a certain demographic that regular police entry work does not – although some respondents have entered the police service through the regular route after completing their university degree. Although "there is relatively little conceptual reasoning offered to explain why, and how higher education matters in the performing of police tasks [...] or indeed what elements are particularly successful" (Brown 2018), interviewees felt that the programme specifically designed for graduates made a difference to them, and in their perception of and decision for police work.

A different type of issue is that of the Austrian special force Cobra. A highly masculine field, the special force has only had three successful female applicants since its inception in 1978. Many attribute this to the high fitness standards applicants have to adhere to, in order to qualify for the physically and mentally rather challenging work as a Cobra officer. Being the first woman to join such an institution, an interviewee remembered the application process as tedious – however, this was not due to the test itself, but rather the backlash she faced from her would-be colleagues.[87] Additionally, she was seen as a sort of outlier by professionals assessing the application process, as her ability to master the athletics parkour rendered her different from other female candidates. In this way, she was not only seen as different from her all-male colleagues at the special unit, but further alienated from her female peers by seemingly deviating from the female norm.

5.3 Police Work

This chapter focusses on the daily police work in general, as experienced by the participants, as well as their perception of policing and any structural issues (apart from discriminatory issues) the police in the respective countries might face. Police internal and external issues of gender and

---

87 To this day she still faces discrimination from her colleagues as well as her subordinates in the special unit – see e.g., chapter 5.4.4.

experiences of sexism are discussed in the next two chapters. The focus of the following part is rather the gendered experiences of policing and police issues that are not directly related to participants' gender.

The material presented was gathered in interviews primarily via the question "Please describe your areas of responsibility, what does a 'normal day' look like for you?"[88] but was also influenced by questions about changes in the culture and everyday work in the police service as a whole.

5.3.1 The Variety of Police Work

As previously mentioned, respondents in both countries are and were employed in various different areas within the police. From working abroad, to being in the detective unit or working with vulnerable people, the range of work experiences within the police resonate with the fact that interviewees had seen the police service as a versatile career option. Even in their current occupation, all interviewees from both countries mentioned the fact that, although there is a rough outline to their day-to-day work, every workday presented them with different challenges.

> "[I]t can be quite varied and you never know what you're gonna come in to in the morning. Which is always a bonus. [I: so, there's no such thing as a normal day] No. No, there isn't. and actually, I don't think I'd ever want a normal day. [S]o yeah, it's quite good. It is a really really good job. Really enjoying it." – Interview 12, England and Wales.

As some have also mentioned this variety and element of unpredictability as something that attracted them to the police service in the first place, their current position in the service and daily work experience was seen as positive by almost all interviewees. Police officers have to fulfil different categories of tasks, ranging from investigating crime to engaging in partnership work with third-sector facilities[89] or connecting with communities (Cockcroft 2020: 18).

The daily responsibilities of respondents range from answering emails and attending meetings to commanding special units and being deployed

---

88 German wording: "Beschreiben Sie bitte Ihre Aufgabengebiete, wie sieht ein normaler Tag bei Ihnen aus?".

89 'Third sector organisations' is a term used to describe the range of organisations that are neither public sector nor private sector.

to critical situations. Many talked about who or what "controls" their daily work schedule – for some it was of course external circumstances, assignments that come in, others praised the fact that they themselves could more or less determine their own priorities in their work. Interestingly, issues of rank seldomly determined to what degree female officers experienced freedom of choice in their daily work.

> "[Y]ou don't get any assignments, but you just go by yourself, we just often drive to [area] and so on, become active independently, so, you don't wait until someone comes and says, I don't know, he stole my handbag but [...] [we act] by ourselves if we just see well okay something doesn't fit or that could be interesting" – Interview 9, Austria.
>
> "[T]he commander [...] sets the strategic direction for the command and I, I'm there to ensure that that plan is carried out, [...] But to be honest normally my day is taken dealing with staff issues, so I just seem to deal with everyday staff, staffing problems, sickness, welfare cases, flexible working, disputes of working, it does just feel like I spend a lot of my time working sorting out staff issues and making personnel decisions and deciding how things are gonna be." – Interview 11, England and Wales.

The experiences described here, one as a regular "Inspektor"[90], the other as a higher-ranking chief inspector, illustrate the contrast between those respondents who frequently had their regular work schedule side-tracked or changed by other matters, and the ones who stated that they could predominantly arrange their working day as they please. Throughout the interviews, respondents were more often associated with the first (non-self-regulating) type.

Additionally, the rota system most respondents used was brought up. More flexible working schedules and rotas were praised, as they offered interviewees the ability to better their work-life balance. However, flexible working, as well as part-time work, was often described as being stigmatised and having a bad reputation – it seemingly stands in contrast with what constitutes "real" police work (see also chapter 5.3.2).

An issue that interviewees at the upper half of the rank structure mentioned, is that of direct contact to police colleagues and citizens.

---

90 Austrian equivalent to a UK constable.

"[A]nd I have to say I miss working with people face-to-face, too. Now my goal is primarily to support my colleagues outside, because I know what they have to do every day, I want them to have the best possible framework conditions. [...] Well, I need the contact to the citizens, and really help actively, where you actually see your impact, that is what I miss." – Interview 13, Austria.

The perception of the daily work is influenced by the period of time it took to achieve said rise in rank – the first quote was given by an interviewee who had gone through the ranks in a very short amount of time. Participants also mentioned that, to them, there comes a time when you actually want that change of scenery and not be "out in the field" for the whole of your career. This shift in type of work comes with a more managerial position, in which officers are responsible for certain teams and their deployment or manage the cooperation between forces and departments.

In addition to their work in various departments, some officers mentioned additional workloads they had to deal with. Sometimes, these were projects that they took part in or managed together with other police departments or even external organisations, special roles they had to fill out, or engagement with differing occupational networks. Being part of the police force's women's or LGBTIQ network is, of course, a voluntary role that respondents take up.[91] In this way, in addition to an already varied workday, some officers also had their "fingers in different pies around the force" (Interview 6, England and Wales), contributing to the heterogeneity of the interviewees.

5.3.2 What Constitutes ("Good") Policing?

As the interviews were ripe with descriptions and information on police work, one can derive a sort of ideal type of police work from it. Standard police work was characterised as being "out on the street", working with people and either helping them or restraining their activities. Respondents often mentioned that the work they carried out was "not really police work", or at least removed from the constructed specific ideal type of real police work. A respondent who, by definition, fitted the narrative

---

91 On the topic of women's and LGBTIQ support networks, their work and reception, see chapter 5.6.3.4 and chapter 5.7.2.

of one doing actual police work out on the streets instead just said "we deal with everything" – this was opposed to the narrow definition of real police work, as she mentioned having to carry out tasks that do not fit her perception of police work. The debate around what constitutes "real" police work does have a history. As mentioned above, there has been a shift in what forms the ideal of police work, and "softer" forms of policing, such as neighbourhood policing and working with survivors of abuse have become more recognised (Frauen im Polizeidienst [1] 2011, McCarthy 2013). The execution of a "hard" policing style, which is historically connected to forms of masculinity, is therefore seldomly the point of reference for female officers when talking about "real" police work. This is somewhat in contrast to findings such as Silvestri's (2003), concluding that only a "masculine man" can fulfil the standards of real police work. Rather, it is an engagement with the community, solving problems with or for them and, most definingly, carrying out active duty on the streets. Many respondents from Austria who had worked for the police for some time mentioned the fact that they themselves had little to do with standard police work.

> "And I have nothing more to do with the normal, I'd say, with the average police work, which is certainly 80% of the job, out on the street; nothing at all." – Interview 7, Austria.

Rather than comparing their day-to-day work with "standard" policing duties, respondents from England and Wales appeared more open in their perception of what constitutes policing. Most importantly, interviewees mentioned the importance of working with the community and their consent, especially in areas such as neighbourhood policing.

> "Neighbourhood policing is all about, well, trust and confidence. And what [...] how can we be visible, how can we be available for people when they need us. And also create contexts where it is not only about enforcement, right. [T]his is just a kind of [policing], well, I couldn't imagine it any other way." – Interview 2, England and Wales.

Policing by consent, which has its roots in Robert Peel's *Principles of Policing* (FOI release. Definition of policing by consent, gov.uk), means that police officers are regarded as citizens in uniform, and exercise their power with the consent of the ones they are policing. Transparency and prevention instead of repression are substantial elements of policing by consent. Almost all interviewees discussed the importance of these principles on their daily work, but also their understanding of what constitutes "good" policing. Consequently, the fact that police officers in England and Wales do not, in contrast to their European counterparts, carry firearms was seen as highly positive, and enforcing the idea of a more level policing in more or less consensus with the public.

"[W]hen I was 22 and wanted to join the police, I would have no interest in carrying a firearm. I think a lot of my colleagues who I know who are police officers in the UK do not want to carry a firearm. I think that makes it more military, for me. If I'm honest. [A]nd I used to feel uncomfortable, when I go on holiday, to other countries and I see other police officers armed. I just think it, I don't know how you feel coming from a country […] but, for me it just like, imposed on you a fear to a certain degree, why do they need to be armed." – Interview 9, England and Wales.

Enforcing the law with the aid of firearms is seen almost as a loss of control – definitely a loss of consent from the public. This is in line with results of a 1994 study, which found that an overwhelming majority of UK police officers were against the notion of routinely carrying firearms (McKenzie 2000). Respondents from the UK talked at length about their view on policing as a service to the public, the mission of the police being to protect and serve. Another aspect of this close connection to the public is the idea that police can and should be held accountable for their actions at all times. It was positively noted that these views on policing have been undergoing some changes over the years.

"I think we're a lot more accountable than we used to be and that's just in the space of 12 years, which is absolutely correct, because the public have to trust us, we're the only police force in the world that, police with the consent of the public, everywhere else is basically army, so we need to be really proud of that and keep that. I feel some people might think negatively and say we're a little bit too account-able, but where do you find the balance" – Interview 5, England and Wales

While interviewees from the UK paint a quite progressive picture of ideal policing and its inception in the various forces across the country, the idea of community policing in Austria is only in its early stages. What neighbourhood policing provides for the police in the UK is being developed in Austria with the project "Gemeinsam Sicher".[92]

> "[W]e always say, affectionately, that is the third branch, so we have repression, we have prevention, and we have Gemeinsam Sicher. For us, Gemeinsam Sicher is, of course, a form of prevention, […] there are many who say that we have always done that in the countryside, well. […] I wouldn't put it like that, because this communication at eye level has to be digested. […] and really make citizens want to engage with [this project], and, that's just the great thing when you notice it works, right. Well, nice and slow" – Interview 14, Austria.

The project works to create a dialogue between citizens, municipalities, and the police, concerning itself with issues of safety. Since its inception in some cities in 2016 it has been expanded to the whole of Austria. Noteworthily, Austrian officers described this level approach to policing as being but one strand of a greater whole, as opposed to the perception of UK officers, who thought it to be the fundamental principle of their understanding of policing. Furthermore, while the Peelian Principles have been, at least in theory, guiding police work in England and Wales since 1829, the recent attempt at policing citizens at eye level is fairly new in Austria. Although "softer" forms of policing have been around for years, this new project is the first to put these ideas in writing and give them a solid platform to develop.

5.3.3 Dealing with the Job

Some Austrian interviewees who were carrying out active duty as a standard officer stated that, in order to keep their private life from their professional one, they took up jobs in districts that are in some distance to their place of living. They do not want their "clients" to interfere with their personal life or be aware of the issues that their residential neighbourhood deals with. Of course, being recognisable as a neighbourhood policing officer while off-duty can be experienced as a nuisance.[93] Only few intervie-

---

92 Literal translation "safe together" (Gemeinsam Sicher homepage, gemeinsamsicher.at).

93 A police officer responsible for the Austrian neighbourhood policing programme in a particular area mentioned the fact that each community building and state-funded residence had her picture in the entrance hall with a slogan saying "Ich

wees discussed the issue of dangers that come with the job as a police officer. Most Austrian officers denied ever having given the dangers of the occupation a second thought, and only one interviewee saw the risks of the job as one of her motives to move up the ranks and resign from standard street policing. A respondent mentioned that a different type of fear can become a danger to officers.

> "[T]here are two different fears, because on the one hand [the fear] that something might happen to me, and on the other hand generally the fear of what I can do at all, legally I mean. And what is abuse of authority, and I think the boundaries are blurring for some people because they are not one hundred percent sure of what they are allowed to do and what they are not." – Interview 10, Austria.

The fear of doing something wrong, and the repercussions of said wrongdoing were discussed as stressors in the everyday work life. According to the respondent, the type of police officer described above was deemed not to last for too long in the profession, as fear is seen as something to be avoided and neutralised if one is to thrive in this job – a view supported by other Austrian respondents. Therefore, the ideal of a true police officer is not associated with any doubt about their work ethics, lest they fear their own occupation.

A connected issue that came up more often was that of a police officer's mental health and the organisation's approach to dealing with work stressors. In Austria, the situation was seen as being on the mend, yet supervision and mental health issues are still not fully integrated into the mentality of the service.

> "But we don't yet have the culture that social workers have, that it's natural to have a profession where you see a lot of negative things, and where it's highly professional to undergo a psychological procedure [...] whether you're doing one-on-one interviews or supervision or whatever." – Interview 7, Austria.

In fact, those Austrian interviewees that did talk about the possibility of undergoing supervision all stated that they themselves had never taken this opportunity. Similarly, police officers in the UK mentioned a cultural change in police perception of mental health issues.

---

bin immer für Sie da" ("I'm always there for you"), to which she responded (in conversation with me) "But I do have some days off".

"Certainly, the last, one of the biggest changes in the last five years particularly has been around well-being. [T]here very much is, until five years ago, and to a point there still is but much less so, a culture of: you just got on with it. So, if you've been to something very traumatic [...] there was no looking after the officers, until five or six years ago. [...] your sergeant now will sit down with you and say, okay, what do you need [...] – and it's officer-driven." – Interview 8, England and Wales.

In both countries, supervision and mental health support is offered to officers, yet the affected people themselves need to request these services. Use of supervision therefore remains considerably rare, even with the awareness around mental health issues being raised. The police historically have had a "strong ethos of controlling emotions" (Brown 2000a: 260), and a more open and tolerant approach towards seeking help in the form of psychological counselling has been aimed at for some time now. In this respect, however, the service seems slow to change in both countries. Some respondents in the UK noted that the change in perception of mental health issues, albeit slow, does have an influence not only on the approach to supervision and inner-organisational issues, but also on dealing with members of the public who suffer of mental illnesses of any kind.[94] As officers learn, or at least aim to learn, to deal with issues of mental health and experiences of extreme stress, there is a potential to a more understanding and calming approach to members of the public who might go through a tough situation themselves. At the same time, officers are asking to respect the fact that they, as police officer, cannot deal with every situation at hand, and that they are sometimes simply not the right institution to address, in addition to a lack of resources.[95] Although there have been efforts to better the situation of stressors at work and dealing with difficult experiences, the police remain a work environment where reflection processes are still not the norm.

---

94 It has been noted quite often that the police might not be appropriate authority in dealing with mental health crises, yet they are nonetheless often called to such incidents as health institutions are regularly too busy to deal with immediate situations – a fact that is also acknowledged by Brown and Silvestri (2020).

95 Interviewees from both countries mentioned the fact that the responsibilities assigned to the police have been growing over the past decades, along with the feeling that the public expects the organisation to deal with any given issue. While the Austrian police service still seems in the process of expanding its duties, respondents in the UK mentioned noticing a certain reversion to police-specific issues.

5.3.4 Structural Issues

In addition to having a wide range of responsibilities, police services struggle with budget issues. Respondents in the UK felt the impact of politics and budget decisions not only influenced their personal day-to-day workload, but also created a rather bleak atmosphere and negative outlook for police officers in the whole country. The cuts in officer numbers throughout the UK (Police Workforce, England and Wales, 31 March 2019 second edition, assets.publishing.service.gov.uk) have created a highly stressful situation, not only for constables, but also their superiors.

> "Because there isn't as many of us so it's harder to support your colleagues. Because somebody might say to me, an officer yesterday, my workload is too high – [sighs] I can't magic more detectives I'm sorry. I can support you in terms of giving you some protective time to plough through that workload, but I can't do what I could have done previously which is share the weight of that workload evenly because there's not enough officers anymore. So that's been the major change."
> – Interview 6, England and Wales.

Some mentioned that they (meaning their immediate work surroundings) were doing good despite these budget changes – the ability to deal innovatively with reductions in officer numbers for example was seen as something really positive about a particular police force. Still, the strain on officer morale is not to be underestimated – some also mentioned a potential influence on officer recruitment. According to respondents in Austria, a similar phenomenon related to officer recruitment can be found in the current demography of police officers: Due to previous freezes in police recruitment, many officers working today are either very senior, or rather young. This can potentially lead to a lack of adequately trained officers while the aforementioned senior officers leave for retirement. Generally, the organisations' skill in dealing with officer numbers is seen as improvable. Many officers leave their permanent post, be it due to pregnancy, further training, or partaking in specific schemes, and these vacant posts will not be covered again by replacement staff. Many officers therefore called for a restructuring of this arrangement or for better recruitment offensives.

Another issue that was found with the organisation of the police service in Austria was that of a high bureaucratisation of the occupation. While filling out paperwork might not be one's favourite part in day-to-day work life, interviewees saw the rigid structure and immovability of the police service as almost hindering to their productivity.

While female officers serving in smaller forces in England and Wales sometimes praised their force's unique approach to policing issues or organisational aspects, interviewees from Austria saw the stark contrast between policing in bigger cities and policing in the countryside as unsatisfactory. This contrast is seen to be especially noticeable in emergency cases, where back-up officers have to be called in: A certain feeling of security comes with knowing that, in case of a situation getting out of hand, additional officers can be called in at a moment's notice in urban areas. Interestingly, however, an interviewee also mentioned the fact that, due to the lack of readily available reinforcements, officers in the countryside would more often aim for de-escalation than their urban counterparts.

5.3.5 Interim Findings

Most respondents found their daily work to be satisfactory and were involved in a range of different roles and projects in the organisation. While only some interviewees currently carried out their job as an out on the beat officer[96], most constructed this part of the occupation as standard policing. Ideal police work is described as being hard but rewarding, while having a sense of purpose in what constitutes your daily work. In accordance with Verro's (2009) results, some participants state that only those who have experienced police work can understand the realities of it.

While standard police work is described as being out on the street, dealing with matters first-hand and being in immediate contact with both the public and colleagues, only some interviewees describe themselves as carrying out such duties. What participants describe as growing in importance in both countries is the concept of neighbourhood policing. While community policing remained marginal in the UK in the 1980s and 1990s, it gained significance in the early 2000s.[97] In Austria, a concept of community policing, called "Gemeinsam Sicher", has only recently been introduced. However, interviewees from both countries mention the importance of the work done in these programmes – there is a certain shift to be noted towards regarding aspects of neighbourhood policing

---

96 "Beat officers" are police officers who patrol a so-called beat – describing a certain territory and time the officer patrols.

97 This was also the time PCSOs were introduced (Higgins 2018).

as similar to elements described as constituting "real" police work, e.g., working with the public. Nonetheless, some associate policing with a certain performance of bravery, an element of action, or use of force, which runs antithetically to the idea of community policing and is deeply interwoven with displays of masculinity (Behr 2008, Brown/Heidensohn 2000, McCarthy 2013). Community policing puts emphasis on skills that are not aligned with traditional ideas of law enforcement and its masculinity (Crank 1998).

The greatest difference in the perception of the police and its culture as such can be seen in the way respondents from the UK describe policing by consent as the primary objective and guiding principle of their work. To them, being equipped with firearms bears no resemblance to a police service that is dedicated to policing the public by consent. In addition to a level approach to policing, interviewees mentioned noticing a change over the years in how far police can be held accountable by the public for their actions. The shift towards more accountability is seen as highly positive, further strengthening the Peelian Principles, the raison d'être of police in England and Wales. In this way, the sentiment that policing is seen as a way of life, not just a job (Reiner 2000) comes through in the interviews. Therefore, the conception of policing as a mission is not only referring to the protection of the public, but also the defending of certain policing values that respondents think inherent to their form of policing. In contrast to this, respondents from Austria talk about their view on policing in rather neutral terms. They address changes in police work responsibilities and link these to greater societal changes – e.g., police officers being called to mental health emergencies. Such developments are not singular to Austria, and interviewees from the UK describe how they have to shut themselves, as police, off from the notion of bearing too many responsibilities, in addition to the police service being understaffed at the moment.

The perception of police work being dangerous is being maintained not only by media, but also social sciences (Lichtenberg/Smith 2001). Nonetheless, respondents seldomly talked about the dangers of their day-to-day job, and even expressed the notion of fear being counterproductive when carrying out their job. This tendency to repress or ignore certain feelings or emotions rather than face them and learn to overcome them is historically common in police culture and highly linked to an ideal type of masculinity (Cf. Behr 2019). Although respondents from both countries mentioned noticing a slight cultural change over the last years, mental health issues are still a sort of taboo topic in the police service. This has to be considered in the context that mentoring programmes can in fact lead to a decrease in stress for police officers (Hassell et al. 2011). Police officers themselves note that the service is slow to change but see that an effort is made, and small steps are being taken – in the UK, for example, officers report feeling more aware of mental health issues as a whole and regarding situations involving mentally ill members of public in a more nuanced way.

When talking about structural issues, officers in the UK inevitably discuss the impact that budget cuts and the resulting weakening of officer numbers had on their day-to-day work life and morale of their colleagues. Some expressed the sentiment that they were doing rather fine, considering the circumstances, with interviewees praising their particular police force for innovative handling of the aforementioned budget cuts. Thus, an element of solidarity in dealing with adverse conditions can be found in these interviewees' accounts.[98] Austrian police officers describe a different type of issue, yet comparable to the experiences of understaffed police forces in the UK, namely, the contrast between rural and urban areas of policing. Respondents note differences in the availability of reinforcements, as well as staffing issues, especially for officers who are seconded or unavailable for a short term. Hence, female police officers' experiences in both countries are not only shaped and informed by their immediate surroundings, but also by wider structural and political issues beyond gender-specific policies.

5.4 Internal Dynamics

The following chapter is concerned with the subjective perception of female police officers gendered experiences of police culture in their respective countries. The responses that were used in the analysis of this chapter were primarily given to the questions "When you think about your daily work (dealing with colleagues/public), to what extent would you say you have had experiences that you would attribute to your gender? To what

---

98 Incidentally, while team spirit is experienced as something highly positive in this instance, the solidarity displayed by members of the police also plays a large role in the continuing hegemony of a particular form of masculinity in the service. On this topic see e.g., Reiner (2016), but also chapter 5.4.1.

extent were you treated differently (by colleagues/public) because of your gender?"[99] and "How is the cooperation between men and women?".[100]

First, the acceptance and admission of female officers in male-dominated places is described. This is followed by a discussion on the theme of equality[101] and perceived differences of male and female policing. In the same sense, the cooperation between police colleagues is discussed under the pretext of gender and rank. Further, experiences of sexism and misogyny in the police force are discussed, before turning to participants' view on internal developments the police has undergone in this regard.

5.4.1 The Acceptance of Female Officers in the "Boys' Club"

The "intrusion" of women into male-connoted occupational areas challenges male and female gender constructions as well as the status and professionalism attributed to certain occupations as well as genders (Riegraf 2005). Participants from both countries frequently talked about the acceptance that male officers held for them, or rather female officers in general. In Austria, those accounts deviate from each other quite regularly. Some did not consider their acceptance any problem at all and held the belief that they were being treated just like any other colleague regardless of gender. Interestingly, these views did not solely come from recent joiners, which would somewhat account for the difference in experiences. Yet, officers who had joined quite a long time ago more often spoke about issues that they had to overcome, and how their acceptance as a female officer had developed over time. As some of my interviewees were among the first women to join the police service in Austria, they described a very different kind of situation, that made acceptance hard at first.

"As I said, it is now difficult to remember in particular, apart from the stories that result from the fact that the 90s were a different time than

---

99 This question was also generating the primary source material for the following chapter 5.5.
100 German wordings: "Wenn Sie an Ihren Arbeitsalltag denken (den Umgang mit Kollegen/Bürgern), inwiefern würden Sie sagen hatten Sie schon Erlebnisse, die Sie auf ihr Geschlecht zurückführen würden? Inwieweit wurden Sie anders behandelt (von Kollegen/Bürgern) aufgrund ihres Geschlechts?", "Wie ist die Zusammenarbeit zwischen Männern und Frauen?".
101 Being an issue of great importance, not least in equality legislation, the subject is discussed in more detail later in chapter 5.6.3.1.

today and that it was understandably difficult for many colleagues at the beginning to accept the fact that women are now joining [the police]." – Interview 7, Austria.

Thus, a narrative is constructed around the peculiarity of the fact that women had gained the same rights as men in joining the police service, therefore making a negative reaction from male officers at the time understandable – they needed a certain time to get used to a female presence in their work environment, which up until then had been unthinkable. The invasion of a male space by female officers is characterised as deviant and threatening, a theme that arises quite often when talking about the integration of female officers in the police (Heidensohn/Silvestri 2012). In trying to justify men's reaction to the inclusion of women in the police service, female officers (subconsciously or not) "play it safe", in that they adopt male thinking patterns and side with their male colleagues, rather than themselves or other early female apprentices.

To interviewees in Austria, the most positive reaction a female officer would generate from their male colleague is that of equal acceptance. There are some determinants for the contingency of acceptance that female officers are faced with: First, there is the element of time – date of entry and developments over time both influence respondents experience of their individual acceptance in the force. Furthermore, the age (and rank) of male police officers also bears importance in their perceived attitude towards their female colleagues.

As mentioned above, the approval of the hiring of female police officers has, of course, somewhat changed with time; respondents mentioned that they noticed a change in behaviour and attitudes of their male colleagues over time. Oftentimes, this change of attitude took an interference from the respondents' side. Thus, the acceptance in a male occupation had to be "earned". Interviewees talked about the struggles of having to prove themselves worthy of the job and their male colleagues' and superiors' acceptance. Respondents from both countries, though to a lesser extent from the UK, describe the fact that they always felt they had to be "better" than their male colleagues, and work twice as hard to achieve the recognition male police officers inherently get.

"And afterwards he observed me, so to speak, as I spoke with this lady and the whole thing then really ended very positively. And with that I have sort of earned his respect, right, so he told everyone afterwards, how great [that was] and that it is perhaps good that women are there." – Interview 6, Austria.

This struggle was certainly even more pronounced when acceptance was sought out from superiors. An interviewee remembers having to carry out secretary's work for her first supervisor:

> "[H]e was, that was (...) quite a struggle with him, so, the acceptance that I'm there now to do exactly the same job as the men, that wasn't there, so his understanding was a little different." – Interview 3, Austria.

Even though this incident took place a long time ago, some interviewees reported that they were still not seen as equal by some of their colleagues – in particular those of a certain age.

Although the police as a whole are a male-dominated field, there are some sections of it that are more heavily afflicted with displays of masculinity. In both countries, certain departments are regarded to still be male domains, while others are more open to female officers. In Austria, this becomes most apparent in the already mentioned special unit Cobra – here, women are visibly absent, and the focus on body issues, acting tough, and carrying big guns leaves very little room for any deviations from the hyper-masculine norm that is perpetuated. It is assumed that no female officer would venture into these depths, and those who do are treated with a sort of exemptive respect.

> "Wicked! [I have the] greatest respect for them [women who joined the Cobra] [...] you have to be an exception to be able to do that. And also psychologically speaking, it's (...) [I: well, it's not that easy] I thought so." – Interview 6, Austria.

In a way, this special unit is seen as the last resort where female applicants still have to adhere to masculine standards[102], an all-male arena where hyper-masculinity is celebrated instead of "feminised". Women have to adhere to those standards if they want to partake in these activities and become even more defeminised as they would in standard policing practice (Cockburn 1991: 69). There are no particular other departments in Austria that are associated with a similar amount of lack of femininity – some mentioned positions in the Ministry of the Interior or other special deployments such as legal service. Generally speaking, the more expertise there is ascribed to a certain position, the less likely this position is taken up by a female officer.[103]

---

102 The admission sports test is the same for all applicants regardless of gender.
103 The issue of rank and power is discussed in chapter 5.4.3.

In the UK, respondents described developments and consistencies in what were seen as male and female domains of policing. Similar to Austria, a special branch of policing, namely that of the authorised firearms officer, struggles with attracting female applicants.

> "[T]here's very very few females on that team, because the firearms team is a very male, macho, you know, if you go visit them, they're all bulked-up, gym, drinking protein-shakes and, you know, it's very very male-dominated, and they really struggle to attract females to that role." – Interview 11, England and Wales.

Different to their Austrian "counterpart", respondents reported being aware of an effort being made to attract more women to the firearms teams. Many spoke about the fact that the police are actively working to recruit more female officers in their firearms teams, be it via advertising or offering special training and information days for female officers. Coincidentally, interviewees also mentioned the fact that the admission fitness test for entry to the firearms branch is higher than the standard test, presumably making it hard for female applicants to comply with the set goals. While the reasoning behind these increased limits was never questioned or even defended by Austrian respondents, some UK interviewees doubted the rationale behind the higher limits for this particular special force. As it seemingly deters women from applying to the firearms team, interviewees challenged the reasoning for implementing considerably high fitness limits – "guns don't weigh much" (Interview 21, England and Wales). According to respondents though, it is of course not only the fitness test that keeps female officers from applying to special units such as the firearms team or the road policing unit.

> "So, because there's virtually no women within the role which I think is enormously influenced by social aspects, my department is generally cars and guns, which, you know, [mockingly] are just for boys. [/] So, I think there are huge barriers, it'd be lovely to say it's as simple as overt sexism and they don't let women in, it categorically isn't, it is about the social stereotypes associated with those departments people don't apply in the first place." - Interview 1, England and Wales.

Handling firearms is described as deterring female applicants, not only because it does not adhere with their ideal type of policing (see chapter 5.3.2), but also due to feminine and masculine stereotypes perpetuated over their lifetime. Interestingly, occupational cultural features are brought up; the issue of different socialisation of men and women is discussed and used as one piece of explanation as to why certain areas of policing seem to lack female participation more than others. Officers' logical response to this issue is to hold the organisation accountable and drive them to creating a less menacing work environment for female applicants, as well as focusing their promotional effort on women (and people of BAME groups[104]).

Respondents also talked about a special branch they felt had changed quite a lot over the recent years. The CID – Criminal Investigation Department – has historically been male-dominated (Holdaway/Parker 1998).

> "A: Yeah, CID used to be a very male orientated role [B: yeah] and that has moved on. [all: yeah] it used to be all about the men, you know, years ago, all these old CID blokes, and there are a lot of women in there now in CID.
> B: It used to be hard-working, hard-drinking men, and now, I think there's a pretty good split in there." – Interview 21-23, England and Wales.

While the culture at the CID is described as still being very traditional, the unit has opened up over the time and cultural processes, even in places such as the CID, seem to have moved on. Today, female detectives are not seen as an alien body in a culture that was not designed with them in mind – at least not to the extent they have been previously. Cultural changes within the branch reportedly have led to a more accepting and open approach of the CID, while still retaining some issues, especially around the area of flexible or part-time work (see chapter 5.6.2.1).

Speaking about the gendered nature of certain police departments or branches, UK respondents discussed what, in their eyes, are female workspaces inside the police. Those spaces have also undergone change over time, and female-connoted areas have become more recognised and are seen as integral to police work. Parallel to female officers getting into stereotypical male areas of policing, the number of male officers in these formerly female-led[105] areas has increased. These areas include working with children and dealing with (female) survivors of sexual abuse. Although these are what can be seen as core issues that police deal with,

---

104 "BME/BAME – Black and Minority Ethnic or Black, Asian and Minority Ethnic is the terminology normally used in the UK to describe people of non-white descent" (Definitions, Institute of Race Relations, irr.org.uk).

105 Not literally led though, as supervisors have still tended to be predominantly male.

their value has historically been underrated (Holdaway/Parker 1998), and only recently its worth has found a place in police culture (McCarthy 2013). According to interviewees, however, these "soft" policing issues gained their status through being recognised as "real", meaning tough, police work.

> "[T]here's other areas of work where we're overrepresented, your safeguarding, and you know, they're dealing with some of the most serious crime we deal with. And so, it's not about being tough, or you know, dealing with softer issues, it's not that, 'cause I think that's probably the hardest area of work we have." – Interview 22, England and Wales.

The fact that some of the work that is being carried out under the guise of "soft" policing, e.g., neighbourhood policing or safeguarding, actually concerns itself with issues that are quite serious, is seen as being misconstrued often. The experience of having one's ascribed area of work downplayed while subjectively feeling the importance of the issues that are being dealt with quite understandably creates a certain bitterness on the part of the respondents.

On their general reception within and perception of the male culture in the police, respondents noted varied experiences. There seems to be a widespread recognition that female officers are an essential part of the workplace – how this manifests, however, differs between colleagues and supervisors. There are still some pockets of male chauvinism or "laddy banter", and it is easy for female officers to feel left out or treated differently in the social side of the job. This seems to be even more pronounced in Austria, where some respondents described not only certain departments, but the police service itself as a male domain – a fact that is adamant to change.

> "And the fact that there are more men than women is somehow obvious, firstly because of the job description and secondly because men have always been there and women since '93? [...] it's somehow in the nature of things that there are more men around." – Interview 10, Austria.

Some interviewees seemed quite content with the fact that their work environment was highly masculinised and unlikely to drastically change in the coming years. Others noted the change that had already happened – one of the most prominent changes they discussed was the shift in atmosphere.

"There were some massive changes, [...] first of all a much rougher tone used to prevail and that was, well, they [men] do pull themselves together now." – Interview 16, Austria.

Respondents remark that they could now engage in "normal" talk – supposedly opposed to the male banter that had prevailed previously. The social standards as well as the approach to female officers have changed for the better. Still, differences between male and female colleagues remain. Austrian interviewees described the male culture they witness to be interrupted when dealing with female colleagues; a certain machismo, exaggerated self-confidence, and a particular diction is displayed by their male colleagues. Other respondents noted that they do not feel that their male colleagues' behaviour is in any way influenced by their gender, and they would not want to be treated differently than other male colleagues.

"Now, they don't really mince matters, and I never wanted that, I never wanted that just because I am a woman sitting there, that my colleagues behave differently, they should behave as they always do." – Interview 13, Austria.

This perceived influence of female officers on their male colleagues' behaviour is discussed in two ways: first, the fact that male officers have to adjust to their female colleagues, but secondly also the issue of female officers having to navigate these masculine behavioural patterns. Thus, female officers likewise have to adhere to some stereotypical masculine practices.

"Well, at our place [of work], we come in and we just banter, actually [laugh] So, yes. You can't be squeamish, that's right, yes." – Interview 11, Austria.

At the same time that male officers apparently have been asked to accommodate for their female colleagues, these female officers try to fit into the male mould that still prevails in policing. The difference they experience is therefore eliminated by copying their male colleagues, a seemingly natural (and safe) way of handling dominant difference described similarly by Lorde (1984). Respondents describe the police as a very tough place, one where you rather not show weakness and verbal insults are the order of the day. It is often remarked that (female) officers need a thick skin to last in the job – this is, contrary to the situation in the UK, not only due to the nature of policing itself, but also the circumstances found internally.

5.4.2 Perceived Gender Differences in Policing

While most respondents concurred that female officers are treated as equals in an occupational context, some perceived (inherent) differences remain. Most officers in Austria, and some in the UK, pointed out the fact that female officers treat situations differently than their male colleague would.

> "I don't know if it's about age or gender but they just like to do it a bit, well, 'the guys they like to fight, it doesn't matter', and as a woman you think well we could solve it differently now and it would work." – Interview 5, Austria.

Broadly speaking, two different approaches to conflicts where constructed: a de-escalating technique and a "tough" approach. Unsurprisingly, the tough approach is seen to be carried out more often by male officers than female ones, while female officers are more prone to use a de-escalating strategy and calm members of the public down.[106] This discrepancy has quite a long history, and the "softer" approach to policing has ever since been ascribed to female officers, creating a legitimate framework in which they could operate as police officers, while still maintaining their femininity (McCarthy 2013). Most respondents attribute these gendered approaches to presumably inherent differences in strength and body structure, as well as a varied caring nature, of male and female officers. While interviewees in the UK acknowledged that the gendered differences in approaches to conflicts are socially learned, most respondents in Austria did not much question the origin of these assumptions. Whereas some officers seemingly accept these differing gendered roles, others made it clear that they were as capable as any male colleague.

> "I mean, again, am I gonna be the first person you're gonna like send in if there's a fight? Maybe not. But if I'm the person there then I'm gonna do it." – Interview 7, England and Wales.

In the perception of people (more so men) who work in inherently violent surroundings that have historically been male dominated "[e]mbodied violence and masculine gender are effectively fused" (Connell 2013: 53). While "violence in military masculinities is a myth that cannot and should not be lived out" (Steinert 1997: 132, my translation), especially in a police

---

106 On interactions with the public and the perceived influence gender has on these reciprocal actions see chapter 5.5.

context where everyday work renders physical violence impractical in most cases, the potential to execute physical confrontations seems still pretty relevant to the ideal type perpetuated by officers of any gender. Violence remains an operational option (Cf. Mochan 2009). Thus, female officers try to conform to a certain type of masculinity. This of course stems from a desire not to be seen as the weak link, demonstrating their equal merit to their colleagues and supervisors in a culture where femininity and other marginalised masculinities are subordinated. At the same time, female officers did acknowledge the gendered difference in general approaches to serious situations, and the different ways in which their simple presence affects members of the public (see chapter 5.5).

An implicit issue that came up quite a lot in respondents' narratives is that of physical strength and body structure. Corporality, especially what can be described as "male" features of corporality, i.e., bodily strength, are of importance to police officers' debates. This can be seen from the way athletic women are almost rendered heroic (Cf. chapter 5.2.4), while stereotypical female acts, such as painting nails (chapter 5.4.3), are strongly rejected in the narratives of the respondents. Inhabiting a "female" body is still associated with shame, and officers (of all genders) who are accused of embodying femininity have to be quick to denounce these accusations or be rendered an outsider. From interviewees' viewpoint, it is a given that male and female bodies differ in strength and size. Therefore, the afore-mentioned divide in adapted roles dealing with the public is perceived as grounded in substantive facts. However, respondents, predominantly from the UK, mention that they do not feel that the ability to win a physical fight is even necessary in good police work.

> "Equally, we have to be relatively pragmatic, an awful lot of the jobs that we do are very physical and physically, women and men are different. And, they are bigger and heavier, and they have more (.) muscles. That said, I don't think that we ever go into a fair fight in the police service, we have tasers, we have pepper spray, we have batons, we're going mob-handed we understand what we're going to do." – Interview 1, England and Wales.

Raw physicality is seldomly described to solve conflicts in policing – even in situations in which tougher measures are considered appropriate, alternative tools and techniques are regarded as being more suitable. This line of argument is almost exclusively found in UK interviewees' responses and encompasses the possibility to alleviate the gender discourse from its focus on corporality.

Respondents are witnessing a change in perception of women in the police. Austrian officers referred to quite recent changes where female police officers have become normalised, and their male colleagues were now seeing them as their (more or less) equal counterparts.

> "And you also notice that it is becoming a given that women are in the police, so where it is never a topic, but where it is quite normal, yes. Where you don't talk about it anymore, and that's the way it should be, not talking about it." – Interview 16, Austria.

At the same time, interviewees desire for equal treatment in the workplace goes along with their want for an end to talks about their gender and its influence on their work life. For them, being treated equally is accompanied by a certain gender-blindness, where no differentiation in any direction is made based on their perceived gender.[107] Some UK interviewees raise the point that an understanding of the employment and promotion processes can lead to an even better recognition of peers regardless of gender. These processes are described as being very fair and equal to all, therefore there is no likelihood of detecting any gender differential. On a related note, Austrian officers stated that there is no gendered occupational aptitude, but rather individual suitability that is to be considered when joining the police.

5.4.3 Getting Along and Getting Ahead

There is a universal agreement on the issue of the cooperation between officers regardless of gender – namely, that it is perceived as very positive. Baring certain exceptions, interviewees regard their work-relations as quite harmonious and constructive. While the direct treatment officers experience from colleagues as well as supervisors is commended, they observed feeling fortunate to be able to do so.

> "I never experienced anything I don't think, because of who I am. [.] So, I've been quite lucky, I feel supported and we all get on." – Interview 17, England and Wales.

Thus, they acknowledged their perceived exceptionalism, as well as open the possibility for other female officers to have made differing experiences.

---

107 A line of argument that feeds into most Austrian respondents' unwillingness to accept the preferential treatment of women, see chapter 5.6.3.

By all means, incidents of sexism are also found in respondents' accounts (chapter 5.4.4), and not only restricted to other female colleagues.

The gender make-up of teams and divisions in the police plays a role in how female officers are perceived by their colleagues – and also how they regard their female colleagues. The discrepancy in experiencing differently gendered teams is best illustrated by a quote from a UK female officer, who remembers a meeting she held with an all-female working group:

> "And my colleague at the end of the meeting: 'that was amazing because we got so much done', 'cause we didn't like yap on about, you know, socially, things, we just got the job done. And we came to a conclusion, we didn't fall out with each other, there was no egos, we just did the job." – Interview 9, England and Wales.

Working with male colleagues is often associated with a certain male egotism that respondents deem counterproductive. In this way, cooperation with female colleagues is constructed as highly positive, and even a stimulating work experience by UK respondents. In other words, a work environment led or primarily occupied by women is in no way constructed as negative here, as all-male environments (see authorised firearms officers) tend to be.

UK respondents overall rated the quality of their cooperation with colleagues, regardless of gender, as very good. At the same time, they acknowledged the fact that they themselves, as female officers, do feel a difference in working with an all-male team. With being the only woman on a team or in a certain division comes a feeling of alienation that respondents say is unique to their gender.

> "[talking about positive action schemes for women] [A]nd the guys are like what about us [...] but when you say to them have you ever walked into a room and thought you looked different to everybody else they say no, so you can't understand where I'm coming from then. So, until you do, and there'll come a time when they will, that's what I deal with every day." – Interview 5, England and Wales.

It is not so much the interaction or cooperation with male colleagues that respondents view as problematic, but rather the fact of the matter that they, as a gender, often are outnumbered, or even the only female officer in the room. With this particular experience, the female officers' difference to the dominant male norm is depicted in an unvarnished way.[108] Incidentally, this feeling of alienation and seclusion can serve as grounds of justification for any actions and policies supporting underrepresented groups within the police service.

Austrian interviewees deemed "their" female colleagues and teams to be highly skilled and generally agreeable, whilst noting that other female officers might not be their idea of an ideal police officer. In order to be considered a valuable member of the team, one needs to present as a "grown woman"[109]; in contrast, female officers who were deemed unfit to the job, or simply negatively received as colleagues, were described as "bitches" (Interviews 10 and 11, Austria). Stereotypically female-associated behaviours such as painting nails or bickering among colleagues were very negatively received by interviewees. At the same time, respondents have not experienced these behaviours first-hand; they were rather treated as given female behaviour or rumoured about other departments. These sort of "ghost stories" about unfavourable behaviour have been trailing around the police since the first female officer joined the force at the start of the 1990s.

What is more, these perpetuated stereotypes often have little to do with the work of a police officer itself – painting your nails does not deter you from fulfilling your duty as a frontline officer. They rather get their adverse treatment simply by being associated with femininity, further proving that there still is little room for the development of a feminine police identity (Cf. Behr 2019). While Austrian respondents acknowledged that they themselves did not experience any kind of problems in dealing with their female colleagues, few also remarked that they see the current number of women in the police as sufficient, not wanting to have any more (potentially "unfit") female colleagues at their station. In contrast, male colleagues are never marked as potentially challenging by default, projecting the treatment respondents got as female officers, namely, to not be outright accepted but continuously tested for job-fitness, on their female colleagues themselves. Austrian Interviewees describe working with men to be easier, owing to their more direct nature and differences in deciding conflict. This seems to be somewhat in contrast to the various instances of sexist behaviour witnessed by respondents – male colleagues

---

108 This difference is of course even more pronounced when other "standards" are taken into consideration, such as race (white), age (middle-aged), or sexual orientation (straight).

109 "gstandene Dame".

are still seen as somewhat preferable by Austrian officers. Respondents further explained that, tactically and socially, going on patrol in a mixed team is most advantageous – which for them individually consequently meant being paired up with a male colleague. Of course, some also state that the nature of their cooperation and team play is not affected by gender but rather the individual officers themselves.

Other, but also more far-reaching, problems arise when one not only considers cooperation among colleagues of the same rank, but also opportunities for promotion as well as interactions with colleagues of higher or lower rank. The issues that present themselves when female officers are, or try to get, promoted are manifold. First, while female officers are generally underrepresented in the police, positions of rank are even harder to achieve for women – the glass ceiling is, if anything, even more pronounced in the police service. Interviewees from Austria acknowledged that there are certain limitations for female officers who want to rise up through the ranks.

> "It gets difficult when you want to have a say in something or apply for positions that are, well, if you say, okay, I'm demanding some kind of claim to leadership, right, if I say okay, I want to become a deputy somewhere, I want to become the head of somewhere, then you notice that you encounter resistance. And some of it very pronounced." – Interview 16, Austria.

It is observed that some women do occupy leading positions within the police service in Austria as well as the UK, however, next to their numbers being limited, those positions often do not come with the same strategic impact as the ones occupied by their male colleagues.[110] This can lead to a feeling of tokenism (Cockburn 1991: 67) on both sides, male colleagues (wrongfully) accusing female officers of benefitting of their gender, and female officers of rank feeling underappreciated and being in a disquieting position. UK respondents also remarked how it is more difficult for female officers to get promoted – not only because of personal predispositions, such as low self-esteem or undervaluing their skills, but also because of socially structured circumstances. For some it is evident that female officers still have to choose between their career or their family.

---

110 A notable exception might be Cressida Dick, the first female Metropolitan Police Commissioner.

> "[B]eing female I do feel that it's harder to get promoted within the police and if you look at all the, not everyone, but if you look at some of the people getting promoted now, they're all either single women or they haven't got children, so I do think that you have to make that choice." – Interview 18, England and Wales.

Accumulating certain evidence pertaining to career advancement, such as number of night shifts and other related work content, is made harder by the twofold burden carried by most women. Additionally, because aspirants have to pass a board in order to get promoted, the issue of white men reproducing themselves in leading roles (Cockburn 1991: 54) is not to be underestimated. Characteristics that are sought out in leading roles are often misconstrued when found in female officers. Female officers noticed a lack of gendered support when it comes to access to higher ranks.

> "As a female in the police if you are, if you're seen to put your foot down, then you're seen as moody or, grumpy, whereas if you're a man it would be seen as good decision-making." – Interview 8, England and Wales.

The behaviour of male and female officials is thus measured with a double standard in this context. Interestingly, it can be seen here that male connotated behaviour can have negative consequences for female police officers in certain cases.

What respondents struggled most with, however, is the different treatment female officers of rank get from their male subordinates as well as their male colleagues of rank. Austrian respondents remarked that (especially younger) male officers are often unable to accept female authority the way they do male authority (Cf. Cockburn 1991: 67). They were perceived to almost test the boundaries of how far they can go in trying to undermine female authority – older male colleagues were, however, understood to value the rank structure itself more than their possible aversion to female leadership. As female leadership has a history of being conceived as not "tough enough" (Silvestri 2003: 132), it is almost inevitable that younger male colleagues follow this structural prejudice in testing out its limits. Some officers in the UK also mentioned that they sensed that their male colleagues are feeling threatened by the rise in numbers of female officers of rank. This is embedded in a prejudiced perception of leadership – it is generally assumed that a male officer is in charge, not only by the public, but also within the police service and in dealing with related institutions. Apart from differentiating comments or outright negative responses women in leading roles get from their male colleagues, some respondents remarked that often the behaviour of their female colleagues is as much of a setback.

> "I've experienced senior women who are up there and they are not interested in helping anybody else get there, and you just think, 'really? after everything you've been through?' and that's quite, that I find the most frustrating. Cause I think, if we could just sort ourselves out as a gender, we'd be absolutely unstoppable. But it's just so, sometimes it's just so petty and it's like really? Really?" – Interview 5, England and Wales.

This quote shows different aspects of certain perceived behaviour and its implications by female leaders: First, an acknowledgement of the fact that, in order to get to the top, as a woman, you have to endure troublesome experiences. Secondly, a lack of solidarity from female officers who, following the achievement of a certain status after allegedly experiencing sexism, are perceived as not feeling the need to look out for their gender peers. Thirdly, the trusting outlook that, if only women would support each other in the workplace, gender equity would be attained in an instant. Female officers in leading roles are hereby made complicit[111] in the continuing oppression of female aspirations for advancement in an inherently masculine environment. The fact remains that "[t]he subject might yet be thought as deriving its agency from precisely the power it opposes" (Butler 1997: 17), rendering any criticism as an end in itself. For those who want to partake in said power, however, this particular form of complicity, bound upwards but never down, is hard to accept.

5.4.4 Incidents of Sexism and Misogyny

While any aforementioned difference in treatment or gendered experiences of female police officers is of course part of and informed by a sexist and/or misogynistic environment, the incidents and experiences discussed in this chapter deal with outright discriminatory behaviour experienced by the respondents – behaviour they themselves classified as sexist. Of course, some respondents, predominantly from Austria, also reported not having experienced any forms of sexism or misogynistic behaviour in their workplace at all. Most interviewees, however, who at first reported no

---

111 On the complicity of women in patriarchy and its controversy, see Thürmer-Rohr (2010).

discriminatory issues, recognised or recalled certain events only over the course of the interview.

Reports from both countries overwhelmingly speak of "small" amounts of sexism in the police service, while some mention having to deal with issues relating to their gender on a daily basis. The sexism experienced by female police officers in both countries mostly has changed forms over the years, and nowadays displays of overt sexism are seen as rare. This, however, does of course not influence people's personal views on the topic, and subtler forms of sexism are quite prevalent throughout different ranks and divisions. Although the majority of respondents mentioned that the sexism and misogyny they experience has weakened both in quantity and quality, they recognised that today's incidents are just as meaningful to them. That "small" issues can have a huge impact on people's perception and situatedness in an organisation is best illustrated by an event that happened in the early 1990s in Austria, shortly after women had been granted admission to the regular police service. A respondent remembered advocating against depictions of (half-)naked women in areas such as locker rooms, but most importantly common rooms.

> "[I]n the beginning they also said, there you go, that's typical female [behaviour] again, they come and make a problem over bullshit such as this, like, whether there is a calendar hanging or not. But for me that had symbolic value, right." - Interview 7, Austria.

The fight for equality and equal treatment in all areas of policing, not only in work-related operational policing but also interpersonal and social relationships and treatment lasts until this day for some respondents. As overt sexist or misogynistic behaviour is more and more considered offensive, interviewees still feared that internally held personal beliefs and prejudice would not necessarily change.

In light of this, many interviewees also mentioned specific individual colleagues who they had troubles with. Rather than experiencing all or even most of their colleagues as discriminatory, many respondents in Austria stated that certain individuals have their problems with female officers. Through this, sexism is constructed as something that is not innate to the police itself, but rather an isolated issue that one can (or must) deal with individually.

As previously mentioned, subtler forms of sexism were seen to be more prevalent in today's police work environment. An example of this is straightforward differential treatment of female and male officers by colleagues or superiors, as well as of female officers in managerial positions.

One or two decades ago, female officers of course also experienced these prejudiced kinds of typecasting of their role in the workplace:

> "[W]hen I came to the police, it was already done by habit that (.) that I made the coffee, right. That I make sure that there's always coffee, so you already adopt this "woman's role" then, I'd say, somehow exploiting the typical female role, or what immediately came was 'Can you cook', well, and then you just cooked a few times, right, and they were really very satisfied, right, then you were one of them, I dare say." – Interview 8, Austria.

Here, outright sexist attitudes of male colleagues were accepted and adopted. By conforming to these values and fulfilling certain stereotypes (cooking), stereotypical expectations are fulfilled on the one hand – on the other hand, this conformity is also framed as a positive means. The resulting acceptance is experienced as an "equation" (of one of them), which in reality is a fallacy, namely simply a subordination to the gendered social constellation. Nowadays, these pressures have subsided somewhat, but there are still echoes of stereotypical allocations in the division of the workload and -quality, or in social work life. These experiences range from being excluded from certain activities at work to male officers ignoring commands of their female superiors.

Sexist behaviour was also experienced in the form of comments or criticism directed at female officers of all ranks. Again, these deal with stereotypical female-connotated behaviour, devaluing female officers' contributions in the workplace. Once more, restricting women's place to their domestic role as opposed to their professional qualifications was a recurring substantial issue.

> "[W]ith the older colleagues, they really had a problem with it, that was really the case, a woman has no place here, that was really the case, right, there's the kitchen, there's the stove, you can go there" – Interview 6, Austria.

This particular incident happened about ten years ago, and it was mentioned that younger colleagues did not behave as extremely. In England and Wales, comments such as these mostly referred to the female officer's "duty" to "put on the kettle" and make tea. There are interviewees who mentioned that to this day, they sometimes receive derogatory comments because of their gender. Furthermore, female officers' achievements are downplayed and sometimes colleagues actively override their decisions simply because they, in their perception, do not see them as equals. This devaluation of female officer's decisions and contributions of course also impacts their standing with other colleagues and sometimes other organisations – a participant spoke of a male colleague who purposefully discredited her work input in front of the public. So, while female officers themselves are devalued simply because of their gender, their contributions in the workspace are also underrated and placed under a much greater scrutiny than those of their male colleagues. Sometimes, these comments were, according to respondents' experiences, intended as "jokes" – however, only a small number of interviewees gave leeway to this explanation.

> "I talked to him again a few days later because I just couldn't leave it alone and he told me it was a joke, but I (..) don't actually consider it a joke. And that's a reason for me to say that I can't work together anymore." – Interview 4, Austria.

Mostly, these so-called jokes have a sexual connotation and originate not only from colleagues but also superiors. In this way, Cockburn's explanation of sexual humour as male control (Cockburn 1991: 153) serves as a fitting explanation of these behaviours. Thus, female colleagues are once again belittled and excluded of equal social relationships in the workplace, such as weighing in on "banter".

Another form of sexism that was received ambiguously by female officers is what they sometimes dub "positive sexism" or male chauvinism. A considerable number of respondents stated that they had experiences where their male colleagues or superiors were trying to protect or cushion them. This type of behaviour is characteristically more prevalent in specialist forces that remain male-dominated, such as the firearms department or riot squad. An interviewee remembered the experiences and reaction of a colleague:

> "[S]he was made to feel vulnerable by some of her male colleagues so she felt that they were having to protect her, or they felt they were having to protect her so she felt awkward because she wants to just concentrate on what she was doing, and she [...] decided not to go back for that reason." – Interview 3, England and Wales.

Some respondents explained this behaviour of their male colleagues with a possible subconscious bias to see women, and therefore their female colleagues, as "the weaker sex"[112]. Interviewees stated that in the sense of team spirit, it is only natural to want to have your colleagues' back, but this type of behaviour does lead to a questioning of female officers' abilities and sense of vulnerability. Of course, the emphasis on stereotypically male-connotated abilities in frontline policing contributes to this culture of benevolent sexism in the police service.

Some respondents also remembered being treated differently, as in beneficially, by their male superiors when they started the job. This "positive" treatment, such as not being sent to possibly critical incidents, is received quite negatively by the affected female officer as well as her male colleagues who deem this type of "preferential" treatment unjust. Especially in Austria, where female officers value equal treatment highly, this behaviour is met with antagonism. Although one might argue that issues such as preferential treatment should not be negatively received, when taking a closer look, these treatments reveal a misogynistic motive. They work to keep female officers' self-confidence down, making them feel vulnerable by insinuating that they could not cope with certain issues on their own – without the help of a man- or at all. Male chauvinism in its core is deeply rooted in misogyny: Steinert finds "the patriarchal protective attitude [...], according to which 'our' women must be protected" (Steinert 1997: 137) to be profoundly misogynist, in that it others and objectifies women in the same way it does the perceived threat.

More open and outright displays of misogyny and harassment were not commonplace for most respondents, yet still remain an issue. Whether it was through the aforementioned differential treatment by superiors or without any obvious reason, female officers experienced exclusion and bullying as immensely hurtful experiences. These occurrences make a stark impression on female officers, no matter however long ago they might have occurred. An Austrian respondent recalls the time immediately after her recruitment in the 1990s:

> "[A]t that time, for example, when they were allocating you to a district, the colleagues of a [...] police inspection, for example, they made a signature list, that they do not want women to come to them, to the police inspection. So, they said, no, we do not want women. And we won't have one at the police station. And, of course that

---

112 As quoted in an interview; research of varied disciplines has shown that these simplistic views on sex and gender do not hold up to scientific evidence, see e.g., Saini (2017).

does something to you, right, if you know, before you go there, well, there are signature lists that nobody wants you, right. Of course, you shouldn't take it personally, but, at 19, 20, 21 years old, it's not that easy." – Interview 7, Austria.

According to this excerpt, there are different layers to these exclusionary practices, as in all cases of prejudicial conduct: that of the group and that of the individual. Women, as a group, are constructed as an undesirable body, which results in the discrimination of the respective individual. This is understood by the officers, as is demonstrated in the phrase and wish to "not take it personally" – maybe they themselves are not perceived as the problem, but rather their belonging to the aforementioned undesirable social group. Similar to the aforementioned prejudicial statements meant as "jokes", bullying and exclusionary practices also often carry sexual, mostly vulgar or demeaning, connotations. These are seemingly even harder to process and overcome, and female officers struggle with the handling of these experiences.

"I remember, being quite young in service, sergeant, so the first rank up, and I told off an officer in the hallway, he'd done something really wrong and he was a difficult officer to deal with anyway and he was very long in service [...], I was going into brief, a big team of officers about a job we would do and I told him off [...] and when we went into the briefing room it was almost entirely male in the room and he said really loudly as we were [entering] 'if you speak to me like that again sergeant I'll put you over my knee and spank you' and the whole room laughed. Everybody in the room laughed. I remember saying actually, sit down I'll deal with you later. And situations like this you can't [...] you know I wanted to cry, but you can't, you just have to crack on because it let's people get what they want." – Interview 1, England and Wales.

The very existence of the all-male environment mentioned makes it even harder for female officers to deal with such serious incidents[113]. Cockburn (1991: 158) considers male-aligned structures at the workplace, from sexual talk to socializing after work, as an essential pillar of the patriarchal regime. Only through the continuous oppression and othering of anything and anyone considered female can these discriminating behaviours contin-

---

113 On the issue of dealing with similar incidents see later this chapter, on reaction to sexist comments and actions from the public see chapter 5.5.1.3.

ue to exist without clear and adequate repression by others. Interviewees treaded carefully when talking about sexual harassment, yet some gave or insinuated examples of superiors or colleagues who regard female officers in an inappropriate way or are no strangers to molesting incidents. Unfortunately, female officers, especially in Austria, felt quite resigned in this regard, with one commenting that "there will always be people like that" (Interview 15, Austria).

Respondents, in trying to cope and to understand their differential treatment, brought forth possible reasons as to why they as female officers were being discriminated against. These grounds differed with the particular individual administering the ill-treatment. When female officers experience maltreatment from male officers roughly their age and of the same rank, most felt that it was competition and envy that drove their colleagues to these behaviours. This was most often the case for interviewees in the UK.

> "B: The guys I struggle with are usually sort of my age. Because I think [hand movements] [A: they're competing?] yeah, they see it as a competition when actually, you can have those conversations you can work together and both, everybody, there's a lot of stuff to do and we're all trying to do the same thing that's what I find quite frustrating." – Interviews 4 and 5, England and Wales.

In light of this, commenting on a female colleagues' supposed professional shortcomings or belittling their contributions can of course be laid out as competitive actions from male colleagues – an action that is in no way potentially problematic for the perpetrator in a male-dominated environment.

Others noted that they rather experienced their older male colleagues as being more sexist and prejudiced against female police officers – in Austria, some might have started their career at a time when it was not possible for women to join the police as an equal. This was, in fact, reported by quite a number of respondents; older colleagues still do not accept female officers the same way they do younger male colleagues. An interviewee described this phenomenon as explained to her by male colleagues:

> "So, I can only say, it's like they explained to me, it's simply a fear behaviour, this "emasculating" of this job, and to be afraid, "oh, a woman can do that too", and that's actually *the* male domain and it's their own male circle and I think that has something to do with it." – Interview 6, Austria.

According to this approach, however, the same underlying reason for gendered differential treatment of any kind seems to be the same for male colleagues of all ages: fear of competition and replacement. As Spasić et al. (2015) find that female officers are more formally educated than male officers, and thus more competitive in promotion bids – a fact that cannot be drawn from this study – this fear might be substantiated.

Last but not least, interviewees discussed how incidents of sexism are handled and dealt with internally, and how they personally dealt with harassing or condescending actions directed at them. Many respondents from the UK claimed that their colleagues and superiors, including those who themselves engage in discriminatory behaviour, would never see themselves as sexist, and be offended at being called sexist – they simply do not recognise their own prejudicial actions as misogynistic. Furthermore, police officers allegedly know that (overt) sexism is wrong, however, as one interviewee noted, this does not necessarily influence their personal thoughts and feelings on the topic. A quote that sums all these issues up quite neatly is that of interviewee 4 when talking about how discriminatory speech and behaviour is constructed in the police service:

> "[Y]ou get some quite invidious sort of undermining comments on the, on the grapevine, from the old [staff] blokes, comments like, you know, it's some kind of political correctness, or it's a lowering of standards, or it's a weakening of the force, or it's going to lead to all sorts of problems or blablabla. It's just cause, I think, 'cause they're threatened by it basically. But they would never use that language. But, to me, that's fairly obvious.[I: So, they're not outright saying that but, it's more like] No, they would never say that, that would show that they had some kind of insight or awareness, which they don't have." – Interview 4, England and Wales.

Again, the possibility of male police officers' as of yet unquestioned sovereignty being challenged is seen as an impetus for their unreconstructed comments and attitudes, along with the unwillingness and inability to detect their own prejudice. A certain lack of ability for reflection and insight is also mentioned by some, rendering it almost impossible to challenge or change individual behaviour.

Respondents note that it does get tiring to try and keep challenging sexist behaviour and comments, a circumstance that surely influences their general job satisfaction and vocational attitudes. Interviewees describe the different ways in which they personally handle situations in which they have been treated a certain way simply because of their gender. First of all, respondents from Austria noted that the predisposition of oneself was not to be underestimated when dealing with these situations. Most importantly, they felt that the younger an officer is, the more these kinds of comments and behaviours get under your skin and make you question yourself instead of the behaviour of others. As some interviewees from Austria have indeed joined the police service when it was still an entirely male domain, they reported being quite affected by the early prejudicial treatment they received. It appears that there is a need to "toughen up" and grow a thicker skin in this occupation, at least from what early female officers described. Interviewees from both countries mentioned that one always has to consider one's reaction to inappropriate behaviour and comments: Some warranted a quick cut off, mostly in form of a strong verbal retort, others were apparently better ignored totally, while individual cases were better talked about in a neutral setting afterwards. While some respondents from Austria noted that they mostly take sexism in the form of jokes or comments with a touch of humour and play along with their male colleagues, others noticed that there is no possibility for change if one does not actively engage with these problematic behaviours and challenge perpetrators as well as their corroborating peers. At the same time, a controversial rhetoric was used, namely, that each individual has to decide for themselves how they want to be treated. Thus, the blame can always be laid at the affected female officer and not the wrongful behaviour of their male colleague(s) or systemic issues. While the singular addressing of these issues is of course to be supported, it must not lead to an atmosphere in which female officers are held responsible for their wrongful treatment.

With more grave issues, such as sexual harassment, female officers felt that, although the situation has improved over the last years and decades, incidents were still not being dealt with adequately. With some noting that incidents were simply ignored or swept under the rug, others further lamented that victim blaming is commonplace. Instead of perceiving the men who perpetrated these transgressions as an issue to be dealt with, female officers were being held responsible and often had to face the consequences of these incidents.

> "We've seen that quite recently with one of our officers who reported that she'd been sexually assaulted, and, she ended up having to move team completely, move out of [area] completely in terms of her work, because [...] the colleagues, one of whom was also female, viewed her as the reason that one of their colleagues had been moved to another area, they liked their colleagues, they saw it as her problem." – Interview 8, England and Wales.

Furthermore, police culture does not view "whistleblowing" in a very good light, as it is a culture heavily reliant on group trust and solidarity (Reiner 2016). In light of this, dealing with incidents of sexism, misogyny and sexual harassment is never easy for female officers, as they do not only have to deal with the issue itself but also with the fallout of a possible reporting or their simple objection to certain practices. Thus, female officers who do rebel against these unspoken rules, for example by reporting incidents of sexual harassment, are othered and outcast a second time, first by misogynistic guidelines, later by the allied patriarchal standards of the police service.

5.4.5 Internal Developments

All respondents noted that their internal treatment has changed over the years, and most found the situation for female officers nowadays to be better than decades or even only some years ago. As mentioned previously, especially in Austria the situation at the start of some of the interviewed women's career was completely different. In England and Wales, some mentioned that female officers of rank were unheard of, if not extremely rare, in certain branches. Interviewees observed that the continued hiring of female officers has brought a positive change to the workplace – "newcomers" allegedly do not face the same or at least not the magnitude of the problems female officers faced years ago.

Respondents from both countries noted that through personal contact and interactions, male officers have learned to see female officers as equal co-workers and to acknowledge that "we are here to stay" (Paraphrase, Interview 1, England and Wales). Furthermore, UK participants remarked that, as pre-conceived ideas about women in the workplace change, female officers' reception changes as well – this could be seen in the way that younger male officers treat their female colleagues as opposed to some prejudicial stereotypes held by older, now mostly retired, officers.

While they acknowledged that the police service has come a long way in terms of gender equality, a large proportion of interviewees from the UK also stated that there was still a long way to go. This, for most, was not limited to the police service and its surroundings but societal pressures in general. It was also lamented by interviewees in both countries that the police service in general was quite slow and adamant to change. Some put this down to the sheer size of the organisation, others saw the roots for this mainly in the culture perpetuated in the police. In light of this, however, female officers overall seemed to have a positive outlook on the changes that had already taken place, and those that will supposedly come to be in future.

5.4.6 Interim Findings

The acceptance of female officers in a male-dominated workspace has improved over the decades since female police officers are hired under equal conditions and have the same powers and duties as their male counterparts. In constructing the equal treatment of women in the police service as incongruous and unusual – something that male officers have to get used to –, not only are female officers themselves objectified and othered, but furthermore the possibility of hostile behaviour from male officers is somewhat constructed as justified (Cf. Heidensohn/Silvestri 2012). It is to be noted that this narrative is much more prominent with Austrian respondents than UK ones, as the complete integration of women in the police service in Austria happened almost 20 years after it did within police forces in England and Wales. Being seen as an equal is still not taken for granted by female officers in both countries today. Many described the need to prove themselves in order to get accepted as a peer, whilst male officers are usually given the benefit of the doubt, and only are perceived as unqualified if proven as such. This can be traced back to the construction of police work as male (Silvestri 2003: 26ff.); with no ideal type of female policing available (Behr 2019: 168), it is almost self-explanatory that female officers are not per se perceived as competent in their work. Female officers are somehow stuck between aligning themselves with the male mould that traditional police culture presents – granting them acceptance within a male-dominated culture – and following their pre-defined gender role in performing femininity (Cf. Holzleithner 2016) – which, to a certain extent, is socially expected of them. Female officers' gender performance is placed under a lot of scrutiny and being perceived as either too feminine or too masculine can become a point of peer critique (Cf. Holzleithner 2017, Müller 2007).

Certain pockets of policing in both countries remain overtly male-dominated: In the UK, this encompasses special units and divisions such as firearms officers or riot squad, while in Austria the largest special unit Cobra – used for crisis management and critical emergencies – is perceived as one of the last domains of hyper-masculinity. While UK respondents talked about the fact that these special units are struggling to attract female officers into their ranks, Austrian interviewees rather viewed this lack of female participation as a given, due to the nature of the work being carried out by the unit. Female officers in Austria also discussed the exceptionalism of those few women who have made their way into the Cobra, while respondents in the UK did not deem the work itself as that much more demanding or impassable for female officers but rather viewed the culture around these special units as deterring women from applying in the first place. An early study from Brown and Sargent (1995) seems to support the latter view. While there is no difference in male and female officers' interest in becoming an authorised firearms officer (AFO), a much higher number of actual AFOs are male. This leads the authors to conclude that, rather than a lack of individual motivation, this gender difference has its roots in "police culture and embedded individual and organizational attitudes" (Brown/Sargent 1995: 13).

Viewing societal issues as the main reason for a lack of female officers in certain special units opens up the possibility to critique the police organisation to actively engage in creating a more welcoming work environment for female officers by developing these units in a more open and flexible way. UK officers also discussed the fact that a previously male-dominated special unit, the CID, has increasingly been accepting more women and made great leaps towards gender equality even over the last few years. Furthermore, there are some areas of policing where female officers have been (and are still) more prominent than their male colleagues – mostly in dealing with children, vulnerable people, and survivors of sexual and/or physical abuse. According to UK interviewees, these areas have witnessed an increase in male officers, along with an increase in allocated importance in police culture. One can argue if these changes in perception of these "softer" forms of policing, which have historically been undervalued (Holdaway/Parker 1998, McCarthy 2013), are due to the fact that more male officers are carrying out these tasks, or if it rather happened of its own accord along with a change in police culture as a whole.

There are differences not only across the two countries but also across respondents on their perception of police culture and masculinity. A small number of respondents, mostly from Austria, reported not feeling different to their male colleagues, or rather concurred with and tried to understand the difference in treatment they receive from colleagues. Still, some female officers, regardless of their area of work, reported feeling alienated and isolated from their male colleagues and the work culture as such. Many also stated that they witnessed change in the behaviour of their male colleagues over the years and decades – as male officers had to "get used to" female officers they had to get rid of certain traditions and practices. Some female officers in Austria do engage in these types of behaviours, such as banter or crass humour, therefore trying to solidify their spot as "one of the boys". Moreover, female officers in Austria often describe the need for (potential) female police officers to be inured to certain comments and behaviours emanating from their male colleagues in order to last in this job, while those in the UK rather described a hostile work environment as something the police service as an organisation has to deal with (i.e., to provide a more positive environment) rather than putting the weight on the individual (female) officer.

Respondents also talked about perceived gender differences in policing. This is perhaps best illustrated when dealing with conflict situations, in which two ends of a scale are used to depict the possible reactions of officers: Female officers are allegedly more prone to de-escalating situations with their presence and their methods, while male officers tend to prolong the situation in having a tougher approach with members of the public. These findings are in line with those by Rabe-Hemp (2008a, 2008b), who finds that female officers view their style of policing as providing more empathy, better communication skills, as well as less forcefulness. This difference in policing "styles" has been a topic of discussion for many theoretical and empirical studies (Bazley et al. 2007, Hoffman/Hickey 2005, McCarthy 2013). This, along with the idea that the difference employers seek when hiring women is that they work harder and are more caring (Cockburn 1991: 68) than men, is confirmed by many respondents.

Following the notion that, when women are employed it is precisely because they are women (Cockburn 1991: 24), one could argue that the recent increase and rise in popularity of softer policing, at least in England and Wales[114], has evolved with the rise in the numbers of female police officers. Respondents from Austria seemed to accept these divisions more easily than their UK counterparts, as the latter pinned these perceived differences down to gendered differences in upbringing and social learning. Instead of questioning the usefulness of a softer approach to policing, they rather disputed the notion that this approach should remain reserved to female officers, while Austrian officers, on the whole, seemed satisfied with the difference in approaches to policing being segregated along a gender-divide.

---

114 Contrarily, as Behr (2019) argues, German police are more and more reliant on notions of masculinity and toughness – a fact that can be argued to reflect on Austrian police as well.

What can be seen from many accounts in both countries is that female officers tried to adhere to male standards – in a policing context this refers to the hegemonic masculinity as described by scholars such as Behr and Connell (Behr 2008, Connell/Messerschmidt 2005). While many asserted their capability of adhering to these standards – being able to physically deal with difficult situations – they also conceded that, physically speaking, female and male officers go into a fight with dissimilar prerequisites. While respondents from both countries were consistent in expressing the idea of gendered differences in physicality, it is predominantly UK officers that mentioned the fact that the actuality of police work is not reliant on the use of force in the traditional sense of the word. The tools and techniques available to police officers effectively render physical strength subsidiary in almost all cases – a fact that was also mentioned by Austria's equal opportunities officer. Regarding gendered differences while at the same time not losing sight of each officer's individuality and an inherent certain want to be treated as equals is a tough balancing act, as can be seen in the accounts of the interviewed officers.

Respondents from both countries unanimously described the cooperation between officers regardless of gender to be highly positive – there inevitably are some individual exceptions. When discussing their immediate work environment, most officers who mentioned being content also remarked on the possible exceptionalism of this circumstance. This perception of working in an environment that is cordial and positive does of course not contradict certain individual adverse behaviour or prevent feelings of alienation and discriminatory practices. Gender diversity in police departments and units influences how female officers are perceived as well as how they perceive their female and male colleagues. Female officers in the UK reported that, while generally perceiving their cooperation with colleagues as good, they did notice a feeling of alienation when working with an all-male team. Conversely, they talked about their perception of all-female teams as highly positive and constructive. Likewise, Austrian interviewees spoke very highly of their immediate female colleagues and superiors. However, a paradox situation presented itself: While Austrian officers did describe being held to different standards and having to prove themselves to their male colleagues and superiors as negative and discriminating, they seemed to hold the same standards for their female colleagues; a priori marking their male colleagues as fit and their female counterparts as potentially "unfit" for the job. Negative preconceived ideas about female officers are often founded in hearsay and gossip about stereotypical female-associated behaviours that have little to do with one's capability and competence as a police officer. In light of this, the progression of a female police identity seems as inaccessible as ever (Cf. Behr 2019).

Interviewees further discussed issues they are facing when moving up the rank structure (or trying to). As female officers of rank are still rare, or at least an aspect worth talking about internally as well as publicly, in both countries, it is not surprising that respondents saw themselves faced with certain barriers when wanting to break this glass-ceiling. The feeling of tokenism (Cockburn 1991: 67) on the side of those female officers who have been promoted stems from the notion that these positions often do not carry the same strategic weight that other positions of similar rank do. While making female officers feel undervalued, this situation also leads to male officers' resentment against female officers for allegedly being promoted because of their gender.

Another issue that many officers see is that women in the police still have to choose between their career and their family life. This is due to manifold reasons: First, certain experience and/or training is needed in order to get promoted in both countries, which is made harder for female officers by social circumstances – women with caring duties are often not able to fulfil these requirements, whereas officers note that, to male officers, having families and children is never perceived as an issue in their career progression. Secondly, research has provided evidence that people in current positions of power do seek out their likeness in future leaders (Cockburn 1991: 54), which makes any deviation from the white male norm a further hurdle to overcome when wanting to progress in the organisation. A third issue is that of perception of female leadership, and male-associated behavioural patterns in female officers. Respondents noted how certain character traits of theirs that would be applauded when looking for male candidates to promote, are negatively received due to the fact that they are female. This also leads to female officers of rank being exposed to a more scrutinising treatment of their subordinates – especially young male officers seem to have a hard time accepting female authority, which is often perceived as not being "tough enough" (Silvestri 2003: 132). Some respondents also lamented the lack of solidarity from individual female officers who have been promoted in supporting other women – they were constructed as complicit in the ongoing oppression of women in an environment that was not designed with them in mind.

While the aforementioned issues deal with underlying and sometimes subconscious prejudices, officers in both countries also talked about what they perceive to be outright sexist comments and behaviours. While the volume of these incidents varied for each interviewee, there are some similarities to be spun from their stories. In both countries, overt sexism seems to decline in frequency, while some interviewees noted that the incident's meaning and importance to them has not lessened due to that. It was also mentioned that the fight for gender equality is not restricted only to operational policing and strictly work-related issues, but also a fight for more recognition and better interpersonal and social relationships with their peers. Sexism was sometimes constructed as something that is not innate to police culture, but rather an issue that manifests itself in individual male officers that are perceived to be problematic. Through this, however, a structural approach in dealing with issues of sexism was not set up to be suitable. If sexism is viewed as a problem on an individual level, rather than an inherent social structure, the rationale behind criticising solutions aiming towards pertaining change on a broader level can be made sense of more easily.[115]

Subtler forms of sexism that seem prevalent nowadays for one deal with gender stereotypes and typecasting female officers in certain roles, socially and professionally. These behaviours include exclusion from certain activities, comments, unwarranted criticism and talking down female officers' achievements and contributions. Devaluing or sexual comments are also often presented in the form of jokes, which leave female officers the choice of either getting along with their male colleagues' inappropriate behaviours or being considered a "killjoy" for calling them out on their actions; most officers in the UK opted for the latter option, while Austrian respondents' reactions were more nuanced. Through this, sexual and misogynistic humour serve as activities of male control over their female colleagues (Cockburn 1991: 153) – either reaction leaves them open to further criticism or shame.

Additionally, many officers reported forms of male chauvinism, or "positive sexism" to be widespread among their male colleagues. From a female officers' perspective, the protection of their male colleague is somehow seen as a given, as police culture values group-solidarity highly, yet the emphasis that is laid on the safeguarding of female officers and the resulting differentiation in treatment of male and female officers caused irritation for respondents. This protective behaviour is ever more prevalent in highly masculinised fields of policing such as riot squads. While "preferential" treatment and being guarded from harm do not seem like harmful actions,

---

115 As these points of view are more prominent among respondents from Austria, their mistrust of positive actions schemes and anti-discrimination law can be made sense of, see chapter 5.6.3.

chauvinistic behaviour is deeply rooted in misogyny: It works to keep women's self-confidence down and others them from their male peers (Steinert 1997).

These othering or objectifying practices also take place in the form of rejection or exclusionary practices in the police service. As can be demonstrated from respondents' accounts, women, as a social group, are constructed as undesirable or unfit, which results in the exclusion of the individual woman. Dealing with these often sexually connotated or demeaning acts while navigating a masculine environment is asking a lot from female officers. These gendered structures, such as sexual talk or "banter", are an essential part of the patriarchal regime as a whole (Cockburn 1991: 158). This circuitry of continuously oppressing femininity with no or little resistance by group members can only persist by constantly reforging itself. An issue that is seldomly talked about is that of sexual harassment. While some felt resignation in this regard, others mentioned that the situation has and still is undergoing positive changes in that women face better follow-up support and are more encouraged to speak up for themselves.

Many, in trying to cope with and understand their situations, were trying to look for reasons for their differential treatment and the discriminating behaviour of some of their superiors and colleagues. For male officers in the same age group as the concerned women, a competitive drive and jealousy was named as a primary drive for their adverse behaviour. In this context, belittling or questioning their female colleagues' actions were most often raised as issues from respondents in the UK. As a tendency, Austrian interviewees more often described older colleagues to be more prejudiced against female colleagues as they were still not accepted as equals by some – they fear an emasculating of the job they view as a male domain. What these notions from both age groups have in common is the fear of competition and replacement. This male concern for being perceived as the superior officer to a female candidate is two-sided: For one, the simple fact of being overlooked or failing to accomplish promotion due to the existence of a better-suited candidate; when bringing in a gender perspective, this also translates to a replacement of male with female officers, in an occupation where men were always perceived as the norm, and therefore the most suitable candidate. This is accompanied by and linked to the fear of an "oestrogen mafia" (Spasić et al. 2015: 265), and serves to explain why some female officers, particularly in Austria, deemed it best to follow the male norm in their behavioural patterns, for fear of being aligned with a malicious construct that attempts to undermine the patriarchal structures of the police profession.

The handling of sexist and/or transgressing incidents internally (by the police) as well as personally (as an affected person) was also an issue of discussion for interviewees. First, respondents from the UK stated that challenging sexism was not an easy task, as the majority of their colleagues would never admit their own sexism and often do not recognise the prejudice in many of their actions and behaviours. Again, the knowledge of sexism and misogynistic behaviour being morally (as well as lawfully) wrong does not deter people from taking a prejudicial point of view. This leads to unreconstructed comments and attitudes, along with a certain inability to detect one's own possible prejudice.

Apart from the fact that female officers perceived the constant challenging and enduring of workplace sexism as highly demanding, they referred to possible intermediating factors. Austrian respondents spoke of a need to "toughen up", referring to the fact that inappropriate behaviour was even more difficult to handle the younger and inexperienced one is. What interviewees from both countries described in a similar way was the possibilities for immediate reactions to sexist behaviours: Interruption and reproof, purposeful disregard, or level-headed discussion afterwards. Female officers have to decide on a case-by-case basis how they react to comments and behaviours they deem inappropriate. Many Austrian respondents talked about the fact that they try to deal with sexist comments or jokes in a humorous way, either getting on their level or rebuking their comments. However, respondents also remarked that it is hard to change problematic behaviours if one does not actively challenge these. As true as that may ring for some, it is a questionable rhetoric as it is making individuals responsible for the treatment they receive and what they are able to bear. While of course individual revolts against unjust treatment are to be applauded, it should not lead to an atmosphere where female officers have to feel responsible for the discrimination they experience. Akin to this, female officers noted that in cases of sexual harassment, next to incidents being swept under the rug, victim-blaming is not uncommon. It is often the afflicted female officer and not the male perpetrator who faces the consequences of these incidents. Again, this is reinforced by cultural issues, as whistle-blowing is frowned upon in police culture which is heavily built and reliant on solidarity and trust (Reiner 2016). In this way, female officers often have no choice but to distance themselves from these cultural standards, continuing the exclusionary practices used by their male peers – a kind of secondary othering, first carried out by the culturally dominant male person adhering to misogynistic code, then by the affected woman in distancing herself further from the culture that rejected her.

There are more similarities than disparities between female officers' accounts in Austria and England and Wales regarding their internal treatment and issues with colleagues and superiors. However, the masculinity encountered in Austrian police culture seems even more pronounced than in the UK – a fact that may not be surprising due to the later involvement of female officers. Some female officers in Austria seemingly still try to adapt to this culture in acting according to masculine standards, becoming defeminised in the process (Heidensohn/Silvestri 2012) – this may help their personal acceptance into the service, yet other female officers who may not adhere to these standards in being "too soft" or "too feminine" are rejected even more (Cf. Brown et al. 2019). These differences are not as pronounced in the UK, yet there remain pockets of policing, notably firearms officers or riot squad, that still exclusively perform hegemonic masculinity (Behr 2008, Connell/Messerschmidt 2005) and in which female officers can feel alienated. The fact that there is little difference between the two countries in the reporting of sexist incidents, while UK respondents seemed to talk more freely about these issues, could be explained by a difference in feminist awareness and political consciousness of the interviewed officers (Brown 1998: 237). In reaction to sexist or misogynistic behaviours and comments, some female officers in Austria tried to take these issues lightly or conform to them either by compliance or disregard. Others, however, seemed to challenge these actions more, while officers in the UK unanimously deemed the tackling of these issues to be the most helpful way of dealing with discriminatory behaviour.

How female officers have been received and treated in the police service has changed in a positive way over the decades and years since respondents joined the service. This is even more pronounced in Austria, where there has been development around the general acceptance of female police officers, while in the UK progress has been made in the introduction and rise in the number of female officers of rank. In both countries personal contact of old-established male police officer with their female colleagues has allegedly led to acceptance in almost all cases. Furthermore, changes in society influence how younger male officers view their female counterparts, and most of the old stereotypes held by older colleagues are not in place anymore. While the UK has had a longer history of female officers in the police, the interviewed female officers also acknowledged that with all progresses that have been made, there is still room for improvement – though they noted that this most likely has to go hand in hand with societal changes. Although the police were described to be quite adamant to change (be it due to its size or culture), female officers in both countries seemed cautiously optimistic for the future of the police service.

5.5 External Dynamics

This chapter, in supplementation to the previous chapter, deals with the reception and treatment female officers receive from members of the public, be they (suspected) perpetrators, victims, or neither. Interactions with members of the public play a vital role in the everyday work life of police officers.

The general acceptance and reaction from external actors are discussed, while focussing on perceived gendered effects on the public and any possible differences in particular groups of the public. Next, prejudicial thinking and actions are highlighted, in particular relating to the questioning of female officers' competence. Following, the influence of an officer's gender is deliberated in the light of witness questioning and protection. Finally, female officers' reactions and their way of dealing with sexism from the public is described and discussed.

5.5.1 Communicating with the Public – Between Respect and De-escalation Strategies

As with experiences of differential treatment and sexism from within the police, female officers' reports ranged from noticing no difference in the public's general approach to them to reporting a great amount of everyday sexism. Some described their perceived gender as something that has aided them in their encounters with the public, while others reported that it reflected negatively on their treatment. In addition to this, many female officers reported no gendered differences in the majority of their dealing with members of the public. Again, officers' gender and its effect on those involved in police-public encounters is highly ambiguous.

First, the issue of respect towards female police officers and (subconscious) prejudices noticeable in police-public interactions are discussed. Then, what can be called positive gendered effects of female-associated or feminine interaction techniques with the public are described and analysed. Lastly, incidents of sexist and prejudiced behaviour from the public towards female police officers as well as potential coping strategies are recounted.

5.5.1.1 The Issue of Respect and Prejudice

First, and perhaps most straightforward of all, female officers from both countries deal with sexist or degrading comments from the public on a varying basis. These comments range from downplaying their abilities ("he's a really big lad you'll need some help love", Interview 1, England and Wales), to insults ("he will certainly not let 'a fucking woman' take away his driving licence", Interview 12, Austria), and sexual comments ("oh look, the strippers are here", Interview 13, England and Wales). Questioning female officers' capabilities is in line with the historical downplaying of women's physical abilities, de-professionalising them as police officers (Brown/Heidensohn 2000: 44ff.). Similarly, the sexual availability of police women has been the topic of discussion and has served as a cornerstone of female police officers' discrimination from within as well as outside the force (Brown/Heidensohn 2000: 62ff.). The contradiction between the sexual knowledgeable woman and the de-feminised police officer has led to varying forms of discrimination throughout the history of women in policing. As a general rule, female officers observed that (predominantly male) members of the public are more condescending or patronising towards them than they are their male counterparts, and many have a hard time accepting female police officers' authority over their own perceived male ego and privilege.

Some officers, predominantly from Austria, further noted that some comments, though they maybe were not intended to be hurtful, still bothered them in their daily work. It was remarked that to many members of the public in Austria, particularly in the countryside, encountering female police officers is still a novelty.

> "P: We just notice that when we get somewhere, people are still totally enthusiastic 'Oh, women in the police', 'two girls here' so.
> B: [unclear] Yeah, you always have to listen to something like that […] when I think [makes annoyed noise] […] [mimicking] 'are there two ladies out and about?' Yes, thanks it's alright we know how to handle ourselves." – Interview 10 and 11, Austria.

In some cases, these comments are perhaps meant as positive reinforcements or support, yet female officers feel that this parading of their difference to male officers, who seem to be perceived as standard, is detrimental to their feeling of inclusion in the workplace. What emerged from many interviews with Austrian female officers was the wish for normality. Many deemed it unnecessary that members of the public were still pointing out their being female, regardless of the action being intended as positive or negative. To most of them it appeared as preferable if members of the public would not address the issue of their gender at all.

An issue many interviewees have to deal with when engaging with the public is stereotyping and prejudice against their gender. When out on patrol or responding to calls, members of the public frequently assume, if there is a male officer present, that he is the one in charge instead of their female colleague(s), often regardless of the age of all officers concerned.[116] People tend to address male officers more often than female ones, as well as addressing them with a higher rank title than their female co-workers. Respondents from both countries addressed this issue, and though not all note it, certain members of the public seem to still hold stereotypically views on what a police officer must look like or be – predominantly, this is associated with masculinity. Interestingly, not only the older generation has problems with this gendered stereotype. An English police officer remembers attending a school event on giving young pupils an understanding of different vocations with two of her female colleagues:

> "[T]he teacher [...] was a man and he introduced us and said, yes and the two 'police (..) police, well you're not police*men*', I'm like (..) you know, he could have just said police officers, but he had such a hard time and he found it fascinating that we are all women and I thought well, how exciting, he is now teaching the children that they can become anything they want [regardless of gender], but he can't even cope with the fact that there are two police women standing in front of him." – Interview 2, England and Wales.

Through this anecdote, the meaning and importance of language as a means of transporting values and beliefs is made clear. Respondents from England and Wales who reported having had to deal with such misconceptions often spoke of a certain feeling of disappointment or bewilderment as to encountering these stereotypes with what they deemed educated and young members of the public – even more so if they are female themselves.

---

116 However, some note that the younger a female officer is, the more likely people are to deem her incompetent to deal with the issue at hand.

"I think, again, even my own GP has commented to me, saying, 'oh, can't believe you're a police officer, you don't look like one', and when I've said, what does one look like, and she says, oh you know you expect a big burly man'. [I]t's quite disappointing as an educated female herself, who has that perception." – Interview 13, England and Wales.

This type of prejudicial thinking often remains subconscious and is only revealed when particular events contradict these assumptions. When addressed directly, as the aforementioned interviewee did, it is made clear that people do carry an ideal conception of a police officer in their minds. This conception, or ideal, does not necessarily have to align the realities of what the "average" officer looks like, it is rather influenced and informed by the same traits and stereotypes that feeds the hegemonic masculinity culture within the police service. The hyper-masculinity is best represented by the focus on body ideals – in order to be a police officer one needs to be big, strong, and manly (See also chapter 5.4.2).

Furthermore, officers spoke about the fact that when members of the public send for the police in order to aid them in their dilemmas, female officers' competence is questioned – a response their male colleagues do not usually get. One interviewee observed that when starting the assignment, she noticed that her "client" did not seem very happy about the fact that his case had been taken over by two young female officers. The interviewee also noted that, although she had particular expertise for this case and was therefore best qualified to deal with the issue, the man in question remained highly suspicious of her during the whole investigation. Interestingly, the actions and remarks made were all quite latent, in that he tried to monitor her work or ask scrutinising questions. The man simply expected to see a middle-aged male – himself – reflected in the officers dealing with his case. Hereby again, the male norm is associated with competence and proficiency, while female officers are questioned and put to the test in order to prove their strengths.

In a related context, female officers spoke about the issue of respect and its varying connotations. First of all, many officers reported experiencing a lack of respect from the public in what they deem ordinary situations, such as traffic stops our routine investigations. Many, almost similar to the behaviour found with some male colleagues, talked down female officers' actions and belittled their deeds. Next to the aforementioned practices of "overlooking" female officers, taking directions only from male officers, and assuming rank structure based on gender, some members of the public also strictly refused to talk and engage with female officers. Almost all officers reported this problem, while the frequency of these incidents range from very seldom encounters to quite regular experiences. These issues are reported to be exclusively restricted to male members of the public – again they seem to refuse the authority of a non-male officer and reject or dismiss orders from female police officers.

> "[O]r in the same way also with deployments, [...] 'no I'd rather talk to the gentleman because he understands me', I say 'no he won't understand you either, you can talk to me or not at all', [...]
> B: Or they overlook you, so to speak
> P: Yes, exactly, so they look [B: look past you], look for the man with whom they can talk at eye level." – Interview 10 and 11, Austria.

To some men's understanding, talking to a female officer is no "talking at eye level", as they rather engage with their male colleague, regardless of said colleagues' expertise or authority. This type of discrimination was, in Austria quite often, in the UK more seldomly, attributed to perceived differences in culture. According to respondents, in situations where men categorically refused to talk to them, these men often were perceived to have an immigrant background, sometimes in addition a religious faith that is different from that of the majority population. Similar to what Müller found about "Turkish family conflict[s]" (Müller 2007:338), female-only patrols are thus constructed as problematic, and the ability of police to adequately handle the situation connected to the presence of a male officer. Female officers experienced this ignorance as very disrespectful behaviour, while at the same time acknowledging that they are incapable of changing a persons' mindset and beliefs, especially if they are grounded in a persons' cultural upbringing. These types of condescending behaviours were familiar to female officers in both countries.

Through this, female officers' competence and authority is undermined, not only as previously mentioned by their colleagues or superiors, but also by those many officers deem their main concern in the job – the public. This disrespectful treatment seems averse to the mindsets of many female officers, who see themselves as equals to their male colleagues, and – predominantly in Austria's case – do not condone gendered differences in treatment of officers internally or externally.

5.5.1.2 De-escalation Strategies

A phenomenon that female officers in both countries addressed is the effect an officer's gender has on certain situations – namely those that involve heated arguments, tension and/or drunk persons. With these types of stressful situations, female officers reported noting a difference in the reaction of the concerned parties attributed to an officer's gender. The, again, predominantly male members of public who at first appeared distressed or threatening were allegedly calmed down in most incidents by the simple presence of a female officer.

> "And actually, to be honest, you can calm situations down a lot better sometimes when you're female, so, in what I would call public-order situations, where people are fighting and drunk, you know, I'm only five foot three, and female, I found that I'm probably more effective at calming men down than men would be, because they see that more as a challenge." – Interview 11, England and Wales.

Some of course also attributed this to the perceived advantage women have in being trained in talking down and calming people, yet often the simple appearance of a female officer was enough to at least let potentially hostile members of the public pause for a moment. Again, it is observed that female and male police officer's competence differ in this regard: Female officers, as a rule, are perceived to be more soothing and relaxed than their male counterparts, while male officers' behaviour tends to be more direct and rasher. This was, with individual exceptions of course, described to be the case in both Austria and England and Wales. Some officers almost disapproved of their male colleagues' behaviour, in that they deemed it inconsiderate and unhelpful in delicate situations. Some even attributed the integration of women in the police as being responsible for the introduction of what they view as a different way of policing.

> "[T]hat there are other ways to solve things and not just drive in at full throttle. Because not everyone thinks they are the big man and can do everything but just talk to the people normally and, well, bring in some calm or something." – Interview 9, Austria.

On the one hand, male officers are perceived to be deemed more "on a level" by and with male members of the public, as described in the above chapter; on the other hand, this leaves them open to be challenged, as well as themselves perceived as challenging the male authority of the affected citizen. Female officers, however, seem to not be perceived in the same way as their male counterparts: They are not a priori understood as a potential threat or competition to male citizens' ego. This introduces the issue of what can be described as chivalry or positive sexism. Some male members of the public address this quite outright.

> "[Y]ou do get treated differently and you know I've had other things where, someone stopped fighting 'cause they punched me in the face and he goes, 'oh I don't fight women', so he stopped fighting." – Interview 7, England and Wales.

Apart from possibly de-escalating situations, female officers seem to have the "benefit" of being less likely to be physically assaulted by male citizens. Some officers reported that, in the eyes of the male member of public who admits reacting differently to male or female police officers, this behaviour is sometimes tantamount to displaying respect. That, of course, is the underlying, yet faulty, logic of male chauvinism, in that it views women as "something different" – something unequal to them – that is to be protected because of its apparent shortcomings. Of course, female officers also reported being physically assaulted by members of the public, yet they note that their male colleagues are disproportionately more affected by such incidents – this may, as previously mentioned, not only be due to the citizens display of male chauvinism, but also male officer's behaviour and demeanour. Out of all issues female officers reported experiencing with male members of the public, this reluctance to engage in physical contact with female officers is, quite understandably, more easily tolerable.

5.5.1.3 Dealing with Sexism

As with internal sexist or misogynistic behaviour within the police, female officer's reaction to detected differences in behaviour towards them is situational and varies from person to person. However, the fleetingness of some encounters with the public as opposed to the continuous cooperation needed inside the police service make certain reactions more feasible. Ignoring or trying to ignore some of the public's comments and behaviours can be either hard work or simply a failure to brace up and react in any other way. As with dealing with police-internal sexism, some respondents noted that when confronted with sexist comments for the first time, they did not know how to react or simply took too long to process the occurrence. At the same time, some officers noted that after a certain time, and with a growing amount of experience, derogatory comments or inappropriate behaviour can simply be overlooked by them. Whether that is down to "growing a thicker skin" and becoming immune to certain actions or becoming oblivious to sexist treatment due to its constant presence is disputable. Female officers in Austria observed that there are certain boundaries when dealing with inappropriate behaviour – at a certain point, for example when insults get too personal or heavy, one should not simply put up with it.

Again, a certain instinctive feeling seems to be needed when dealing with sexist behaviour from the public. Especially with men who do not wish to engage or talk to a female officer, respondents vary in their advised method of response. Some observed that you cannot and will not change a person's learned behaviour in one interaction, and therefore deemed it best to let a male colleague deal with these people. Officers spoke of a certain respect and need to tolerate other cultures in accepting their preference not to engage with a female officer in charge. However, there were also those who deemed it best to simply carry on with the act and speak of a need to claim authority of the situation. In any case, female officers in both countries seemed to have learned not to take this particular behaviour personal, a circumstance that seems to be alleviated by the fact that this unwelcome attitude is attributed to differences in culture. Additionally, Austrian officers also spoke of the fact that they and their female colleagues know how to assert themselves. Some, however, also criticised the behaviour of some of their female colleagues and deem it too harsh, almost as if they try to overcompensate for their gender. Interviewees in the UK spoke about the fact that one needs to trust and support your colleagues' decision regardless of gender – thus male officers are obligated to support the decisions and actions of their female colleague when dealing with prejudiced people, so as to not undermine her authority any further. Some UK respondents further put responsibility on the police service as an institution: By visibly placing more women in leading position and advertising their advancement, a change of consciousness in the public could be achieved.

5.5.2 Witness Questioning and Protection

In the same way that an officer's gender influences interactions with members of the public or presumed perpetrators, it shapes and influences the communication with vulnerable groups such as presumed survivors or witnesses to particular crimes. Although some of the participants noted that performing empathy and sensitivity is not restricted to one gender, many acknowledged that they notice a change in, particularly female, victim's approach to the police. Some participants also displayed an awareness of the fact that the police itself is sometimes to be held partially at fault for vulnerable people not coming forward and reporting certain issues, especially in cases of domestic violence. A police officer in Austria recalled a particular event, back when the integration of female officers in the police had just started.

> "I [...] can remember one of the first women who experienced a rape who actually wanted to report something else. [...] And I took the transcript with her and she told me about it. And [...] she was so positive, she came back the next day, or a few days later, and thanked me again, because she said that it was so great, that she certainly wouldn't have told that to any man. And, that it is in fact easier for her to talk about it, and that it was just something different, that you tell a woman rather than a man." – Interview 7, Austria.

Through these kinds of experiences, the presence of women in the police is constructed as something highly positive, in that it brings to light certain cases that otherwise would have fallen between the cracks. In this way, gendered experiences with potential victims or other vulnerable people are – as opposed to those dealing with presumed perpetrators or offenders – predominantly constructed as positive incidents.

Police officers from both countries noted that certain groups of people react more positively to a female than a male officer, which highlights the need for female officers across many different sections of policing. While most officers spoke about the fact that female members of the public who are in distress of any kind tend to react better to a female officer, some also noted that (small) children, elderly people, or sometimes even vulnerable men tend to prefer interacting with female police officers rather than their male counterparts. A respondent from the UK theorised that this preference for a female police officer, also on the part of the male citizens in distress, comes from an underlying desire for a "mother figure" (Interview 17, England and Wales) – dealing with a female rather than a male officer, from officers' experiences, calms an otherwise stressful situation and the involved persons.

A special issue in this regard is the handling of cases of domestic and/or sexual abuse by the police. In the UK, officers stated that there is no statutory basis for the use of female officers in regard to questioning and dealing with female survivors of abuse. However, policing in England and

Wales, as previously mentioned, is fundamentally based on policing by consent (FOI release. Definition of policing by consent, gov.uk). Thus, officers noted that the victims' preferences when giving statements is the basic principle to which the police adhere when dealing with any kind of case. Many officers noted that female survivors of sexual abuse almost exclusively prefer dealing with female officers, and, as the police is reliant on survivors' report in order to pursue certain cases, the person's needs and wishes will be respected as a matter of principle. Similarly, Austrian officers reported that the existence of female police officers often makes it easier for women who have experienced sexual violence to come forward or to be more at ease when giving a report. Older officers also noted the difference in the legal frameworks they have to work with. Since 1997, a so-called Protection Against Violence Act is in place, which allows officers to handle restraining orders for premises in cases of domestic violence, an act that has been extended in 2009 in order to improve victim protection (Weiss 2009). Additionally, vulnerable victims have the legal right to demand being questioned by an officer of the same sex according to § 66a par. 2 STPO (Strafprozeßordnung 1975, ris.bka.gv). This was often supported by female officers who noted that it is almost necessary to have these legal guidelines, as not everyone is fit to deal with issues of domestic violence. An officer remembered a time when restraining orders were not legally enforced, and female survivors of abuse either had to leave their home or continue staying in their household.

> "[T]he male colleagues, they don't question it, it's just an assignment like any other, the law says so, and how to protect the victim [makes indifferent hand gestures] well, I don't have to worry, right, it's not my job. I do what the law says, but, beyond that, that's it. And I, as a woman, just thought to myself, that I understand how it is, […] that it's not so easy as to go to a women's shelter and get protection, it's not that easy." – Interview 7, Austria.

In the absence of legal guidelines, it is assumed that female officers are more understanding and able to empathise with the struggles of women suffering from abuse or the possible dilemmas that arise when seeking help. The fact that these legal guidelines have now been established was therefore seen as convenient and worth to uphold.

In this sense, respondents also noted that, if there is a report of a sexual or violent incident involving female victims or children, sometimes female officers are almost automatically sent out to deal with these issues. Officers from the UK noted that this also happens without any clear reasoning behind it, but simply because it is assumed that female officers deal better with these kinds of incidents. Naturally, given the positive response of members of the public some officers get, this is understandable. Yet some interviewees feel that this "typecasting" is in some cases excessive – being sent out of their precinct for example – and further puts the strain on female officers rather than holding their male colleagues accountable and providing them with a reason to educate themselves on improving their interpersonal skills as well.

5.5.4 Interim Findings

Female officers from both Austria and the UK reported having to deal with differentiating and sexist treatment from the public. The effect that an officer's gender has on relations and dealings with members of the public is highly ambiguous. What respondents viewed negatively is the degrading or sexist comments they sometimes get from predominantly male members of the public. These comments all aim to discredit women as police officers, either by downplaying their (physical) abilities (Brown/Heidensohn 2000: 44ff.) or by sexually objectifying them (Brown/Heidensohn 2000: 62ff.), which leaves a discrepancy between the feminised woman and the de-feminised police officer. Both approaches serve as a means to de-professionalise female police officers, a fate that they also reported encountering in various other settings, as (male) members of the public generally seemed to be more condescending toward them than their male colleagues. Additionally, in the Austrian countryside, female police officers are still seen as a novelty by some, leading to comments that may have been intended as positive, while still other female officers reported rather negative experiences. In this sense, many wished for a kind of normalcy, where members of the public would not see the need to comment on their gender at all. As this is not yet the case, many interviewees from both countries reportedly experienced gendered stereotyping and prejudice in their daily dealings with citizens. When having to deal with the police, people tend to address male police officers more frequently and with a senior title, assuming their male counterpart to be in charge regardless of their behaviour. This is very probably associated with an underlying stereotypical view that most people may still hold about what a police officer should look and act like; a view that is influenced predominantly by hegemonic masculinity and is not only reserved for older, male, or less educated members of the public, as officers have found out to their detriment. Often, these assumptions remain subconscious and are only revealed when addressed directly. The ideal type many people tend to have in their minds when it comes to police officers does not have to align with the realities of what an average police officer might look or behave like, but is rather informed by masculine stereotypes similar to those that prevail police-internally. This hegemonic masculinity is here defined by the focus on outer factors such as physique – a need to be big, tough, and manly. Furthermore, female officers' competence is questioned more often than that of their male colleagues, predominantly by male members of the public. This phenomenon can be explained by the circumstance that men, deeming themselves as highly competent sometimes simply due to their gender and age, expect to find themselves represented in the aid they call. As the male norm is associated with competence, dealing with younger, female officers often leads to a questioning and testing of their abilities.

In explaining the troubles in dealing with some members of the public, female officers raised the issue of respect and its connotations. Many interviewees reported the fact that in what they deem routine interactions with the public, such as traffic stops, they witnessed a certain lack of respect towards them from the public. Some, especially male, members of the public tend to be overcritical of female officers' actions and treat them dismissively, undervaluing their contributions. A special issue female officers reported having to deal with is that certain groups of people simply refuse to talk to or deal with a female officer. That certain individuals seem to deny the authority of female police officers and therefore ignore or dismiss orders was reported by almost all respondents in Austria, and some in the UK. Respondents perceived this as a certain inability of male members of the public to perceive women as being "on the same level" as them, rather engaging with a male officer with whom they think they are equal. This particular type of discrimination female officers experience was often attributed to perceived differences in culture, such as having an immigrant or a marginalised religious background. The handling of such an attitude is difficult for the officers, as most acknowledged that differences in culture should be respected and attitudes can seldom be changed by a single interaction, while at the same time there is a need to assert one's authority in particular cases. Having their authority and therefore competence undermined by members of the public is no small feat for female officers, and many reported a certain wariness in dealing with these issues. Based on the belief that they are equal to their male colleagues, female officers' convictions are opposed to the difference in treatment they receive from the public, be it with or without ill intent.

An officer's gender not only has a direct effect on people's behaviours, but sometimes also subconsciously affects the atmosphere of certain situations. Respondents noted a difference in how female officers are perceived in tense situations such as potentially violent arguments or dealing with drunk male persons. Officers from both countries reported that in stressful situations, the simple presence of a female officer can lead to the respective persons calming down or appearing less aggressive than before. This appears to be the case for two reasons: First, female officers reported that in most cases they are more experienced and better equipped to talk people down and handle emotionally complex situations than their male colleagues. The gendered socialisation they received helps them to be capable to deal with people in crisis. At the same time, the predominantly male member of the public being in a heightened emotional state might not regard a female police officer in the same way they do their male counterpart. While a male officer might be deemed as equal to them, making them open to challenge, female officers are – as a general rule – not perceived as that much of a threat and therefore addressed in a less aggressive and confronting manner. The indicated display of male chauvinism was at times subconsciously, at other times addressed quite directly by members of the public. This is, of course, a broad over-generalisation, and there were instances where female officers were treated with the same aggression as their male colleagues, yet officers' differences in handling emotionally heated situations is still dominated by debates around femininity and masculinity.

Female officers' reactions to received differences in treatment by the public were varied yet influenced by the fleetingness and urgency of each situation. Most respondents noted that one needs a certain amount of experience in order to be able to react, appropriately or at all, to sexist comments or behaviours from members of the public. At the same time, female officers remarked that with a growing amount of experience, certain comments or behaviours can be more easily overlooked or disregarded, as they tend to become normalised. In any case, respondents perceived there to be a certain threshold – for example personal insults – where it was no longer possible to ignore comments from members of the public. Some sensitivity is required in dealing with incidents of sexism and misogyny with members of the public in finding the appropriate response that enables officers to continue carrying out their duties while at the same time not giving too much leeway to inappropriate behaviour. In the particular case of male members of the public ignoring female officers and not wishing to engage with them in any way, respondents' reactions notably varied. Some deemed it best to let male officers handle this type of situation, adopting the concerned party's attitude because, as they put it, they will not be able to change a prejudiced mindset deriving from cultural differences in a single interaction. Others saw it almost as their duty to assert their authority in this type of situation in continuing to carry out the official act themselves. According to respondents, a very important feature of learning to deal with sexist actions by the public was to not take these actions personally, a rule that applies to any unpleasant experiences one may have in encounters with the public.

In Austria, interviewees described their female co-workers as highly skilled and tough, knowing how to deal with any issues that might arise, while others regarded some of their female colleagues' behaviour as too harsh and hyper-masculinised. In this context respondents from the UK noted that as a police officer, one needs to be able to trust and rely on your partner regardless of gender, and male officers therefore need to support any actions female officers might take in scenarios where members of the public undermine their authority simply because of their gender. Furthermore, some argued that a change of public perception can be best achieved by improving the visibility of women in the police service.

Another group's actions and interactions with the police that are influenced by officer gender is that of witnesses or survivors. In particular in dealing with survivors of domestic violence or sexual violence, officers noted that a lot of tact and empathy is needed in order to gain the most insight while putting those members of the public at ease. Although sensitivity is not only performed by female officers when dealing with such incidents, many stated that they noticed a change in a (female) victim's approach to the police. As with (suspected) perpetrators, the simple presence of a female officer can influence not only the tone and manner of an interview setting, or even if victims of violence do come forward at all. Thus, the existence of female police officers is constructed as something highly positive, in that certain crimes would not surface without them present. Female officers themselves also viewed this issue as deeply positive and sometimes even reassuring in that their presence in the police service is somewhat endorsed by this treatment, ensuring their right to carry out this profession. There are certain groups of people that, on average, reportedly react better to a female than a male police officer: Female members of the public who have experienced (intimate) violence, (small) children, elderly people, and sometimes even male members of the public who experience distress of any kind (i.e., psychological emergency situations, suicidality, etc.). As with (presumed) perpetrators, the presence of a female rather than a male officer has the potential to calm a situation down. From a legal viewpoint, there is no statutory basis in the UK that sees to the fact that female survivors of abuse are questioned by female officers. In practice, however, officers noted that the wishes of persons to be interviewed are followed as much as possible, as policing is inherently based on consent in the UK. Officers seemed content with these regulations and mostly see no need for change in this regard. In Austria, a Protection Against Violence Act that mostly deals with issues of restraining orders is effective since 1997, having been extended in 2009. Vulnerable victims additionally have the right to ask to be interviewed by a person of the same sex according to the code of criminal procedure (§ 66a par. 2 STPO). Female officers in Austria viewed these legal guidelines as very helpful in dealing with issues of domestic violence and intimate partner violence in particular. Some female officers from Austria again described some of their male colleagues as being almost blind to these "female issues", rendering the involvement of a female police officer as almost necessary in certain cases. However, some officers from the UK reported that this typecasting of female officers also has negative connotations. When female officers are assigned certain cases simply because of their gender and not their competence or skills, it puts a strain on the female officers while their male colleagues are "let off the hook" instead of trusting them to build up their interpersonal skills as well. Walklate (2000: 239ff.) suggests that the introduction of domestic violence units has not only led to a large number of women joining these units and thus being absent from mainstream policing but has also led to the issue being devalued as a "women's issue"; this also leads to the sidelining of a broader discussion of male violence and aggression as a societal norm. Further research argues along similar lines with respect to female survivors of rape (Brown/King 1998: 277) - gendering these investigations could at the same time lead to their marginalisation. This, along with the findings of Jordan (2002) that an officer's gender per se does not matter as much as providing survivors with adequately trained and experienced officers, actually speaks for an increase in training options and further education for officers of all genders. This can be achieved alongside the promotion of women in policing and improving support for survivors of rape and intimate partner violence (Cf. Jordan 2002).

5.6 Gender Dynamics

The next few subchapters deal with issues relating directly to gender yet are not based in interactions with either colleagues or members of the public, such as the previous two chapters. These are issues that are predominantly police-internal, yet sometimes influenced by various societal and/or legal matters. Furthermore, this chapter, although it acknowledges the intersectionality of most of the described problems, focusses on gender as the main determining factor in the matters described.[117] The data used in the following chapters is derived from answers to various questions, including "How has the way women are treated in the police force changed? How has the job itself changed?", "Do you think that the police as such has/will change due to the presence of (more) women?", and finally "Which (governmental) measures/policies of gender equality (in the police workforce) do you know of OR may already have experience with (e.g., encouraging women to apply for certain positions)?".[118]

The first subchapter deals with what are described to be "women's issues" by interviewees, excluding issues of maternity or parental leave. Being female in a masculine environment and the problems that might arise from gendered stereotyping and performances. Related to this, issues of maternity, parental leave, workhours and equal pay are discussed in the next subchapter. The repute of part-time or flexible work schedules in the police service, which is often linked to care work, seems to still provide difficulties to the integration of female officers in the police. The subsequent subchapter deals with the countries' respective equal opportunities policies and their reception among (female) police officers. Related schemes, such as women's networks or recruitment/training days are also discussed. Associated with this is female officers' perceptions and opinions on gender equality as a concept, as the implementation of gender equality policies is sometimes incompatible with officers' conceptions of equality. Last, improvements and changes in the police service as a whole are discussed in relation to issues of gender.

---

117 Broader issues of diversity and inclusivity in the police service are discussed in chapter 5.7.

118 German wordings: "Wie hat sich der Umgang mit Frauen in der Polizei verändert? Inwiefern hat sich der Job der Polizistin verändert?", "Denken Sie, dass sich die Polizei als solches durch den vermehrten Einsatz von Frauen verändert hat/verändern wird?", "Welche frauenfördernden Maßnahmen des BM.I kennen Sie BZW haben Sie eventuell selbst schon Erfahrung damit gemacht (Beispiel Quotenregelung)?".

5.6.1 Women's Issues in a Male Environment

Female officers in the UK did take issue with the fact that, to them, the police are still very much a male-dominated culture. Although respondents in both countries noted developments inside the police service, opening it up to female officers and different practices, there are still some pockets of policing, mainly special units, that value masculinity exceedingly. Women, many respondents argued, do not take a vital part in the formation of police culture. As stereotypical male qualities are emphasised and strengthened, officers, regardless of gender, are expected to fit into the mould created for them. Some UK respondents illustrated this in the example of their police uniform:

> "So, you know, things like that where they're looking at equipment and what we wear, we're still not quite there, cause we're still wearing men's tops which continues to infuriate me. There's no such thing as a unisex, they just put us in men's clothing. And it's just little things like that and the message that comes with them." – Interview 22, England and Wales.

As described in the quote, the issue of clothing might not seem very grand, but the message transported with it influences, if only subconsciously, how female officers feel about and are welcomed in the police service. Contrarily, some interviewees' preconceived ideas about masculinity and gender in the police service were not confirmed, as they found the police to be a rather welcoming place, not encountering any issues because of their gender. What all respondents agreed on is the fact that the public's perception of police work is still very much associated with masculinity. As previously mentioned, some officers were of the opinion that the media should actively work against these prejudices and show more women in policing – not only carrying out care tasks such as interacting with elderly citizens, but also "tougher" aspects of police work such as "going into a dangerous situation" (Interview 13, England and Wales). At the same time, showing all aspects of police work seemed to be an important issue for female officers in the UK, as, according to respondents, public perception of police work as violent and potentially dangerous does not aid in trying to attract more women to apply for a job with the police. A clear line of argument for or against the portrayal of (female police officers in) dangerous situations is therefore not to be found. Media representation is thus said to play an important part in people's perception of the police, and potentially influence not only prospective officers' decisions but also their social contacts, which in turn can influence prospective applicants.

> "[P]eople's families, we've talked about this, the difference of people thinking of joining the police force for women and men are different, because for women you've got fathers and partners saying 'oh it's really dangerous are you sure it's something you wanna do', the odd mother might say that to a son, but not to the same extent." – Interview 22, England and Wales.

In fact, respondents from both countries reported some doubt or incomprehension on their family's or friends' side regarding their decision to join the police. Regarding dangers in the job, most respondents agreed that the public perception regarding exposure to hazardous situations is overstated. An interviewee in Austria regarded fear of the job itself as the biggest danger, as it hinders you in correctly and calmly carry out tasks and official acts, as well as leaving you unhappy in your profession. In this way, officers have to learn to deal with exceptional circumstances in order to be able to perform their best professionally, but also be personally content with their career choice.

To this day, female officers, rather than embodying a female ideal type of police officer, have to adhere to "male" standards when it comes to being validated as a police officer. Although many described a change in policing styles, beside the growing representation of women in the police service, a certain archetype of police officer still is perpetuated as the norm. As an Austrian officer put it: "If you're normal, you'll be respected" (Interview 15, Austria). Respondents in Austria, in their respective notions of what a female police officer should and should not do, helped create an image of said "normal" woman. First, one should stand up for themselves and not hide away; at the same time, one should not expect any special treatment because of one's gender. The ideal type of a policewoman in Austria is represented by her complete equality to her male counterpart, not asking for favours, hard-working, relying on the fairness of the system to acknowledge their achievements. In her perception, thinking and behaviour, the female police officer does not differ in any way from her male colleague – the only acceptable deviation from this norm seems to be the performance of empathy when dealing with certain members of the public. What differs, however, is clearly how officers are perceived by their colleagues as well as the public – the previous chapters have presented examples of these treatments. The ideal type of female police officer in the UK, in contrast, seems to be a bit more multi-dimensional. First of all, respondents acknowledged an inherent difference between male and female officers, rendering an equal performance of the two improbable. The focus on diversity as a marketing tool seems to exert its influence, as possible differences between genders, ethnic backgrounds, and so on, appear to were taken for granted as well as embraced as valuable assets. In line with this thinking, a difference in treatment is much more explicable. However, respondents also acknowledged that in most cases, officers of any background are still held to "male" standards, and the police service as an organisation is only now slowly learning that it is acceptable to behave differently and "not have to perform as if you're a different person" (Interview 4, England and Wales). In both countries, this leads to female officers doing things "the men's way" (Interview 4, England and Wales) and trying not to over-perform their femininity, as their performed de-feminisation helps with peer-acceptance. The potential for performing individuality increases with time spent in the service as well as when advancing through the rank structure – after trying to fit the male mould, resilient female officers might get a chance at performing individuality and, for example, engage in a more level management style.

As UK respondents tried to perceive personal differences as structurally influenced by social factors such as gender or age, they addressed what to them are inherent differences between genders. Women's issues are at times ignored, or simply not thought about. Examples of these were providing appropriate toilet facilities, fitting clothing options, sanitary wear, and issues of menopause. The latter has grown in importance as the police service is now confronted with an aging female workforce, still, the only appropriate setting in which a discussion on the topic can take place is the local female support group. A UK respondent describes noticing positive changes in the service's approach to women's issues:

> "[B]ut I still think it's done because you know, they've all got sisters and daughters you know, not because women are people, but because we should, because of benevolence." – Interview 1, England and Wales.

The actions themselves are not condoned so much as the assumed reasoning behind them. As with some interaction issues reported with colleagues as well as members of the public, the organisation itself tends to display signs of male chauvinism in dealing with what are perceived to be "women's issues".

Aside the obvious shortcomings in accommodating female police officers, respondents in both countries reported what can be described as underlying problems of the service that might make it harder to deal with, or even reinforce existing problems female officers face.

UK respondents, for example, mentioned the fact that the police service does not have an adequate system to filter out talent and people with potential are often not supported enough. Additionally to what a respondent called the "chronic problems with women's career paths" (Interview 4, England and Wales), these issues around promotion might further influence female officer's progression through the ranks in the service. In this sense, interviewees also felt that smaller forces are better suited to support individual officers, as well as accept them for who they are regardless of potential societal differences in background. The police organisation's inflexibility was also mentioned as an issue that affects female officers' integration by respondents in both countries. Thus, the police service seems slow in adapting to changes (see also chapter 5.6.5), as exemplified by the treatment and struggles the first female officers in Austria had to face. Female officers, in these times, of course, had to suffer the consequences of this adamant refusal to change; even nowadays social change often only slowly seeps into police practice and policies. A related issue typical to Austria is that of the urban-rural-divide in terms of acceptance of female police officers. According to interviewees, in urban areas the public is more "accustomed" (Interview 11, Austria) to female officers, while it was only recently that female officers have come to work in some rural areas. When considering the realities of women in the police service, one has to consider not only the social and political context of the respective country, but also factor in possible organisational issues.

5.6.2 Equal Pay – Equal Workload?

A considerable factor in participants' discussion on gender and their workplace is the division of labour as well as respective salaries. Austrian female officers made a point of the fact that they, as women, are receiving the same payments as their male colleagues. This is of particular importance to them, as female police officers in Austria did see themselves as equal in almost any regard to their male colleagues and took pride in carrying out the same duties as their co-workers. They framed their equal payment as an inevitable consequence of the fact that they performed their job in the same way as their male colleagues did, and vice versa. Equal pay was also brought up in comparison to working in the private sector, where, according to interviewees, getting paid less because of your gender was the rule. Conversely, interviewees from the UK might address the issue of being paid rather fairly – again, in comparison to the private sector – as an incentive to join the police service. However, some addressed the issue of the gender pay gap in the police service as a serious issue and measure of gender equality in the respective force.

The gendered mean average difference in hourly rates in the 43 police forces of England and Wales range from 0.4% (City of London Police) to 31.5% (Leicestershire Police) for the year 2018.[119] For the year 2018, the median income of women in the Austrian police service was on average 20.2% below that of men.[120] These figures cannot be compared adequately – for one, each individual police force in England and Wales produces their own gender equality measures and works under different preconditions such as force size, whereas Austria does not provide gender pay gaps broken down by states. What can be said, however, is that police services in both countries still struggle to close the gender pay gap (some more than others). Furthermore, the awareness of unequal payment seems to be more pronounced in England and Wales, where participants talked quite freely about their perception of the gender pay gap and how their respective force handles the issue. Contrarily, in Austria, interviewees did not seem sensitised to the topic, assuming that, because of the clarity of the rank structure and its related payment scheme, the gender pay gap is a non-issue for the police as an employer. Related to discussions around remuneration, participants further discussed the gendered division of labour and responsibilities within and outside the job and its implications for female police officers.

---

119 See Table 9 on page 163 (Employer Comparison, Gender Pay Gap Service, gender-pay-gap.service.gov.uk).
120 See Table 10 on page 164 (Lercher, 2019).

Table 9: Gender Pay Gap, Police Forces in England and Wales, 2018, sorted by % difference in hourly rate (Median)

Employer	Employer Size	% Difference in hourly rate (Median)
City of London Police	500 to 999	0,4%
Cleveland Police	1000 to 4999	0,4%
Metropolitan Police Service	20,000 or more	9,7%
West Midlands Police	5000 to 19,999	11,0%
Lincolnshire Police	1000 to 4999	11,1%
Gloucestershire Constabulary	1000 to 4999	11,7%
Sussex Police	1000 to 4999	12,4%
Northumbria Police	5000 to 19,999	13,9%
Cambridgeshire Police	1000 to 4999	14,1%
Avon and Somerset Police	5000 to 19,999	14,4%
Norfolk Constabulary	1000 to 4999	15,0%
Greater Manchester Police	5000 to 19,999	16,2%
Merseyside Police	5000 to 19,999	16,5%
Surrey Police	1000 to 4999	17,2%
Nottinghamshire Police	1000 to 4999	17,6%
Thames Valley Police	5000 to 19,999	17,9%
Bedfordshire Police	1000 to 4999	18,1%
North Wales Police	1000 to 4999	19,0%
Staffordshire Police Headquarters	1000 to 4999	19,1%
West Yorkshire Police	5000 to 19,999	19,5%
Suffolk Constabulary	1000 to 4999	20,1%
Wiltshire Constabulary	1000 to 4999	20,2%
West Mercia Police	1000 to 4999	20,3%
Northamptonshire Police	1000 to 4999	20,3%
Hampshire Constabulary	5000 to 19,999	20,6%
Hertfordshire Constabulary	1000 to 4999	21,5%
Warwickshire Police Authority	1000 to 4999	21,6%
North Yorkshire Police	1000 to 4999	22,2%
Dyfed Powys Police	1000 to 4999	22,5%
Humberside Police	1000 to 4999	22,5%
Gwent Police	1000 to 4999	22,7%
South Wales Police	5000 to 19,999	23,2%
Cumbria Constabulary	1000 to 4999	23,4%
Cheshire Constabulary	1000 to 4999	24,3%
Essex Police	5000 to 19,999	24,4%
Devon & Cornwall Police	5000 to 19,999	24,5%
South Yorkshire Police	1000 to 4999	26,8%
Dorset Police	1000 to 4999	27,9%
Kent Police	5000 to 19,999	28,6%
Derbyshire Constabulary	1000 to 4999	29,0%
Durham Constabulary	1000 to 4999	31,0%
Lancashire Constabulary	5000 to 19,999	31,4%
Leicestershire Police	1000 to 4999	31,5%

Table 10: Gender Pay Gap, Austrian Police Force, 2018, sorted by occupational rank

Tabelle 2 Einkommensbericht gem. § 6a Bundes-Gleichbehandlungsgesetz (Datenbasis: Kalenderjahr 2018): Bundesdienst

Berufs-gruppen/ Verwendungs-gruppencluster	Beschäftigte Männer	Beschäftigte Frauen	Brutto-jahresein-kommen Männer	Brutto-jahresein-kommen Frauen	Durch-schnitts-alter Männer	Durch-schnitts-alter Frauen	Medianein-kommen der Frauen liegt um ... % unter dem der Männer	Durch-schnittsalter der Frauen liegt um ... Jahre unter dem der Männer
Allgemeine Verwaltung	24.372	27.889	47.003	37.759	49,1	46,0	19,7 %	3,1
Exekutivdienst	28.378	6.066	52.832	42.157	44,3	34,5	20,2 %	9,9
E1	642	38	86.951	68.957	53,5	46,0	20,7 %	7,5
E2a	9.406	1.101	60.919	49.366	50,4	40,1	19,0 %	10,3
E2b, Greko	15.977	4.036	49.744	42.387	42,9	34,8	14,8 %	8,1
E2c, Aspiran-tinnen/ Aspiranten	2.313	891	22.967	22.957	26,6	25,4	0,1 %	1,2
Dienstklasse Exekutivdienst	40	0	56.673	-	56,8	-	-	-

5.6.2.1 Part-Time Work

An issue that is simultaneously associated with and delegated in responsi-bility to women is that of part-time or flexible work. There is consensus in research literature about the fact that part-time work is not valued or seen as equally contributing as their full-time counterparts, not exclu-sively but especially, in police work (Charlesworth/Whittenbury 2007, Ed-wards/Robinson 2001). Indeed, the introduction of flexible work in the police service in England and Wales, starting with the Met Police, in 1992 was (officially) due to the need to retain (more) female officers (Dick 2006: 41). The change in policy was, however, also "vital for the avoidance of sex discrimination claims" (Edwards/Robinson 1999: 12) from those female officers applying to work part-time. Female officers from England and Wales reported feeling that part-time work was still not accepted in many areas of policing; those that carry out their work part-time were rather considered a burden. Although female officers noted a culture change in some departments around the issue of flexible working – incidentally, this often went along with more male officers applying for flexible work patterns – the negative preconceptions of flexible work prevail. Female officers considered the circumstance that male officers are increasingly applying for flexible work as positive, not only because, as previously mentioned, it normalises i.e., masculinises the existence of part-time work in the police service, but also because in the course of it, female officers feel that the weight of performing an undervalued task is shifted partly away from female and onto male officers. In Austria, interviewees regarded the possibility for part-time work within the police service primarily as aimed at women with care duties. In a complementing manner, from an organisational standpoint, the issue of gender was sometimes brought up under the guise of discussing part-time work.[121] In a similar way to the UK, part-time work in the Austrian police is not yet fully integrated and accepted by superiors and colleagues of equal rank alike. The reciprocal relationship between the facts that part-time work is female-connotated as well as undervalued still proves to be true in both countries, albeit in some corners of UK police to a lesser extent.

5.6.2.2 Care Work

What is often directly linked to the issue of part-time or flexible working schemes is the matter of parental/maternity leave and care work. In both countries, a compulsory mother's leave exists[122], with co-parents being able to apply for parental leave on a voluntary basis. In the UK, parental leave is an individual entitlement (Blum et al. 2018: 16), and it was noted by interviewees that co-parents are entitled to less parental leave than mothers.[123] In Austria, parental leave has the same maximum length for both parents regardless of gender and is therefore regarded a family entitlement (Blum et al. 2018: 21). However, in both countries it is still women who face the negative job consequences of a pregnancy or adoption. Even the mere mention of planning to have a child sometimes has a negative impact on

---

121 According to the head of the ZOG (Centre for Organisational Culture and Equal Treatment).

122 In Austria, the compulsory mothers leave consists of a total of 16 weeks (§ 3 ff Mutterschutzgesetz 1979 – MSchG BGBl. Nr. 221/1979), while mothers leave in the UK consists of a considerably shorter time period of two weeks (Section 72 (3)(a), Employment Rights Act 1996).

123 For example, for North Wales Police, maternity support or paternity leave can last up to two weeks, following 18 weeks of unpaid leave in blocks of 4 weeks per child per year. Maternity leave can be taken for a maximum of 15 months (with continuously decreasing pay) (Duties and Leave for Police Officers, northwales.police.uk).

the interaction and relationship with police superiors. An Austrian officer recalled a conversation around her application for further training:

"I said 'well maybe next year I'll have a child and can't do [the training] anymore and then the statement was, 'so you want to have children', […] and...'then you don't need to do any more training anyway', so it was very misogynistic. [...] he told me it was a joke, but I don't think it was a joke. [...] I now have two pregnant colleagues at my department, I was present in one situation where said colleague reported it (..) the facial expression and the reaction, I would have up and left because (...)." – Interview 4, Austria.

Debates around pregnancy and maternity were experienced as very negative by respondents in both countries. Interviewees in Austria talked more about the detrimental impact having children has on their relationship to superiors and co-workers, as well as their potential career paths. In the UK, respondents in a similar fashion brought up the feeling of "not pulling one's weight" when having care duties and the stigma of childcare, that further leads to difficulties in achieving certain ranks. Additionally, pregnancy leads to a restriction of duties in both countries which often leaves pregnant officers doing desk work instead of carrying out their usual duties. As soon as a pregnancy is announced, these restrictions take effect and often an additional risk assessment is necessary to determine which tasks can still be safely carried out (See for example: North Wales Police 2020/022 Maternity & Paternity Leave, north-wales.police.uk, BMKÖS, Rechtliches, oeffentlicherdienst.gv.at).

As some women I spoke to already experienced (or were in the midst of experiencing) pregnancy and maternity leave while working for the police, their tales show some poignant similarities. The maternity benefits offered by police forces in the UK, for instance, are considered to be detrimental to those of other civil service employers. Female officers in the UK who reported having been pregnant during their employment with the police all stated that they had saved money and planned ahead a long time before deciding to have a child or start a family, in order to be able to reconcile their income with the ability to care for their child(ren). In Austria, respondents also noted that there is a discrepancy between the recognition of an officer's performance and the reception of their intention to go on paternity leave; for women it often is a case of deciding against promotion/progression or against having children. The sensation of being perceived as and feeling unequal to childless colleagues carries on after maternity leave and often stays as long as female officers still have caring duties for their child(ren). The aforementioned rigorous shift work patterns of police work do not allow for flexibility in care work, and as previously mentioned, flexible or part-time work is still negatively received within the organisation. Often, these negative experiences are more common in historically male-connotated pockets of policing such as detective work.

> "[M]y son was sent to school in [city], but I didn't live in [state], I was living slightly outside of [state], so I put a plan in, a request to do flexible hours, so that I could get him to school, cause we lived outside [state], and my boss said 'if you want to be in the CID, you will make it work. It's not *my* fault you've got children'" – Interview 14, England and Wales.

Respondents, primarily from the UK, lamented that it is still the mothers who have to carry most of the negative occupational repercussions when having children. To them, some jobs in the police are simply not compatible with being the primary carer of children, and the struggles of deciding between career and family almost exclusively fall on the side of the female officer. As one respondent put it quite simply: "Men don't have that issue" (Interview 18, England and Wales). Although a few interviewees saw a positive change in how paternity leave is received within the organisation, it can still hardly be passed off as a non-issue inside the service. An organisational change for the positive in this regard is the availability of a "pool" of officers to stand in for deployed officers on paternity leave in Vienna (Polizei aktuell, "Schaffung eines Karenzpools", polizeigewerkschaft-fsg.at). In the UK, partial changes to some forces' maternity/paternity leave policies have also taken place, and the issue of flexible working has (in some parts) received more acceptance. It is still undeniable that care work is an issue that disproportionately affects female officers and their career (progression), a circumstance that is not helped by the rather rigid organisational structure of the police service. It is evident that the police is an organisation that was not designed with the reality of having a family and related duties, let alone women, in mind.

5.6.3 Equal Opportunities Policies and Related Schemes

The focus of this part of the study is on the participants' position on (perceived) equal opportunities policies and their perception of the current state of (gender) diversity in the police service. These opinions and positions are inevitably influenced by and linked to their countries' respective social and cultural environment. Relating these opinions and experiences to actual legal frameworks and interpretations is a vital part of the research.

The responses this section predominantly references where given to the question, "Which (governmental) measures/policies of gender equality (in the police workforce) do you know of OR you may already have experience with (e.g. encouraging women to apply for certain positions)?".[124] What is to be noted is that the policies implemented under the guise of securing gender equality differ between the two countries, as well as marginally between the individual police forces in the UK.

5.6.3.1 Equality, Equity, Diversity

Almost all Austrian participants discuss which policies are seen as promoting equality and what "equality" really means to them. The issue repeatedly comes up when discussing the Austrian police's gender quota. In most police job advertisements, the phrase, "Women are given preferential treatment/employment if they have the same qualifications" is displayed. This phrase is cause for much debate among police officers themselves and in the interviews. Some think it unwise, even unfair, to prefer equally qualified female over male applicants. Others find this to be a good thing, ensuring that more female officers are getting promoted and therefore being able to influence decision-making processes. In the same way, in England and Wales positive action allows for an employer to favour someone who shares a protected characteristic[125] over someone who does not. Similar to Austria, positive discrimination is unlawful in England and Wales.[126] As positive action in both countries refers to equal qualifications as a prerequisite for positive action to be effective, many Austrian interviewees

---

124 German wording: "Welche frauenfördernden Maßnahmen des BM.I kennen Sie BZW haben Sie eventuell selbst schon Erfahrung damit gemacht (Beispiel Quotenregelung)?".

125 According to the Equality Act 2010 c 15, Section 4 these are: age, disability, gender reassignment, marriage and civil partnership, pregnancy and maternity, race, religion or belief, sex, and sexual orientation.

126 Although it has been the topic of discussion quite recently regarding the introduction of positive race discrimination backed by some police leaders as well as politicians (see: Dodd 2020, theguardian.com).

discussed the problem of how to assess what 'equal qualifications' mean and how they are perceived.

> "I don't know if it's a good thing. That you say you have to give women preference. [...] I think first and foremost the qualification should be right." – Interview 12, Austria.

Equality, to most of them, means to treat everyone equally, regardless of the circumstances. This is why it is hard to understand for some of them what the "preference of women over men" has to do with equality. Being treated as an equal, having to adhere to the same guidelines and requirements, is of enormous importance to most of the participants. This approach reflects findings of previous research which shows that female officers have a hard time adjusting to a male-dominated field, and some therefore (have to) adapt their behavioural patterns to fit into the dominant culture, and not be seen as "other" (Cf. Rabe-Hemp 2008a, 2008b).

Conversely, when interviewees from England and Wales talked about positive action schemes, they frame it as a sort of corrective justice. In lieu of positive discrimination policies, all police forces follow the national Equality Act of 2010 which prohibits any discriminatory behaviour at work based on age, disability, gender reassignment, marriage and civil partnership, pregnancy and maternity, race, religion or belief, sex, and sexual orientation (Equality Act of 2010 Section 4). Further, all police forces are encouraged to have positive action schemes in place in order to "level [...] the playing field" (College of Policing [6]: 6, college.police.uk). These include positive action in recruitment and promotion, for example holding special training days for female applicants. Rather than talking about perceived equal qualifications, interviewees in the UK addressed the inequalities of predispositions in reaching said qualifications.

> "[B]ecause I think per definition, she would probably have to struggle harder to get to that standard. She's got more of what it takes, depends what you're measuring doesn't it." – Interview 4, England and Wales.

Structural inequalities, not only regarding gender, were taken for granted in most officers' arguments and any impact from positive action schemes therefore justified in trying to counteract these inequalities. Thus, female officers in the UK framed the existence and influence of these measures as something very positive. The perception of the interviewed officers' colleagues and superiors in both countries regarding positive action schemes were considerably less favourable.

5.6.3.2 The Reception within the Police Force

What was being brought up by participants and discussed in every interview is the reception of equality policies within the police force. What is to be noted is that, in Austria, the issue that was talked about most was that of so-called quota rules. Other provisions, such as mentoring programs, were not mentioned at all, or, like parental leave, only sparsely. Regardless of this narrow perception of equality policies, strikingly, all Austrian interviewees seemed to have an opinion about quota rules. Almost all officers mentioned that they had to deal with what they believed to be the negative outcomes of a gender quota, as perceived by their (male) colleagues.

> "[O]r with the women's promotion plan, that they are now saying, with equal qualifications, a woman will get the job because we are so underrepresented. That is of course also a topic which always creates a big wave of heat, right. Because, of course, it is very difficult for a man to understand why, if the two are of equal value, the woman is preferred, right. If there is no reason for him other than that it is a woman. – Interview 7, Austria.
>
> [W]hich will never be the case, because the men always complain about it, [mockingly] ugh [/], well, not complaining but, you have to listen to it, of course, [mockingly] the women are being preferred." – Interview 4, Austria, on the topic of female applicants getting a job because of quotas.

In most cases, the state of view of the male colleague is taken and made comprehensible. At the same time, it is not assumed that male officers can understand and empathize with the concept of equal treatment. Being emphatic and being able to reconstruct different points of view is a characteristic that is once again attributed to female rather than male officers.

Interestingly, female officers in the UK did not bring up the issue of preferential treatment of female applicants in the case of equal qualifications in this detail, but rather talked about other measures such as training days or workshops catered towards marginalised groups. What is to be noted is, that any aforementioned practice, e.g., recruitment days, often is aimed at different groups simultaneously, e.g., special training days for people of BAME groups and female officers. While the general attitude did not seem as averse as in Austria towards these equality policies, officers remarked that some of their colleagues do find the provisions made for certain marginalised groups to be unfair. Interviewees, however, noted, that straight white able-bodied male applicants might not get additional support by the police as an employer, yet this group already sets out with certain privileges that they themselves might not be aware of.

> "And seeing it that way, yeah well, you did it because you know 5 different people who are in the special forces, and mentors who sort of told you step by step what to write and what to say, but well, no, the other person didn't deserve it. [...] Yeah, well, nobody wants to see it that way, especially if you took advantage of the fact that you had help. But as I said, some people get the help, others don't, and it's, it's all about making up for that. [...] is it a perfect system? I don't know. But it definitely meets with (.) negative reactions." – Interview 2, England and Wales.

In this way, negative talk about equality policies is met with a clear and rational refutation, namely the fact that every person's prerequisites differ from one another, rendering the additional support some get a mere side-factor to their success. However, the negative reactions of some officers to these measures will most likely prevail in any case, leaving those associated with them with a felt obligation to justify their professional progress.

A number of Austrian interviewees lamented that, if they were hired for a particular job, some male colleagues would joke about them being a quota-woman. This, of course, goes hand in hand with ascribing lesser qualifications to female officers in general, questioning their professional abilities simply because of their gender.[127] Female police officers are therefore not accepted as equals, but rather mocked for needing assistance – in the shape of quotas – to acquire the same positions as men. Most, of course, saw this state as something to be criticized.

> "What of course (..) is actually counterproductive for women in the police force, in my view, are all these provisions with equal treatment. I think it is important, but it's no use for women. Because, I hear that even now, even from young people, if you talk about it, there's this passage "if women are equally qualified, women are preferred" only this passage is read as "as soon as a woman applies for the position, she gets the position" [...] Well, there (.) I can still see that it is going slowly, because I believe we have had the Equal Treatment Act since 96 [1993 AN] now, and (...) they still don't want to understand it properly." - Interview 3, Austria.

---

127   See chapter 5.4.1.

The cause for complaint here is not merely the fact that these equality provisions exist, but rather the circumstance that most officers (male and female) misunderstand the situation. This is an issue that (former) equality commissioners as well as most senior female officers brought up and is seen as a predicament to them (see also chapter 5.6.3.5). The different approach and viewpoints of female officers in differing spots on the hierarchical order is something that needs consideration.

5.6.3.3 Self-Perception

In relation to perceptions of gender quotas and other equal treatment policies of male colleagues, the interviewees' own perception and opinions on these measures were voiced equally often in Austria and the UK. Often, these views came up in relation to other colleagues' perceptions of these policies. In Austria, this was discussed controversially, as some felt that the differential treatment they are presumably being given was something to be avoided, rather than embraced.

> "Because that's what I wouldn't want, for example. So, I wouldn't apply somewhere because I know, [...] there are only men and they're sure to take me because I'm the only woman. So just to get anything because of that, I wouldn't want for myself. Not at all. See, that's where everything in me bristles, because either I want it because my performance fits, but not just because I'm a woman. [...] So, they are not doing us any good with it." – Interview 11, Austria.

Others see it as an insult to their pride.

> "I don't believe in quotas. I also do not think anything of, or little of, equal treatment. If it says (..) that if a job is advertised, women who are of equal value are to be treated particularly preferentially, right. That is not good for us. If we, we are good, right, [...] we are in a position when we have achieved something and then we do not need to put something like that in." – Interview 14, Austria.

Quotas were mostly seen as something rather negative, at best to be ignored, sometimes avoided and in some cases even something to advocate against. This does not only stem from negative reactions of male colleagues that female police officers have to deal with, but also from an inherent wish or desire not to be treated differently than their male colleagues. After all, interviewees argued, they are doing the same job and getting the same salary.[128] Conversely, participants from the UK did not share the negative outlook on positive action that some of their colleagues held. To them, the need for these policies is evident. However, some interviewees admitted to not having engaged with any positive action policies, presumably because they felt no need to partake in activities. In any case, female officers often tried to distance themselves, some quite overtly (Austria) others less often and more subdued (UK), from the marginalised group in question and the perceived aid they receive. To not position oneself clearly while still having to deal with one's own situatedness as a woman in the workplace is presumed a safer move than to fully engage and support equality policies within the police. Actively advocating against these policies was perceived as a valid option by female police officers in Austria to uphold the illusion of sameness with their male peers. In England and Wales, however, a rejectionist attitude towards equality actions in regard to gender was scarcely found in female officers.

The issue of justice and equality, in contrast to equity, is a cornerstone of Austrian policewomen's work identity. Throughout their accounts, their perceived sameness to their male colleagues overwhelmed their alleged gendered differences. This serves as the main reason as to why, to them, it was often not clear on what grounds they should receive work-related preferential treatment. Some even went as far as judging quotas as unjust.

> "Yeah, well, there are quota rules. It's even the case that now I'm actually saying as a woman [...] [it's] actually unfair to men because when a job is advertised, it even often says 'women are preferred, or given priority." – Interview 8, Austria.

From their viewpoint, the current situation in the police service presents itself as equal regarding gender issues – same pay, same work, same conditions. The preferential treatment is therefore deemed unfair or unjust – at least from their perspective on equality as discussed above. Similarly, some UK respondents mentioned that they perceive those who do not belong to a marginalised group, as defined by the Equality Act (Equality Act 2010 c 15, Section 4), to feel left out.

> "I think they have preconceived ideas about positive action sort of thinking of getting benefits [...] people might need more help to get to that start line. That's how I see positive action." – Interview 15, England and Wales.

---

128   A view that is not supported by official numbers, see chapter 5.6.2.

However, UK interviewees themselves did not follow this line of argument, and rather followed the explanations given by those officials that initiate policies regarding the Equality Act. It is hard to say whether these positions were acquired due to a personal examination of the topic, or simply a repetition of learned patterns of explanation as they are given by equality policy makers. Regardless of the origin of this position, UK respondents seemed to distance themselves from critics of equality policies, while Austrian interviewees deemed it better to align with these critiques. This is particularly interesting in view of the fact that respondents on both sides have indicated that they are affected by the negative reactions of others to equality policies.

The issue of the problematic reception of gender quotas was also discussed from an organisational point of view, by interviewees working on or with equal treatment issues, such as equal treatment commissioners or women's network representatives. They all acknowledged that there is a problem in the reception of such policies among police officers. One of them voiced an opinion about a possible explanation of the overall negative reception of equality issues among female police officers in Austria.

> "[B]ut I also have, I also know a lot of women who are opposed to these women's promotion policies [breathes heavily] which is of course problematic. Because they misjudge the situation a bit. They don't want to be treated differently, they believe they have to act like the men do so that they are recognised. [...] They have a different point of view because everyone wants recognition. That's the way it is, right. And they just think they can get recognition from men if they act like men. And that is why they reject these measures to promote women." - Interview 16, Austria.

This view and its rather simplistic explanation are backed by the data gathered from the conducted interviews in Austria. Most female police officers in Austria tried to liken their behaviour and thinking patterns to that of their male colleagues, whether it was in order to be accepted or out of an unreflecting acquisition of (male-connotated) stereotypes. But this reasoning is only one of many factors and circumstances that could explain the lack of acceptance gender equality policies are being shown by female police officers. Another, rather large part is played by the aforementioned negative reaction such policies get from male police officers, and the way they then reflect on female officers.[129] This, in rare cases, also reflected negatively on UK respondents' view of gender equality policies.

> "I don't want to say that everyone thinks like that, right, but in reality, you hear that again and again, that's not really great for me, right. They didn't do the women any good." – Interview 14, Austria.
>
> "I mean that's one of the reasons I imagine we don't have a positive action policy, is because the backlash from it, particularly in a small force like ours, we don't need it. We have some policies that are female-friendly, around maternity and the likes. But in terms of, you know, I wouldn't wanna go down the lines of positive action. Because I don't think it helps." – Interview 21, England and Wales.

Wanting to be treated without what, in their eyes, appears to be a bias towards women and the specifics of the environment in which they had to operate are the reasons given by Austrian participants on why the majority of them do not favour equality policies. While most Austrian respondents deemed these policies counterproductive in ensuring gender equality, personal critique of positive action within the police service was found only seldomly among the reports from UK interviewees. The negative issues related to gender equality measures (existing or potential) in the police service were very similar in their basic features in both countries, although the extent of these problems varies.

5.6.3.4 Women's Networks and Equality Commissioners

Beside quotas, another issue that was discussed quite frequently was that of equality commissioners and "contact women" in Austria, or women's networks in the UK. None of the Austrian interviewees had actively sought counsel with such a commissioner or contact woman, although most of them knew about the option at the time. Local policewomen's networks, among other things, serve as a similar intermediate body to address complaints or problems in the workplace. An issue that equality commissioners or women's contact persons face in Austria is the reluctance of female officers to raise any work-related issues they might experience with the relevant representative body. As can be concluded from the previous chapters, this is not due to a lack of perceived gendered issues that female

---

129 The backlash surrounding equality policies in both countries and its implications for (affected) female police officers is further discussed in chapter 5.6.3.5.

officers encounter. Rather, female officers seem to have developed their own method of dealing with such issues.

"There is a women's representative [...] if you probably have problems such as I myself had with my boss, in truth I could have gone to a contact woman and talked about it." - Interview 4, Austria.

Most Austrian officers reported to rather deal with the problems they were facing themselves than taking them to a contact woman. Some justified this by believing it to be less hassle to tackle the issue themselves, for example requesting to transfer to another police station. This of course also means that, if the underlying issue is one that (also) affects people other than the officers in question (such as repeated sexist behaviour from a supervisor), these issues will not be raised with management. Therefore, equality commissioners are not able to provide assistance on a larger scale or take steps to prevent further discrimination. This reluctance to report incidents was also experienced by an officer who used to work as a contact woman for 10 years (up until some years ago).

"I have never had any incidents, so no one has ever approached me. I would have been there for it if, as a contact and counsellor in cases of sexual abuse or, like., harassment or, appointments to posts, but, in that time, I never had a case in the sense that I was approached." - Interview 3, Austria.

Female officers acting as contact women or equal treatment officers today reported that the situation is undergoing changes. According to them, this is due not least to initiatives on the part of the organisation.

"[T]here frequently are inquiries, but this has a lot to do with our level of awareness, so initially there were few, there are now more and more. That's simply because we do everything we can to say okay, we want people to know that we exist, so they know what equal treatment is, so they know what their rights are." - Interview 16, Austria.

Raising awareness and promoting the work of equal treatment commissioners seems to be a priority at the moment. This tactic, at least from what reports say can be seen so far, works quite well in shedding light on equality issues and making people less reluctant to address issues of gender-based injustice with the responsible organisational authorities.

The involvement in (local) women's networks in the UK can similarly be challenging for some. The reason given by respondents on why many female officers feel no need to join their respective network (aside from the additional work/time factor) was, again, possible repercussions from (male) colleagues. "[T]hey'll be perceived by their male colleagues as being a feminist" (Interview 8, England and Wales) seemed to be the main ideological reason why women's networks were often not very popular. Regardless of people's personal ideologies or whether or not these networks serve a feminist purpose in any sense, association with these organisations that carve out a space reserved solely for women, especially in a male-dominated – previously exclusively male – environment such as the police serves as another alienating factor for female officers and was generally met with resentment. This can also be seen by the way in which some women's groups have allowed access to male participants on certain occasions such as internal development days.[130] Not wanting to alienate male colleagues while furthering women's causes and implementing equality strategies presents as a narrow tightrope walk for female officers in both countries.

In the same sense, getting in contact with equal treatment commissioners can also be a rather alienating experience for female officers in Austria, as a particular interviewee recalled. She was contacted by an equal treatment commissioner during her maternity leave, to check for possible re-entry options into the service – an offer the interviewee declined, as she did not deem it necessary to receive additional help in re-entering the service.

> "I thought to myself, what kind of impression does that make if she calls there [at the police station] and says I want to go there or something, right. [...] And I also told them back then that I don't think that's okay and [...] a bit exaggerated, because, everyone knows that there are women's representatives, and then I can still turn there or not if I want to, but [getting contacted by] them, that was already a bit too much. Because if a male colleague is somewhere else he will not be called, right. 'Can we help you with where you want to go.'" - Interview 8, Austria.

As with quota rules, the main issue female officers find with this kind of service seems to be the differential treatment of male and female officers, as well as the possible reaction from other colleagues. Being equal to their male colleagues is, again, of great value to female police officers in Austria. Although, as some equality commissioners have pointed out, these kinds of services are available for all police officers, as they deal with issues

---

130 See for example the curriculum provided by the College of Policing (Initial Police Learning, college.police.uk).

such as sexual harassment and maternity/paternity leave, they are seen as something carried out by women for women. Some noted that this misconception can in part be attributed to the name of the responsible official – "contact woman" – which evokes certain associations. The further clarification of areas of responsibility and creating awareness for the service is a currently ongoing objective of the Centre for Organizational Culture and Equal Treatment. This is mainly done via workshops and lectures within the training courses for all police ranks.

Similar issues can be observed within women's associations for the police service in England and Wales. As mentioned previously, these associations and groups sometimes struggle with their police-internal acceptance. Many have undergone changes in names and focus over the years due to various reasons. The national women's association, BAWP[131], does not play a major role in the accounts of the interviewees. Local women support groups, however, were mentioned by almost all interviewees as providing an important service to the policing community, although not every police force in England and Wales has their own local women support group. Each local group is characterised by various workstreams, such as flexible working or wellbeing. Much like their national counterpart BAWP, these groups are mostly open to officers regardless of gender – the focus, however, lies on furthering women's issues within a policing context. The reception of these organisations is predominantly positive, even if interviewees noted that some do have issues with the presumed unjust preference of some social groups over others. Interviewees did note that officers overwhelmingly seem to interact with these associations once they personally encounter a work-related problem. There also appears to be a tendency for these organisations to be engaged with more frequently by female officers of a higher rank. Through regional meetings, individual groups can meet and exchange their strategies and ideas, though the individuality of these local groups has both pros and cons.

> "[I]t's not as high-profile as it used to be, it used to be very comfortable very open marketplace, now I don't see an open marketplace I think people do it as quietly as possible. Which I think is a little bit sad

---

131 The British Association for Women in Policing is represented on the Equality Subcommittee of the Police Federation and seeks to address women's issues in policing in England and Wales, Scotland and Northern Ireland. Membership is open to police officers regardless of gender (British Association for Women in Policing, bawp.org).

because there are a lot of women out there who need more encouragement." – Interview 4, England and Wales.

What is reflected in this quote can be sensed in many other narratives. Associations and groups aimed at women in policing are under a lot of scrutiny by officers, the fear of appearing too feminist or anti-male leads to a dilution of the groups – this can also be seen, for example, in the attempt to keep male colleagues "on board" by not excluding them from activities. A reformist approach is often missing in these organisations today.

5.6.3.5 Perceived Gendered Difficulties

In the interviews, some issues arose that, in the interviewees' perception, did not receive enough attention, or were left out completely by equality policies or strategies. These matters differ slightly in their significance in the two countries, yet can be broadly compared to each other.

The first issue is the compatibility of family and career. Many interviewees mentioned that the police in particular do not provide an ideal background – shift work, long working hours, and on-call duty being some of the main aspects that curtail a potential family life. The fact that the police as an organisation have failed to implement better strategies around flexible working and part-time employment is a serious source of frustration for female officers. As mentioned previously (chapter 5.4.3), these schemes have improved over the years, yet still fall short in providing adequate support for female officers. This is exemplified by the accounts of an interviewee who described the incompatibility of receiving a promotion while simultaneous taking care of her children.

> "I love my policing career, I wish I could do both, the promotion and the children, but right now, I can't. it frustrates me, it frustrates me that I can't, and you see people getting promoted and thinking [sighs] I can't get my evidence to do that promotion." – Interview 18, England and Wales.

The negative effect shift-work can have on family life (Jensen et al. 2018: E705ff.) is mirrored by the decision to prioritise family life, and therefore has a negative impact on possible promotions and career progression. The circumstance that departmental policies do little to reverse these detrimental effects, as stated by interviewees, is also supported by previous research (Ellis 2016).

Furthermore, the difficulty of finding replacement or substitutes for officers going on parental leave was brought up by Austrian interviewees. This is due to the special deployment and work rotas of police forces in the country.

"I must say, they should start to think about something because of, if you get pregnant. [...] [I]t is currently, I mean for the [pregnant] woman herself, yes. But there is just no pool where people are taken from, for a colleague who is pregnant, she is on maternity leave and is still listed up here [points to duty rota] so everyone thinks she is there, but you lack the people." – Interview 5, Austria.

It was noted that in Vienna, Austria's capital and most populous city, this kind of 'pool' of officers to be deployed where they are needed already exists. Still, in other regions, and especially in the countryside, police forces often struggle with this problem. This does not only create organisational issues but reinforces the negative attitude and resentment that many in the organisation have towards (pregnant) women in the workplace. Similarly, issues revolving around childcare and flexible working are attributed to female officers, and the often too rigid guidelines and circumstances of police work make it hard for (future) mothers to adequately combine their work and home life.

As well as parental leave, the issue of later child support, such as a kindergarten, was also brought up by Austrian officers. Currently, there is the possibility to leave small children with a ministry-internal kindergarten if you are employed with the Ministry of the Interior.

"And as far as the support of women is concerned, I believe we have room for improvement. So, I know here in the BMI [Ministry of the Interior, AN] there's a childcare facility, there's a kindergarten, I think that's very good, but that should be expanded. We should make it possible for women to be really flexible in the whole area of childcare, for them to receive support from the federal government, and for them to be able to hand over their children to an institution so that they can really be fully reintegrated into the service. So, we certainly still have some [.] need for action." - Interview 13, Austria.

The fact that these internal services are not offered for officers regardless of the location of their current workplace, is, again, an issue that seems restricted to female officers. Furthermore, the divide between gainful employment and care work was made clear in the statements of officers demanding the right for female officers to cede/outsource one while furthering the other. What is particularly striking is that the full commitment to police work in this sense can only be seen in the complete opposite of care work. So, one of the two must always step back in this relationship. This is a phenomenon that can generally be found in both countries, and, due to the arguments presented above, is inherent in police work.

The second big issue is, again, the reception of equality policies and legal frameworks within the police service, and their limitations. In Austria as well as the UK, the issue was not only discussed as one that elicits a certain amount of annoyance or resentment among police officers – the fact that certain policies are ill-received was in itself seen as a problem by some respondents in Austria and by all in the UK.

According to some Austrian participants, the equality policies themselves are a fair and just measure and the negative reception they receive is down to the lack of awareness on the issue. Regardless of their own opinion about such policies, lots of interviewees wished for more information and clarification on that topic. Some interviewees mentioned that the negative attitudes towards such things as quota rules displayed by male (and sometimes female) police officers was mostly due to the organisation not providing enough information and insight into the topic of equality policies.

> "So, I really have to say it would have rather bothered me that colleagues were not briefed there, or respectively create awareness. […] That it's not so easy, "she's a woman and that's why she gets it", right." - Interview 6, Austria.
> "I know it from my boyfriend who has already told me, right, I won't apply to this job at all because two women applied there already, then I'm not getting it anyway. And I said, no, exactly that is not it, right. But it's really that, it's in most people's heads. That is, that is really bad yes." - Interview 17, Austria.

Raising awareness, and briefing officers from the start about such issues as the quota rule, is desired by most interviewees in Austria. Recently, this situation might have improved due to there being more mandatory courses on issues such as gender equality. Still, there is a lot of reluctance within the police service to deal with these issues, as one participant remembers.

> "And with the Equal Treatment Act, in truth no one cared, you have been able to argue, it is a federal law like any other, a *federal* law, and the police are there to uphold and enforce laws, but this federal law has simply been ignored for a long time." - Interview 3, Austria.

The circumstances, of course, have changed from back when the Equal Treatment Act was coming into force, but there are obviously still some issues around the reception and awareness of gender equality policies. This was also noted by the head of the "Centre for Organizational Culture and Equal Treatment" (ZOG) in the Ministry of the Interior. He is well aware of the issue surrounding the reception (and rejection) of equality policies such as quota rules or mentoring programs. He believes, in accordance with what many female officers have stated, the most headway is to be made by education and providing information on the subject.

> "[A]nd that is precisely what we have to work on, right, there is now training [in all courses] so that [officers of] all hierarchies have at least one time heard about the subject of equal treatment. And in these lessons we always also address the subject of "quota women" and quota regulations, so that perhaps one day they will understand what it means in the first place. [...] And with that one could, if one looks at the organisational culture, perhaps bring about a change in this thinking in a few years' time." - Interview with the head of the ZOG, Austria.

While acknowledging the amount of work and time necessary for such a shift in perception of gender equality issues, educating officers is seen as the best possible option for both female officers and organisational staff. As mentioned earlier, there seems to be an awareness of this issue in the organisation, and an attempt to rectify the situation. The data suggests that a re-invention or better integration of some measures of gender equality in the police service seem necessary.

UK officers likewise stated that, in some parts, providing additional training courses or mentoring programmes is received as "unfair" treatment by some colleagues. What was, however, only noted by interviewees from the UK, is the view that these policies and legal frameworks can, due to their nature, only go so far in furthering equality within the police service. The emancipatory effect of law and directives and their limits were experienced quite often by female officers in the UK, who may have received a state of legal equality earlier than their Austrian counterparts, but due to this also see the downfalls of change which is ordered from the top.

> "[I]t's more about helping these disadvantaged underrepresented groups, helping them pass through into the environment that wasn't designed with them in mind. When, actually, it's the environment that should be changing." – Interview 4, England and Wales.

This view is not expressed by many interviewees[132], yet it is immensely important in the argument surrounding police cultural change. Throughout the interviews, a certain dissonance between inherent police culture and modern approaches to policing as well as equality policies or actions of any kind can be identified. This, of course, is nothing new when looking at the literature (Brown/Heidensohn 2000, Heidensohn/Silvestri 2012, McCarthy 2013), yet it leads some officers to question the ability of equality policies or a simple increase in (female) numbers to provoke a greater change within the police service. This insight, however, can only be derived through an extensive examination of the subject matter and further reflecting, which is often only possible through an external perspective.

5.6.4 Improvements and Changes in Police Culture

When talking about changes to police and police culture through a gendered lens in their respective countries, many respondents mentioned the increase in numbers of female officers over the years. Further, there is an acknowledgement of the achievements of the first female police officers and interviewees carry a deep sitting respect for these early pioneers. Some attributed any positive changes to police culture to an increase in the numbers of female officers, others only saw it as coincidental, the change and improvement in police being inevitable. What is similar in both countries is the fact that female officers saw the police service as being slow to change, regardless of which direction that change might take. Interestingly, respondents from both Austria and the UK, figuratively speaking, likened the police service to an oil tanker: massive in size and therefore hard to stir off its path. The less overt sexist climate within the police service, the fact that the numbers of female officers of rank has increased over time, and the general bettering of representation of female officers within all areas of policing was unsurprisingly described as positive, yet necessary and often seen as a sort of the bare minimum, especially for interviewees from the UK. The humiliating tradition of the "station stamp" (Garavelli 2017, heraldscotland.com), the othering practice of being registered as "WPCs" (Women Police Constable) rather than PCs (Police Constable), as well as other discriminating, excluding, and harassing processes are, according to all respondents, a thing of the past in

---

132 The particular quote stems from the interview with a Leadership Development Officer for Police Now.

the police services of England and Wales. Likewise, Austrian respondents noted a decline in outright sexist practices within their workplace. Yet there is a certain dissatisfaction with the current stagnation of the discussion around diversity issues and the breaking up of the traditional police mentality, which according to some has even turned into a backlash.

Although all interviewees remarked noticing a positive development of police culture, valuing female officers and female-connotated work more highly than years or decades ago, the further development of a different, namely more open and progressive, sort of police culture also seems to have somewhat stagnated. Again, it was noted that certain value judgements and practices still have little or no chance of gaining a foothold within police culture.

> "[W]e used to talk about the advantages of de-escalating violence and avoiding conflict and defusing it, and all those things. And it's kind of well-established, well-known, and yet it's still not given as much weight. As if the ultimate test is, 'oh but if you had to would you be able to knock them all out' [laughing] so there's still, there's a little bit of a cultural (..) lag, that's the wrong word 'cause it implies it's moving at all, I don't think it's moving at all, I really don't." – Interview 4, England and Wales.

Of course, the positive impact equality policies and the furthering of women's issues within the police service already had on internal developments and the surrounding police culture cannot be denied. Yet, while some may argue that "if equal opportunities initiatives did not exist we would have to invent them" (Cockburn 1991: 16), it seems fair to say that they have seem to reach an impasse.

> "For the master's tools will never dismantle the master's house. They may allow us temporarily to beat him at his own game, but they will never enable us to bring about genuine change." (Lorde 1984: 112)

The theoretical and political assumption that regulations and concepts implemented from above can never reach the root of the problem, let alone eliminate it, is found here in practice. Regardless of the label that is put on policies – such as equality or diversity – one can argue that these seem to only work as an organisational tool, serving and feeding the same system they profess to change or even improve for those that feel alienated and/or repressed by it. To put it bluntly: While the police as an organisation try to recruit people who are not white, male, heterosexual or in any other way enjoy social privileges in Western society, it is not possible for the police to redefine itself as an organisation from the ground up – in a way that does not support the current dominant culture while excluding and suppressing certain groups. This may also be due to the police's unique position in the social and political fabric (chapter 6).

5.6.5 Interim Findings

It is acknowledged and noted by female officers that the police service in both countries remains a very male-dominated field. The male mould that exists to a different extent in various work areas of the police is something that officers regardless of gender have to adapt to, even if some respondents noted feeling welcomed in general. What all respondents could agree on, however, is the fact that the media portrayal of police (work) and with it the public perception still very much focusses on displays of masculinity. In this respect, masculinity is aligned with prestige, showing the "dangerous" work (male) police carry out, while female officers are left to carry out less prestigious tasks.[133] This in turn can not only directly influence potential applicants' decision to join the police service, but also indirectly take an impact through their social surroundings. What can be seen from interviewee's accounts is that a certain ideal type of police officer exists in Austria, which, regardless of subtle changes to policing styles or a growing representation of marginalised groups within the police, adheres to male-connoted standards such as assertiveness and toughness. The ideal female police officer in Austria is therefore defined by their lack of differences to their male counterpart. In England and Wales, conversely, the notion of diversity leads to a highlighting of potential (gendered) differences which theoretically make it acceptable to present as other than the predefined male standards, yet this notion has not taken hold within police culture quite as much as many would wish. For both countries it can therefore be said that the "safe" option for female officers still remains, and adherence to stereotypically male-associated qualities in order to gain acceptance from their peers as well as superiors.

In England and Wales, some noted that dealing with specific female-dominated issues such as appropriate toilet facilities or menopause often remains restricted to female-led workgroups or organisations, which makes it hard to fight for change on these issues. Furthermore, a certain display of male chauvinism can be noted from those in charge of implementing

---

133 For example, assisting elderly people (Compare also Fejes/Haake 2013).

said change, establishing female officers and their issues as "less than" in a surrounding designed by and created for men. Some problems that potentially underly and reinforce issues surrounding the full integration of female officers into the police are also noted in both countries. The inflexibility of the police organisation, for example, is a factor that may contribute to the circumstance that many female officers struggle in retaining or progressing in their job in both countries. For the UK, a failure to adequately assess people's potential was mentioned, while Austrian officers often discussed the divide between rural and urban areas of policing, the latter providing a more welcoming conditions for female officers.

Equal pay is a topic of tremendous relevance for female officers. In Austria especially, respondents pride themselves in presumably receiving a salary that is equal to their male colleagues due to the fact that they carry out the same tasks and duties. In the Austrian interviews, no evidence of knowledge around a gender pay gap within the police service emerged, conversely to UK officers, who often noted the gathered statistics examining an unequal distribution of salaries. Although there is not adequate means to compare the different statistics available in both countries, not least due to the different organisational nature of the police services, what remains clear is that the organisation still struggles to close the gender pay gap. The difference in awareness around this particular issue, however, is quite striking and most likely has to be attributed to a divergence of information dissemination.

Issues around part-time or flexible work remain closely connected with assumptions on (a police officer's) gender. Negative preconceptions about flexible working are still prevalent in both countries' police services, ranging from officers being perceived as not "carrying their weight" to being considered an active burden on the organisation. A possible bettering of the reception of flexible work within the police service seems to be linked to the fact that the number of male officers applying for flexible work, in the UK maybe more so than in Austria, is increasing. A masculinisation of part-time or flexible work patterns not only seems to normalise their existence but also shifts the social pressure surrounding these practices away from female officers. Yet, broadly speaking, the gendered nature of flexible work and its overwhelmingly negative reception within the police service remains. Previous research has noted that flexible working arrangements and better management of sick/parental leave are areas the police have to improve on with regards to employing and retaining more female officers (Brown/Woolfenden 2011: 362). Not for nothing is the topic of flexible and part-time work described as a key target for future reform in policing, especially with regards to gender (Silvestri 2017).

Closely related to the topic of flexible work is that of maternity/paternity leave and care work. Compulsory mother's leave is considerably shorter in the UK than in Austria, and parental leave also differs slightly in its design. Regardless of these preconditions, in both countries the negative occupational consequences and associations of pregnancy and care work are almost exclusively linked to female officers. In both countries, female officers reported to have "the shadow of future motherhood cast upon them" (Müller 2007: 333), and, although parental leave options are in place in both countries, the negative occupational consequences of a pregnancy (inability to work) remain exclusively linked to female officers. A certain feeling of alienation was described by (would-be) mothers, who, in various contexts, depicted the incompatibility of childcare and police work. Furthermore, maternity benefits in the UK are seen to be insufficient, as many reported a need to save money and plan ahead before deciding on their family life. As with experiences around flexible work, there is a sense of devaluation of an individual's work that comes with the reality of a pregnancy or parental leave. Again, a progression through the ranks was considered hard or even impossible, in addition to experiencing a feeling of letting your colleagues down while not being able to work or even entering flexible work patterns. While, structurally, there have been some partial positive changes, such as the introduction of a "maternity leave pool" in Vienna, or a bettering of parental leave policy in some forces in England and Wales, it is still indisputable that parenthood and care work disproportionately affect female officers' career and its progression (Schulze 2010).

The topic of equal opportunities policies and gender equality is of importance to Austrian as well as UK police officers, especially female officers. They have to deal with what can be seen as the repercussions of these policies and measures on a day-to-day basis. Of course, equality policies are not the only issue these female officers have to manage, but evidence suggests it is still a relevant factor in their everyday work-life.

First of all, policies relating to (not only female) officers' care work or better organisation of work-life balance, such as offers for part-time work, flexible working schedules and childcare institutions were, unsurprisingly, received very positively. These measures are applicable for both male and female officers, yet they are part of the Austrian Ministry of the Interior's "women's promotion plan", highlighting the fact that managing childcare and household chores are still predominantly "women's issues" in Austria.

Likewise, parental support policies for police forces in England and Wales do allow for time-off for mothers as well as for co-parents, yet mothers are often granted support which is further-reaching. Furthermore, departmental strategies that appear gender-neutral can often be found to be gendered after all (Ellis 2016: 11) – as is the case with these regulations. Research has further shown that care work is in fact more stressful for female police officers than their male counterparts (Holdaway/Parker 1998). Trying to soften these stressors for all officers has naturally been welcomed as a positive measure. In Austria, other policies relating strictly to female officers only, are being placed under more scrutiny. This is to a great part due to the defensive attitude Austrian female police officers display when they are being or should be treated any differently than their male colleagues. This dire need to fit in with dominant police culture presents as difficult for female officers, as they have to adapt to certain behavioural patterns in order to not be excluded from a male-dominated field (Rabe-Hemp 2008a, 2008b).

The data show that "equality" is of utmost importance to female police officers in Austria. To them, equality is signified by treating all people in the same way. This rather simplistic view does not account for differing backgrounds or even structural inequality. As Ben-Galim et al. put it: "Treating everyone in the same way does not protect women from oppression in societies where differences and inequalities exist" (Ben-Galim et al. 2007: 21). Regardless, one of the most important things for female police officers in Austria is not to be treated differently than their male colleagues. That their notion does not coincide with that of authorities responsible for issues of equality is one of the reasons why they deem equality policies, in particular quota rules, as unnecessary or even discriminating against men. This harsh view of stately regulation almost exclusively comes to light when talking about quota rules. The need for other policies and provisions, for example regarding parental leave and childcare, are seen as absolutely self-evident – here the differing positions of male and female officers in the police service is not disputed. However, the constricted notion of equality policies equalling quota rules accounts for the general negative reaction when talking about issues of equality in the police service. In trying to explain and understand this predicament one must factor in the prevalent (hegemonic) masculinity in the police service and its culture. If there is no alternative "female" conception of police culture (Behr 2019), it comes as little surprise that female officers (have to) try to adapt to the male-dominated culture they find. In doing this, they keep their female viewpoint but act as an "ally" to their male colleagues in understanding their behaviour and worries about a "feminisation" of the police service. This also aligns with the findings of Jacobs (1987) that female officers have to navigate their gendered performances in the workplace, where disassociating their femininity and trying to become "one of the boys" is of importance to some female officers. In this way, they might gain entry to the restricted male dominated space that policing still represents. The fear of reprisal ("othering") for being associated with their female peers can lead some to distance themselves and align their performance with the dominant male-oriented police culture (Rabe-Hemp 2008a, 2008b). Conversely, UK respondents generally regarded the diverse nature of people of different social backgrounds as a given, rendering a difference in support and approach of particular marginalised groups as a prerequisite to being able to perform as an equal. Structural inequalities are therefore seen as something to be overcome by means of supportive policies, which are framed as quite positive. Although there is no overwhelmingly hostile environment towards equality provisions to be found, it is noted that some officers still lament the fact that they are presumably being excluded from certain supportive actions, deeming these arrangements unfair. It can therefore be concluded that the negative connotation of these policies in police internal talk are somewhat similar in both countries yet differ in their levels of distribution and intensity.

Incidentally, what is illustrated in the respective countries' respondents' arguments is known in feminist theory as the infamous Wollstonecraft dilemma (Pateman 1989). According to this notion, drawing on women's struggle for full citizenship, understandings of "sameness" and "difference" prevent the advancement of gender equality by trapping it within an ideological discussion (See e.g., Lombardo 2003): Demanding equal rights as equal citizens leads to more citizens living by and following patriarchal standards – the current situation of female officers in Austria can be seen as a prime example of this, as female officers liken their perceptions and opinions to those of their male peers, focussing their debates on the perceived gender equality within the police service. Conversely, claiming female officers, as women, have specific needs and abilities opens the discussion to a certain othering, a difference from the male norm. In both scenarios, men are perceived as the norm to which women must aspire or subordinate to.[134]

---

134 A logic that is also found in the rejection of equality policies, see later in this chapter.

What is to be noted is that interviewees from England and Wales, broadly speaking, do not follow the negative line of argumentation around equality policies. Quite the opposite, there are many justifications and explanations of these provisions (which often resemble the official position of the respective police force) to be found in their accounts. Some Austrian participants, however, see quota rules as an affront to their proficiency and performance – they could "make it on their own" and would not need any outside help. This behaviour, as Scharff argues, is typical within a postfeminist, neoliberal discussion, as the presentation of one's own empowerment often goes hand in hand with the portrayal of other women as "victims of patriarchal oppression" (Scharff 2011: 119). It is very important for female officers in Austria to be seen as a full and valuable member of the police service, rather than relying on aids that aim to balance any structural inequalities. Similarly, support structures provided by police (such as equality commissioners) are rarely, if at all, contacted by policewomen – respondents from England and Wales show a greater acceptance of these institutional aids. This may suggest an improvement of the situation as Brown[135] described it more than 20 years ago. However, evidence seems to suggest that the more intimately one is familiar with the process and the more personal a complaint procedure in the context of equality policies, the less trust in the credibility of the procedure is present (Brown/Gillick 1998: 130).

Furthermore, there is, as of yet, very little education and clarification about most equality provisions that are carried out. These factors, combined with the simplistic view of what "equality" means and entails, lead to a rejection of certain equality policies that work with so-called positive discrimination. Thus, it can be observed that, while female officers in both countries have to deal with the detrimental attitude some colleagues display towards issues of diversity and equality, UK interviewees predominantly distanced themselves from this criticism, while Austrian respondents often aligned their opinions with these critiques. It may be noted, however, that in both countries, although progressive views and opinions were voiced by some of the interviewees, "feminism is not an identity easily claimed" (Scharff 2011: 119), as these forms of collective thinking and organising contradict the individualised perspective most respondents

---

135 The findings report that women officers who experience harassment or discrimination are most likely to use self-help strategies, and least likely to make use of equal opportunities policies (Brown 1998: 237).

have on issues of gender within the police.[136] Furthermore, the inadequate nature of equality legislation as a feminist concept is pointed out by these discussions. As legal measures to promote gender equality have to live with the seeming paradox of treating unlikes alike or likes unlike (MacKinnon 1987: 37), their problematic or at the least ambiguous reception within both countries' police forces illustrates this dilemma further. When officers, regardless of gender, are still held to male standards and have to adhere to male norms in carrying out their profession, "sex equality is conceptually designed never to be achieved" (MacKinnon 1987: 44).

A further problem that can be observed in Austria is the general lack of information on gender equality issues. Sometimes, respondents only gave their opinion after specifically being prompted about a certain measure, as they could not come up with any themselves. But quite as many times, respondents instantly pointed to quota rules and their (often negative) perception of it. This perception, and the description they gave, however, does not correspond with the legal workings of the policy. There are a lot of misconceptions on how and when quota rules come into play, respondents often misconstruing the policy's effect as enabling any female applicant to get the job, regardless of their qualifications. These issues have also been discussed in courts, and the currently existing legal text is very restrictive in whom to grant preferential treatment to, in order not to put male applicants at a disadvantage (Holzleithner 2002). What these misconceptions show, however, is that gender as such is seen as the weighing quality rather than qualifications or expertise. Once again, the acknowledgment of structural inequalities, or even solidarity with their own gender, cannot be shown or performed by respondents who are trying to align themselves with the male peer pressure that encompasses police culture.

A line of argument that shines through in a handful of UK interviewee's accounts is that the underlying problem of an existing male-dominated workplace can only peripherally be touched by policies of equality and diversity. The traditional police culture is seen as standing in contrast to what can be described as modern approaches to policing, including the recruiting of (more) female (and/or other socially marginalised) officers. Consequently, there are limits to how much change equality policies can bring to police culture.

---

136 Illustrated best by a quote from Interview 9, England and Wales: "Now, I'm not feminist at all, by any means, so, I really respect men, and you know, so I'm not one of those".

While many note a change for the better in regard to the previously all-male police cultural environment in both countries, there is also a certain stagnation to be noted when it comes to further progress and what some participants regard as "true equality". The root of the problem, namely the inherently white and male culture of the police service in both countries, seemingly cannot be eradicated by a perfunctory modification such as the hiring and retention of e.g., female officers. While circumstances might have improved over time, and the social climate within the police service allows for a more welcoming atmosphere for people of differing backgrounds, this change cannot be seen as absolute and all-encompassing. It remains impossible to change personal attitudes and opinions simply via the introduction of legal measures or rules (Cf. Crank 1998). Male officers' rejection of gender equality measures almost seems self-evident in a highly masculinised environment – as outside threats to the masculine system increase, so does the inner solidarity of the group (Crank 1998). This leads to the fact that female police officers still have to position themselves in relation to this dominant group, especially in terms of the acceptance and reception of gender equality policies.

5.7 *Intersectional Aspects*

> "There was a hierarchy in the police. First came the white straight male, then the white straight female, then white (male) gay officers, then white lesbian officers, then straight officers of colour. Black gay officers didn't make the list. Disabled officers weren't even considered." (Maxwell 2020, theguardian.com)

The "analytical tool" (Carbado et al. 2013: 303) that intersectionality provides cannot be overlooked when considering and analysing the realities of female police officers within their workspace. Intersectionality is a term first coined by Crenshaw in 1991 (Crenshaw 1991: 1241) to describe and analyse the topic of male violence against women of colour. It is important to note that intersectionality refers to "particular forms of intersecting oppressions" (Collins 2000: 18) rather than the simple intersecting of social categories as such. Although this text does focus on the lived experiences and perceptions of female officers, the intersectionality of discriminatory experiences cannot be ignored. Furthermore, a broader discussion of all aspects of diversity is necessary to grasp the state of current gender debates in police culture. Gendered differences are often overlapped with other factors of inequality (Riegraf 2005). Therefore, this section explains and analyses issues of diversity and discrimination that do not limit themselves to the sphere of gendered experiences.

The aspects raised in the following subchapters do not exclusively refer to intersectional discrimination (e.g., race and gender), yet they have to be considered under the lens of the highly gendered surroundings the police service and its culture provide. The issues addressed in the following are those raised by the respondents themselves. These do not stem from an individual question on the interview guideline, but are rather informed by circumstance, such as interviewees being part of LGBTIQ-organisations within the police, or having experienced e.g., racism themselves. It is to be noted that not all interviewees discussed these issues, and that not all aspects of intersectional discriminatory practices can be treated in the same length or depth. The discussion is therefore limited to those issues that participants deem worth mentioning or discussing during the interview process. Within intersectional issues of discriminatory experiences, there are two dimensions that derive from participants' accounts: First, the seemingly key factor of diversity within the police organisation which go hand in hand with a sense of inclusivity. Second, a more personal approach and practices emanating from the persons involved.

5.7.1 Diversity and Inclusivity

What can be derived from the interviews is that UK female officers' views on and definitions of diversity are defined by their notions of perceived difference as a resource and tools to better experiences of policing. Difference can manifest in various ways, ranging from speaking a second or third language to displays of empathy – difference here clearly is the differing from masculine standards. Mostly, these perceived differences come to light and are spoken about when dealing with members of the public, rather than police internal. All participants view this notion of diversity as highly positive, especially in a police environment. This is due to the notion that police should represent the society they aim to serve and protect. This is an argument found not only among UK interviewees, but also Austrian female officers. In the UK, this is further embedded in a debate around police professionalisation – some see the representation of the policed demographic within the police organisation as further proof of a "good professional police service" (Interview 3, England and Wales). Similarly, although not many Austrian respondents spoke about the topic, diversity within the police service is seen as a challenge as well as a chance.

A challenge, because the inclusion of various groups into the institution brings up a lot of questions around ideals of policing as well as practical implementations of creating accessibility to the organisation. However, diversity is also perceived as a chance, namely to better relations with the public and create an environment of reciprocal trust. What goes along with the notion of representing society within the police organisation, is the consideration to accept people "as they are" (Interview 7, Austria). Not only is the goal to better relations with the public and seem more representable of society, but also to further organisational culture in practicing acceptance and creating a non-discriminatory environment. This leads to the concluding thought that "in the end, police officers are just people" (Interview 2, England and Wales). Following this line of argument, it is the police organisation's responsibility to reach people from all backgrounds and create a positive working environment for all.

What can be noted in arguments from UK respondents' accounts is that the organisation often falls short of providing adequate tools to ensure a positive handling of diversity. Rather than embracing the complexity of people's realities, the police seem to have adapted a "one-size-fits-all" (Interview 4, England and Wales) approach that transgresses the reality of many people. Conversely, Austrian police seem only to have started working on issues of diversity, and as of yet there is no organisational implementation plan on trying to recruit or retain people of different backgrounds, e.g., people with disabilities. It is noted that the desired acceptance within one's own ranks is often lacking, and people of a different religion or sexual orientation can therefore feel alienated. Similarly, some UK interviewees state that for anybody who is perceived as "different" in any way it is still hard to get accepted by peers. That the sensibilisation and adequate representation of all people in the police is an important issue can best be illustrated by a personal example a respondent gives. As previously mentioned (chapter 5.1.3), the interviewee struggled with experiences of racism as a member of the public from Austrian police, while she feels for the most part accepted within the police service in England and Wales. Although there are high reports of racism found within the police force in England and Wales (See e.g., Warren 2020, theguardian.com, Maxwell 2020, itv.com), the personal experience of said interviewee does not match these accounts.[137] However, it is possible that an acknowledge-

---

137 It has to be stated that this is potentially due to the fact that the interviewee, unlike the persons involved in the cases mentioned, has only spent a short time with the police and not gone/tried to go through the ranks.

ment and admission of an organisational culture's problem, in this case institutionalised racism, can lead to an overall more positive outlook of potentially affected people on the organisation. This example, albeit very specific and personal, exemplifies the need for Austrian police to develop a diversity strategy that goes beyond the already existing integration of women in the workplace. Although the implementation of such strategies can entail manifold problems and will of course not be able to eradicate any existing issues completely, as can be seen from the example in the UK, yet a simple acknowledgement of this issue from a managerial standpoint can lead to a more positive work environment for many (Cf. Van der Lippe et al. 2004).

This can further be illustrated by an issue brought up by participants from England and Wales: the inclusion of Muslim women into the police service. The Metropolitan Police has been offering its officers the possibility to wear a headscarf since 2001.[138] For female police officers in Austria, this option is currently not available. Arguably, this practice discriminates against women wearing headscarves on the basis of their gender and religion (as well as ethnicity) (Holzleithner 2017). Furthermore, as participants argue, this potentially deters Muslim women from applying to the police in the first place. Incidentally, this argument was the reasoning behind the changes in strategy of the Metropolitan Police, striving to create a more diverse workplace by eliminating restrictions put on particularly marginalised groups, such as Muslim women.

A further issue that is brought up is the difference in branding and reception of equal opportunities policies. Some respondents in the UK noted that programmes aimed at underrepresented groups within policing often focus on both women and people of BAME groups. This is criticised, as the specifics of each group's potential needs seem to be discarded in favour of "inclusivity". These managerial failings are argued to be stemming from a lack of sensibilisation of diversity issues as lived experiences.

"I have frequently been the only female officer [...] in the room [...] and therefore I'm supposed to talk on behalf of women which is worrying cause [sighs] I don't speak 'woman', you know, it's not a Mel Gibson film, it's very difficult, they have to have this understanding, and I don't think underrepresentation affects a lot of the people who

---

138 Hopkins 2001, theguardian.com. The article further mentions the possibility to wear turbans for Sikh officers as well as wearing dreadlocks (Rastafari).

are making these decisions, they do not understand what it feels like to be the minority." - Interview 1, England and Wales.

This perceived shortcoming is counterbalanced by an apparent feeling of tokenism in being expected to speak on behalf of the marginalised group one is associated with. The inability to provide adequate provisions to non-white, male, heterosexual and able-bodied officers is underpinned by a further lack of acceptance of these provisions by the majority of officers. Those affected often deem them lacking in suitability, while others critique the apparent unfairness of these policies (chapter 5.6.3.2). Yet even within these critical groups a certain hierarchy prevails: "I hear it [critique of support programme's unfairness, AN] most from white men. [...] and then from white women" (Interview 2, England and Wales). In the discussions, it seems that especially the support of people of BAME groups is received very badly among (white) officers. Taking a closer look at the reception of equality policies and diversity programmes while taking into account intersectional issues of discriminatory experiences is an important issue that cannot be discussed in full here, and therefore needs to be addressed by further research.

5.7.2 Networks and Visibility

In both countries, networks have been established to support different groups of officers. The following discussion focusses on LGBTIQ networks, as members and representants of these networks were interviewed in both countries. For Austria, there is a national LGBTIQ group called Gay Cops (Gay Cops Austria, gaycops-austria.at)[139], in England and Wales, there are some local groups[140] as well as a national organisation made up of existing local groups called National LGBT Police Network (The National LGBT+ Police Network, lgbt.police.uk). To the chairs and members of these groups, the networks are important not only in supporting their peers within the police, but also create a positive representation of the police as an organisation to the LGBTIQ community. Historically speaking, the LGBTIQ community and the police seem to rather be opposites – one might only think about the Stonewall Riots and the police raid

---

139 The organisation has recently (10/2021) been disbanded (Gay Cops Austria. Der*Die Letzte macht das Licht aus, gaycops-austria.at).

140 For example, the LGBT+ network for North Yorkshire Police (twitter.com/ NYP_LGBT).

that initiated them (Stonewall Riots, history.com). It is also suggested by research that, as a perceived social group, homosexuals are the most disliked group by police officers (Burke 1994). Respondents from both countries acknowledged these existing barriers between the police and the LGBTIQ community and strive to better these relations.

> "I think as the police we need to have a responsibility to go out there to the community and break down those barriers and show that, you know, you can be LGBT and police." - Interview 24, England and Wales.

For the English and Welsh police forces, these engagements include community events as well as taking hate crime seriously, providing a safe environment for people to report their experiences to the police. In Austria, participants also saw a need to establish better trust and relationships between members of the LGBTIQ community and the police. However, there is a disparity that some noted between being urged to create a positive connection towards the LGBTIQ community, while not providing adequate measures or instruments to do so. Even simple steps are sometimes seen as potentially aiding in the trust-building process yet are somehow not acknowledged by management.[141]

On a police-internal level, LGBTIQ networks are seen as a way to be yourself at work, as sexual orientation is understood as part of a person's personality. Being out[142] can remove some social heteronormative pressures from LGBTIQ officers (Miller et al. 2003). The psychological distress that not being "outed" at the workplace can create was experienced by a respondent themselves.

> "[W]hen I came out, my mother could still tell me I'm going to lose my job, and I'll end up under the bridge, right, and I believed that to

---

141 In a particular case, a respondent was not able to hoist the rainbow flag in front of a police station in celebration of Pride Month due to the bureaucratic process associated. As this involved an application form, which simply does not feature this "type" of flag, she was not able to complete the application process. A little while later, she was asked by her superior to propose actions to better relations between LGBTIQ communities and the police. To her, this exemplified the disconnect and lack of understanding from a managerial position on these issues.

142 The concept of "being out(ed)" refers to a person acknowledging their own sexual orientation as well as disclosing this information to others. Of course, this is a continuous process that can never be fully accomplished in a heteronormative society. In this context, reference is made to outing in one's workplace.

a certain extent. Because I just did not know how the police deals with gays and lesbians." - Interview 7, Austria.

In this way, visibility is seen as immensely important in so far as it simply shows officers and (potential) applicants that there are others like them. This lessens feelings of alienation and can lead to a more positive work environment for the people concerned. Especially in an organisation like the police, where officers spend long hours at their workplace, have to work together closely and a certain familiarity between colleagues is formed as well as expected[143], it can be very hard for people who feel like they cannot be themselves for whatever reason. Some respondents also mentioned incidents of discriminatory behaviour or comments regarding their or their colleagues' (perceived) sexual orientation.

> "[O]ne of the guys that I used to work with [...] he went 'hey J., I heard you moved up here so you could be nearer your boyfriend is that right?' and our sergeant was a lesbian, and she said 'D., my office' and she took him into the office, cause J. had moved to [area] to be near his boyfriend, but actually D. hadn't realised that that was the truth, he was just sort of mocking him, but it was, that would have been [19]98, 99. But it was nipped in the butt immediately, and I think possibly because our sergeant was a lesbian as well, she was very quick to deal with it." - Interview 14, England and Wales.

Here, the fact that the person responsible for ensuring a safe and welcoming work environment is a lesbian, and therefore presumably more aware and sensitised towards issues of homophobia, plays a large role in their dealing with inappropriate commentary. Likewise, the sensibilisation of all police employees towards diversity, be it via the work of networks, organisational guidelines (College of Policing [2], college.police.uk), or in personal settings is believed to bring about a positive change within police culture. Generally speaking, incidents of discrimination or difference in treatment due to (perceived) sexual orientation have lessened over the years, similar to issues around gender. It seems that, as stereotypes associated with the job as a police officer lessen and change, so do stereotypical views of different social and personal backgrounds. Issues around the acceptance and reception of LGBTIQ officers are strongly linked to displays of masculinity and gender stereotypes. An interviewee remembers the public discussion of the 1970s:

---

143 "[Y]ou become like a little family" - Interview 9, England and Wales.

"And at the time I firmly believed that all I was seeing was that if you were a police officer, a female police officer, you were probably a lesbian.[...] Whereas the other way, you know if you were a gay bloke nobody would [assume that] [...], most of my schoolmates if you were heading for 6 foot and very good at hockey [chuckles] or things like that, very rugged and outdoorsy, people would say, ah do you want to join the police, you know,[...] Mad, isn't it? It's mad. Yes." - Interview 4, England and Wales.

The fact that non-heterosexual women might experience less direct discrimination from their peers than their male counterparts is noted by most interviewees discussing LGBTIQ issues within the police service. As demonstrated above, displays of masculinity are still highly valued within police culture. This, in turn, creates a hostile environment for any possible deviations from this masculine norm. The hegemonic masculinity still prevalent in the police organisation is, amongst other things, reliant on distancing itself from the emasculation that is associated with being a homosexual man (Cf. Connell/Messerschmidt 2005). Conversely, the existence of lesbian and bisexual women apparently is not perceived as that much of a threat to the current balance of power within police culture – indeed, historically, "[b]utch women have been accused of being complicit in maintaining the oppression of women through their masculine-like behavior" (Nguyen 2008: 667). Although this simplistic position is to be disputed (Nguyen 2008), the acceptance into male dominated spaces, at least as demonstrated by the police, theoretically appears to come more easily for non-heterosexual women than for men. What has to be kept in mind, though, is the fact that these women still face the discriminatory experiences female officers live through due to their perceived gender, on top of their possible rejection because of their sexual orientation.

That the police as an organisation is only beginning to grasp LGBTIQ matters in Austria is exemplified by one respondent by the failing to provide adequate guidelines for both trans officers as well as members of the public who identify as transgender.

"[W]e are at the very beginning of this process with trans police officers, right, we haven't thought about how we are going to do it if we search a trans person. Like, searching a person. [...] Or with admissions. Now if someone comes along, he began [his career] as a woman, and now he's a man [...] that has consequences, of course." - Interview 7, Austria.

The various difficulties that arise from these debates are not yet adequately covered by policies or internal regulations. This is also noted by a trans officer, who states that he simply stopped carrying out searches for a while, due to the "ambiguity" of his gender presentation (Meyer/Mestrović 2017, dasbiber.at). Evidently, the inclusion of LGBTIQ people has not come as far as that of women into policing in both countries. Especially the insufficiently researched area of trans officers within police culture (Cf. Panter 2018) seems to have been somewhat of a no-go area for those involved in creating and furthering diversity policies in both countries.

5.7.3 Interim Findings

Diversity, as understood by interviewees from both countries, is first and foremost a tool to enhance the police as a professional body and its practices in engaging with members of the public. Respondents describe this in a very positive way, in that the more diverse the police become, the more it represents the people it is supposed to serve – after all, "police officers are just people" (Interview 2, England and Wales). In England and Wales, it was noted that the organisation often does not follow the best way to ensure that people of all backgrounds are welcome within the service. The "unisex" approach that is sometimes noted in relation to gender issues within the police can be found in regard to other diversity measures as well, leaving many individuals feeling left out. Indeed, in the implementation of equality policies and regulations, gender issues have a tendency to get lost in general ideas of diversity (Ben-Galim et al. 2007). In Austria, discussions around diversity – other than gender equality policies – have not yet reached an organisational level or are reflected in any policies.[144] For both countries, it is noted that being (perceived as) "different" is still proving difficult. Although the integration of people of diverse backgrounds into the police along with organisational provisions supporting these changes cannot eradicate persisting issues within police culture (completely), it provides a starting point for a potential bettering of the work environment provided for future officers. Alongside this, the current state of equal opportunities policies and/or related schemes within UK police has been criticised as not providing sufficient support for vari-

---

144 Similarly, Behr notes that German police have no real notion of diversity apart from gender and ethnicity, as they are seemingly not of relevance to them (Behr 2016).

ous individual groups and rather addressing diverse issues as one big issue. This is attributed to a lack of understanding of issues that marginalised groups face, an understanding that can only be gained by lived experience. In short, inadequate schemes designed by non-marginalised groups may lead to a slight bettering of numbers of officers of all backgrounds or a marginal shift of police cultural practices, yet in the overall context they reproduce the same inequalities they profess to eradicate. The data support Angela Davis' statement she gave at a speech in 2015: "Diversity is a corporate strategy. It's a strategy designed to ensure that the institution functions in the same way that it functioned before, except now that you now have some black faces and brown faces. It's a difference that doesn't make a difference" (Eckert 2015, dailytrojan.com). This can also be seen by the continuous critique and negative reception of said schemes by police officers.

To further support and also provide representation for marginalised groups, police officer networks have been established in both countries. Focussing on local and national LGBTIQ-networks, the bettering of relations between the police as an organisation and members of the LGBTIQ community seems to be an important issue for those involved. Again, at least for Austria, it is noted that the support and framework provided from an organisational standpoint is lacking in adequacy. As LGBTIQ officers view themselves as particularly qualified to deal and connect with marginalised communities (Miller et al. 2003), their input regarding a bettering of relations with the LGBTIQ public should be given a higher value than it currently receives, at least as told by respondents in Austria. A service that networks can provide nonetheless is an advanced feeling of inclusivity for officers in the LGBTIQ community. In a close-knitted social group such as the police, being able to "be yourself" at work is of immense importance to the psychological well-being of officers – by lessening feelings of alienation and normalising difference, LGBTIQ networks seemingly provide a valuable contribution to ensuring a positive work environment. Discriminatory incidents relating to (perceived) sexual orientation of officers have lessened over the years and decades, much like discrimination associated with gender. Much as the inclusion of women in the police service, LGBTIQ issues are strongly linked to displays of hegemonic masculinity and gender stereotypes. In a highly masculinised surrounding such as the police, potential threats to male heterosexuality are quite naturally rejected. However, it seems that male homosexuality is perceived as a higher threat – more prone to a need to distancing oneself – than female homosexuality. Furthermore, displays of masculinity by non-heterosexual women can be perceived as a lesser threat to heterosexual male officers than that of heterosexual women (Miller et al. 2003). If this is due to the fact that female homosexuality is more closely associated with masculinity, or female officers as such are denied participation in the hegemonic discourse cannot be said definitively. However, research has confirmed that male homosexuality is generally perceived to be more of a threat to the hegemonic masculinity culture of policing than female homosexuality, paradoxically leading to a better integration of (white) lesbians than gay men (Miller et al. 2003).

Not unlike debates around BAME groups or diversity as such, LGBTIQ issues seem to only have started getting a foothold in Austria. This can be seen most prominently by the failed integration of trans officers as exemplified by the issue surrounding the occupational fitness test – as of yet, no official guidelines have been developed to handle the dealing with trans officers as well as trans members of the public. According to Holzleithner (2017), one could further argue that trans- and intergender people are discriminated against per se by the binary provided by such tests. Indeed, both countries' police forces do currently not have provisions and regulations for the hiring and retaining of nonbinary or intersex people.[145] This specific issue seems to be another area where further research will be necessary if the police are to provide adequate support for trans people.

---

145 Although police in England and Wales currently employ (at least) one nonbinary person (See: LGBT Police Network UK. "As it's International Non binary People's Day" Facebook. facebook.com).

6. Conclusion

While earlier studies focus on quantitative assessment (Kofler 2011) or male experiences within a male-dominated culture (Behr 2008), this research contributes to police studies in adding female experiences and their subjective viewpoints of gender-relations in the police service. In adding a transnational comparative perspective, issues that otherwise may have been missed or interpreted differently were able to be regarded in a different light.[146] Legal provisions, such as the countries' respective equality legislation as well as equal opportunities policies within the police can also be adequately assessed through the qualitative approach this research has taken. The police are an organisation in which differentiated organisational cultures emerge through which the guidelines coming from "the top", such as equal opportunities policies, are not only applied but also interpreted (Stölting 2009). The current state of the discussion around gender, equality, and diversity within the police can therefore best be grasped by the study's approach, generating results through analysing current debates and reported everyday work life of female police officers. Through this, police sociological research can be enriched in the field of comparative police cultural analysis.

On the basis of the exploratory study presented here, I have endeavoured to gain empirical insights into the extent to which the constitutional and legal claim to equality between men and women has already led to lived equality. However, the gender-specific problems that become apparent in this study on the implementation of e.g., gender mainstreaming are not only to be seen within the police force, but also in society as a whole, and the wider discussion and debates around equality, diversity, and inclusivity. Yet the specific nature of police culture cannot and should not be overlooked when discussing matters of gender within policing.

In answer to the research question, it has to be stated that the similarities between female police officers' lived experiences and attitudes between the two countries in general do outweigh the differences. This can be seen in the analysis of the themes that arose from the interview data. The limitations of the study are, of course, its lack of generalisability due to the

---

146 For instance, the issue of firearms and its link to hegemonic masculinity, which presents differently in the two countries.

qualitative methodology used – nevertheless, the study makes a valuable contribution to a better understanding of the working environments of female police officers, and deepens the knowledge on gender and policing.

The desire to enter the profession is based on similar motives in both countries, first and foremost the wish to help people and contribute to the community, as well as the variety within the job as a police officer. In attracting interviewees to join the police, personal experiences with the police played a role in the accounts of interviewees from both countries more often than not. A difference can be found in the formal qualifications received by interviewees before joining the police – respondents from England and Wales reported attaining higher levels of formal education than their Austrian counterparts. Regardless of this, the police service in both countries was constructed as a promising career path in the accounts of the interviewees, often not despite but because of its connotation of cultural masculinity while at the same time offering (formal) equal treatment and fair working conditions.

A topic that generated much interest and debate in the two countries can be found within the issue of recruitment and training processes: Both gendered and "gender-blind" sports and fitness tests received criticism – finding an option that would suit all police officers is constructed as an almost unachievable task. The applicability of police training to every-day experiences in the profession was, of course, priced highly among officers from both countries, while they also mentioned experiencing their day-to-day work as continuous training, and spoke of a steep learning curve – a possible indication of the masculine nature of police work – especially in the first months on the job. A major distinction between the two countries arises when focusing on special recruitment issues, as the sample drawn made it possible to compare two very dissimilar processes: on the one hand, the Police Now programme in England and Wales – a community-driven programme that draws their recruits from university graduates –, on the other hand, the Austrian special force Cobra – a high-ly masculinised occupational field within the police service, focusing on corporality. While recruitment processes for the Police Now programme were experienced as highly positive by the interviewees, the recruitment and training for Cobra can be described as a rather alienating experience – this highlights the difference these processes can make in attracting and retaining female police officers.

What can be derived from respondents' accounts of their day-to-day work experiences is the notion that what constitutes "real" police work has seen a slight shift towards a more eye-level approach to policing in both countries. With the aid of the concept of community policing, the more "ground level", everyday police work gains importance over a tough, masculine policing stereotype – these implications, however, are very faint. A disparity between the countries can be seen in the way that interviewees from England and Wales hold police accountability to the public in high regards, and the Peelian Principle of "policing by consent" remains a steadfast mantra in respondents' accounts. This is counterposed by a more neutral approach to policing ideals in Austria, where e.g., the carrying of firearms is constructed as self-evident in its necessity. In both countries' police services, mental health issues remain a taboo topic, yet England and Wales' officers see small steps taken towards a better approach to dealing with (potentially) threatening or unsettling events. Structural differences within the police services are discussed by respondents in the two countries: In England and Wales, this is exemplified by the differing effect budget cuts have had on the various individual forces, while Austrian respondents take issue with the contrasts between rural and urban policing, especially with regards to staffing issues.

On a structural level, there is a positive change to be seen in both countries regarding the better integration of women into the police service. The numbers of female officers have increased over the years, and although vertical segregation by gender is still prevalent in both countries' police forces, there has been some modest progress in the promotion of female officers. In terms of horizontal segregation, in both countries there are still pockets of policing that are very much male-dominated (almost male-exclusive) – these are inherently linked to displays of hegemonic masculinity such as the Cobra (Austria) or authorised firearms officers (England and Wales).

The acceptance of female police officers within the police service is still not a given, as respondents in both countries recount the struggles they faced in their strife for (equal) acceptance into their workplace. At the same time, their gender performance is placed under scrutiny – appearing too feminine (or too masculine) can have an adverse effect on their social standing within the police service. The difference between the countries can be found in the fact that female officers react differently to these challenges: While many Austrian respondents try to cope with this "othering" by adhering to male standards and trying to take up the viewpoint of their male colleagues, UK respondents view a detrimental work environment more as a structural issue that the police service as an organisation has to remedy.

In terms of ideas around (ideal) policing, it is to be noted that in both countries' respondents' narratives, "softer" forms of policing (de-escalation, rhetoric, empathy) are associated with femininity – and therefore female officers – while tougher, more aggressive approaches are linked to displays of masculinity. Again, a subtle difference between the countries can be noted in their approach to this discursive link: While most UK respondents assert that sensitivity and empathic approach to policing should not be gendered, and therefore do not believe that it should be reserved solely for female officers, most Austrian respondents seem more resigned to the fact of these supposedly gendered differences (with a few exceptions) and view them positively. This can also be observed in the debate around corporality, and the alleged gendered differences between bodily strength – respondents from both countries view these differences as a given, yet UK officers are more prone to mentioning the fact that actual police work overwhelmingly does not rely on bodily strength (alone).

Another slight difference can be perceived when looking at the issue of the reported cooperation between colleagues. Although all interviewees (across the two countries) spoke highly of their colleagues, UK respondents sometimes remarked a difference in working with either an all-male or an all-female team – the all-female team being perceived as highly positive, while male-dominated work groups can create an alienating experience for the female officer. Conversely, Austrian interviewees focused their narratives on potentially problematic (in the sense of "suitable for police work") individuals. Interestingly, they hold their female colleagues to the same standards they had to meet (namely a higher standard than their male colleagues), creating a sort of anti-type of police officer – one that is strongly linked to images of femininity. This typification occurs exclusively in Austria and hinders an emergence of a possible ideal type of a female police officer.

In terms of career progression, three issues emerged from the accounts of the respondents: First, the fact that a (police) career and family life seem hard to balance – in both countries, women are still held responsible for the majority of the housework and care work, making police-specific stressors such as overtime, and shift and night work difficult to comply with. Secondly, respondents (mostly from the UK) note a certain bias in the promotion processes, with (white) male officers often seeking their likeness in potential candidates. Lastly, respondents report that masculine behaviour, such as assertiveness and rigour, is often framed as negative for women (as opposed to men) in leadership positions.

Outright sexist behaviour and practices are understood to be in decline in both countries, while respondents note varying degrees of personal experiences with such incidents. Sexist behaviour, broadly speaking, is mostly not framed as a structural issue in both countries, yet more as an individual issue that some officers have to deal with. This can be seen in the fact that only specific male colleagues are often portrayed as being problematic, which shifts the problem to the individual level. What are described as subtler forms of sexism seem more prevalent in the accounts of female officers in both countries. This is often demonstrated through othering or objectifying practices, such as chauvinism, "positive" sexism, or banter. Female officers in both countries struggle to navigate these forms of sexism, sometimes because of their double-edged nature (seemingly preferential treatment) or because of their ubiquity. Sexual harassment is seldom, or only very carefully, mentioned in accounts of respondents, with some observing positive changes (e.g., follow-up support) while others feel more resigned and allude to a potential high number of unrecorded cases and the struggles female officers face in bringing these issues to light.

In dealing with issues and incidents of sexism, respondents from both countries note that one has to decide on a case-by-case basis on one's reaction. The options respondents report to draw from are the possibilities of interrupting and rebuking comments, deliberately disregarding them, or a later discussion of the incident. Austrian respondents tended to favour the first option, often addressing the apparent need to respond in kind in order to prohibit future digressions. UK respondents reported trying to address any issues in a later setting, mostly with incidents that they perceive to be serious in nature. In this regard, some respondents also brought up the perceived unjust treatment many female officers who come forward about experiencing sexual harassment or abuse face. This can be seen in accounts in both countries, in which the female officer often faces harsher consequences than the male perpetrator (e.g., being transferred) – a fact that is supported and reinforced by a police culture that is strongly based on solidarity and rejects whistle blowers.

In interactions with the public, a commonality between respondents from both countries is the fact they reported that the effect that their gender has on relations with members of the public is highly ambiguous. Degrading or discrediting comments from (predominantly) male members of the public serve to de-professionalise female officers, either by objectifying them or by putting their professional abilities as such at question. Apart from these rather confrontational reactions, female officers in both countries reported a general stereotypical attitude displayed by many members of the public when dealing with female officers.[147] In respondents accounts, these attitudes are inherently linked to the fictitious ideal type of a police officer (big, tough, manly) that many members of the public seemingly retain – a culturally hegemonic masculinity that is not different from the one prevailing police-internally. As with police-internal issues of gendered differential treatment, respondents note that there is no universally applicable reaction to such incidents or displayed attitudes. Here, female officers report having to decide between asserting their authority (especially in cases they deem important) or otherwise withdrawing from a situation and/or letting a male colleague handle the respective person(s).

Next to these rather negative implications, officers from both countries further observed that their presence can have a positive effect on people's behaviour, or even shift the quality of certain interactions. This seems true for (predominantly) male members of public in tense or aggressively charged situations: They, generally speaking, seem to react more positive to female than male officers, which can help diffuse potentially threatening situations. This is partly due to the (perceived) better, namely de-escalative, conversation skills of female as opposed to male officers, and partly due to them not perceiving female officers as being their equal – and therefore non-threatening. Likewise, participants report sometimes noticing gendered differences in interactions with victims, especially survivors of sexual abuse or domestic violence. Here, again, the presence (and existence) of female officers is constructed as highly positive, which confirms many in their right to carry out their profession. However, a critique that comes from UK respondents is the fact that, through their assignment and handling of certain cases (e.g., vulnerable survivors) some supervisors automatically typecast female officers as the assigned officers to these cases – an additional strain that is put on female officers, which furthermore takes their male colleagues out of the obligation to contribute or educate themselves in this regard. Along with conclusions drawn by previous studies (Brown/King 1998, Jordan 2002), these findings speak for a bettering of training options with regards to vulnerable survivors for officers regardless of gender.

When looking at the issue of gender not only from a structural, but from a discursive perspective (Müller 2007), it seems that the conversation

---

147 Examples of this include addressing male officers with more senior titles, more subtly questioning their competence, or even simply framing the existence of female officers as something unusual and alien.

around gender within policing has not really progressed much over the last years. The police remain an inherently masculine institution, and the prevalent culture can be argued as "predicated on the oppression of women entering the police force" (Franklin 2007: 5). Although one could argue that in the case of the UK, the shift in policing styles (i.e., towards community policing, evidence-based policing) might promote more "feminine values" (Brown/Silvestri 2020: 471), these indications are, as Brown and Silvestri have found, fragile (Brown/Silvestri 2020). Internal and external pressures are likely to put a stop to any progress made in terms of a "feminisation" of policing, and rather revert these changes. In Austria, it seems, these different approaches similarly work in opposition to each other – any attempt at a feminisation (as exemplified by community policing) is countered by opposing procedures such as budget cuts. These processes seem similar, but it should be noted that any cultural change of the police in the England and Wales towards an integration of "feminine" standards is more long-standing and deep-rooted than in Austria, where the processes are more recent and not as thorough, and the structures of hegemonic masculinity in the police remain ingrained in the culture.

Kofler's (2011) report on the situation of women in policing in Austria finds that there are a lot of knowledge gaps, but also a fairly negative reception of gender equality policies among male as well as female police officers. This research, among other things, focuses on the reasons behind officers' apparent disapproval of gender equality policies and found what can be seen as two main factors: female police officers' perception of "equality" and a lack of information and education about the issue of gender equality, resulting in highly negative responses from colleagues and consequences for female officers themselves. Similar to the situation of women in policing in the UK in the late 1990s (Brown 1998: 238), equality policies remain the least likely source of support for female officers in Austria; they are still heavily self-reliant.

However, some female police officers also lament the fact that some policies, in particular Austrian quota rules, are received badly by (male) police officers, creating a hostile space for female officers getting a new job or being promoted. Dworkin (1977) also mentions this problem of equality policies: By (re-)producing categories, resentment against certain groups is made possible and even partly encouraged. What is to be noted is that, in Austria, any criticism directed towards female officers reacting in the same way as their male colleagues comes from female officers either carrying out the role of equality commissioner, or those in senior ranks. This is not surprising, as female officers of rank do have a different position in the hierarchy structure of the police service as their lower-rank peers. Using what O'Connor Shelley et al. (2011) found about Acker's four processes of gendered institutions, one could argue that female officers of rank had to overcome more hurdles than their male peers of rank, but also than their female peers working in lower ranks. Due to this, they might have a different point of view and perception of policies that positively influence female officers' chances of promotion and recruitment. Another possibility is that these respondents simply had more time and information available to them to get acquainted with gender equality policies. Some respondents even predicted that education about gender equality policies would render the negative comments they receive now void. Of course, such a linear impact on personal perceptions can be ruled out due to the complexity of the issue at hand, nevertheless do these findings strengthen the possibility that the more officers are being educated about these issues, the less they reject or denounce them. In light of this, the recent attempt of responsible authorities to further and broaden the education on the subject of gender and equality issues in the police service is to be welcomed.

A possible strategy to better the situation by providing education and information on the subject of gender equality policies and gendered in-equalities in general, is trying to change the viewpoint of the affected parties. In understanding that "[t]he flipside of gender discrimination [...] is the privileging of men" (Flood/Pease 2006: 119), male officers can be held accountable to do their part for a better integration of women into the police service. This would offer a shift in the strains connected to gender equality issues, taking some of the burden from female officers on to their male peers who would then (possibly) be better suited to deal with and process structural inequalities and their role in it.

With regards to intersectional issues, the aspects most talked about were that of people of BAME ethnic groups and LGBTIQ issues. Respondents understand diversity in this regard first and foremost as a tool to be used to further a bettering of the police service. However, the perceived "unisex" approach UK police services adapt with regards to these issues was often a point of critique by respondents: They felt that the support for specific individual groups was lacking, addressing diverse issues as one common topic. A lack of understanding for certain issues was professed by respondents from both countries, and a real influence on or change of police culture described as very rare or even impossible. In dealing with these issues themselves, female officers report being members or even leaders of various police networks, be they focussed on gender or the LGBTIQ community. Discussions on LGBTIQ issues are strongly linked to displays of hegemonic masculinity and perceived as threats to the male heterosexual norm. Paradoxically, however, female homosexuality seems to be perceived as a lesser threat to this male heteronormative system than male homosexuality – the reasons for this may include the notion that female homosexuality is more closely associated with displays of masculinity, or the fact that female officers as such are denied participation in the hegemonic discourse – a definitive conclusion, however, cannot be drawn. Issues of diversity, especially with regards to people of BAME groups or trans- and intergender people, are only slowly becoming relevant in policing discourse in Austria, and have not yet been addressed by legal measures, among other things.

All these issues suggest that the culture of the police service in both countries is still dominated by masculine themes and it is hard for women to enter or succeed in this domain. This research cannot give an answer to the question of the feasibility of quota rules and other equality policies in aiding the path to a more equal workspace for female officers – their potential is often diminished by their poor execution and failed integration into the field. Nevertheless, the law can make an important contribution to gender equality – but it cannot and should not be the only contribution. Rather, the interplay of legal empowering mechanisms and the reshaping of the police service is necessary to bring about fundamental change in the organisation. However, the study once more highlights the fact that the field of policing remains one of male dominance and masculinity, that restricts the complete integration of women.

The manifold issues arising when dealing with the situation of women in the police necessitate further in-depth research. The data and information gathered in the present research can be used to develop a questionnaire aimed at (female) police officers in the respective countries, focusing on issues of gender within the police. In generating subjective responses and opinions towards the police service and its culture, I was able to gain a unique access to issues that influence female police officers and their work environment. The singling out of issues that affect female police officers provides an adequate guideline for developing a tool to assess the wider situation of female police officers in the UK and Austria respectively.

Figuratively speaking, Austrian police are lagging behind England and Wales in the pursuit for gender equality, but the one hurdle that both seem unable to overcome is that of police culture. As Behr notes, both police and cop culture and heavily reliant on homogeneity – they explicitly are not cultures of diversity (Behr 2016). This is also reflected in the data collected for this research project. Despite slight changes and shifts towards a more open police culture, there seem to be certain intrinsic barriers within the organisational culture that work against the full integration of female (as well as non-white, non-heterosexual) police officers. Equality is often synonymous with conformity to the given masculine ideal. This further reflects negatively on police legitimacy (Silvestri et al. 2013: 70) – the absence of certain groups (non-white, non-male, etc.) from policing raises the question of the extent to which the organisation may claim social legitimacy.

References

Online Sources

70% of BAME police staff say they have been racially abused on job, exclusive ITV News survey finds. Available at: https://www.itv.com/news/2020-06-23/70-of-bame-police-staff-say-they-have-been-racially-abused-on-job-exclusive-itv-news-survey-finds/, Accessed on 24.06.2020.

Austrian Center for Law Enforcement Sciences (Hrsg, 2018): *ALES-Studie über den Umgang mit Misshandlungsvorwürfen gegen Exekutivbeamte.* Available at: https://www.justiz.gv.at/file/2c94848a66ede49101671cc760ff1142.de.0/ales%20studie%20endfassung%20nov18.pdf, Accessed on 06.05.2020

British Association for Women in Policing, Available at: www.bawp.org, Accessed on 10.06.2020.

BSC Code of Ethics, (2006) Available at: http://www.britsoccrim.org/docs/CodeofEthics.pdf, Accessed on 28.01.2016.

Bundes-Gleichbehandlungskommission, Available at: https://www.bundeskanzleramt.gv.at/agenda/frauen-und-gleichstellung/gleichbehandlungskommissionen/bundes-gleichbehandlungskommission.html, Accessed on 07.01.2021.

Bundesministerium für Kunst, Kultur, öffentlichen Dienst und Sport, Rechtliches. Available at: https://www.oeffentlicherdienst.gv.at/moderner_arbeitgeber/elternkarenz_wiedereinstieg/rechtliches/rechtliches.html, Accessed on 19.05.2020.

Bundeministerium für Inneres, INNEN.SICHER. FÜR SICHERHEIT.FÜR ÖSTERREICH. GEMEINSAM.SICHER in Österreich, available at: https://docplayer.org/74054391-Innen-sicher-fuer-sicherheit-fuer-oesterreich-gemeinsam-sicher-in-oesterreich.html, accessed on 15.04.2021.

Büchner, B. (2019) Vom "Fräulein Polizeiassistentin" zur Kriminalbeamtin https://bm15blog.wordpress.com/2019/10/21/vom-fraeulein-polizeiassistentin-zur-kriminalbeamtin/, Accessed on 04.01.2021.

College of Policing *(1) – Am I eligible?, Available at: https://recruit.college.police.uk/Officer/Pages/eligibility.aspx, Accessed on 05.01.2021.*

College of Policing (2) - *Code of Ethics (2014)* Available at: https://www.college.police.uk/What-we-do/Ethics/Documents/Code_of_Ethics.pdf, Accessed on 29.06.2020.

College of Policing (3) – *Entry routes for police constables.* Available at: https://www.college.police.uk/What-we-do/Learning/Policing-Education-Qualifications-Framework/Entry-routes-for-police-constables/Pages/Entry-routes-for-police-constables.aspx, Accessed on 05.01.2021.

College of Policing (4) – *Information for students for the CKP.* Available at: http://www.college.police.uk/What-we-do/Learning/Certificate/Pages/Information-for-Students.aspx, Accessed on 29.06.2016.

College of Policing (5) - *Policing education qualifications framework (PEQF)* Available at: https://beta.college.police.uk/career-learning/learning/PEQF, Accessed on 05.01.2021.

College of Policing (6) *Positive Action. A guide for police recruitment,* Available at: https://www.college.police.uk/What-we-do/Development/Promotion/Document s/College_of_Policing_Positive_Action_Guidance.pdf, Accessed on 20.05.2020.

Die Ausbildung zum Polizisten bzw. Polizistin. Available at: http://www.polizei.gv.at/ wien/beruf/berufsinformation/4/ausbildung.aspx, Accessed on 13.04.2017.

Definitions, Institute of Race Relations, Available at: http://www.irr.org.uk/research/ statistics/definitions/, Accessed on 27.05.2020.

Dodd, V., *Labour backs positive discrimination to close racial gap in policing,* Available at: https://www.theguardian.com/uk-news/2020/feb/24/labour-backs-positive-dis crimination-to-close-racial-gap-in-policing, Accessed on 20.05.2020.

Durham Constabulary – Who are we? Available at: https://www.durham.police.uk/A bout-Us/Documents/PUBLIC%20INFORMATION%20AS%20AT%2001%2001 %202016%20To%20circulate.pdf, Accessed on 14.11.2019.

Duties and Leave for Police Officers, Available at: https://www.north-wales.police.uk/ media/344639/duties-and-leave-policy.pdf, Accessed on 14.05.2020.

Einstellungsvoraussetzungen prüfen, Available at: http://www.polizeikarriere.gv.at/ein stellungsvoraussetzung_pruefen.html, Accessed on 07.07.2020

Executive Summary, European Committee for the Prevention of Torture and Inhu-man or Degrading Treatment or Punishment (CPT) Available at: https://rm.coe. int/CoERMPublicCommonSearchServices/DisplayDCTMContent?documentId =090000168069d4f5, Acccessed on 11.05.2020.

Eckert, M. (2015) *Civil rights leader Angela Davis speaks at Bovard.* Available at: https://dailytrojan.com/2015/02/23/civil-rights-leader-angela-davis-speaks-at-bova rd/#:~:text=Diversity%20is%20a%20corporate%20strategy,a%20difference%2C% E2%80%9D%20Davis%20said., Accessed on 30.06.2020.

Employer Comparison, Gender Pay Gap Service. Available at: https://gender-pay-gap.se rvice.gov.uk/compare-employers/2018, Accessed on 04.05.2020.

Equality and Human Rights Commission [1], Available at: www.equalityhumanrights .com, Accessed on 22.09.2017.

Equality and Human Rights Commission [2] - Inquiries, investigations and wider powers, Available at: www.equalityhumanrights.com/en/our-powers/inquiries-in vestigations-and-wider-powers, Accessed on 07.01.2021.

Fitness Standards, College of Policing. Available at: https://www.college.police.uk/ What-we-do/Standards/Fitness/Pages/default.aspx, Accessed on: 20.01.2020.

FOI release. *Definition of policing by consent.* (2012) Available at: https://www.gov.uk /government/publications/policing-by-consent/definition-of-policing-by-consent , Accessed on 07.02.2020.

Garavelli, D. (2017) Ex-policewoman: 'They would lift up your skirt and use the office stamp on your buttocks'. Available at: https://www.heraldscotland.com/news/1568 3849.ex-policewoman-they-would-lift-up-your-skirt-and-use-the-office-stamp-on-y our-buttocks/, Accessed on: 16.06.2020.

Gay Cops Austria, Available at: https://www.gaycops-austria.at/, Accessed on 24.04.2020.

Gay Cops Austria, Der*Die Letzte macht das Licht aus, Available at: https://www.g aycops-austria.at/newsroom/vereinsarbeit/der-die-letzte-macht-das-licht-aus, Accessed on 09.11.2021.

Gemeinsam Sicher homepage, Available at: https://www.gemeinsamsicher.at/index.h tml, Accessed on 06.02.2020.

Hopkins, N. (2001) *Met lets Muslim policewomen don headscarves.* Available at: https://www.theguardian.com/uk/2001/apr/25/ukcrime.religion, Accessed on 08.07.2020.

Firearms. Police Federation homepage. Available at: https://www.polfed.org/our-wo rk/firearms/, Accessed on 07.09.2020.

Frauen im Polizeidienst (1) (2011) Available at: http://www.bmi.gv.at/cms/BMI_Oeff entlicheSicherheit/2011/11_12/files/Polizistinnen.pdf, Accessed on 10.12.2015.

Frauen im Polizeidienst (2) (2011) Available At: https://www.bmi.gv.at/magazinfiles/ 2011/11_12/files/polizistinnen.pdf, Accessed on 11.09.2019.

Gleichbehandlungsanwaltschaft – Unsere Aufgaben. Available at: https://www.gleich behandlungsanwaltschaft.gv.at/wir-ueber-uns/aufgaben.html, Accessed on 07.01.2021.

Gleichbehandlungsbericht des Bundes 2018, Available at: https://www.bundeskan zleramt.gv.at/agenda/frauen-und-gleichstellung/gleichbehandlung/gleichbeh andlungsberichte/gleichbehandlungsberichte-des-bundes.html, Accessed on 09.09.2019

Gleichbehandlungsbericht des Bundes 2020, Available at: https://www.bundeskan zleramt.gv.at/agenda/frauen-und-gleichstellung/gleichbehandlung/gleichbeh andlungsberichte/gleichbehandlungsberichte-des-bundes.html, Accessed on 04.01.2020.

Gleichbehandlungskommission, Available at: https://www.bundeskanzleramt.gv.at/ag enda/frauen-und-gleichstellung/gleichbehandlungskommissionen/gleichbehand lungskommission.html, Accessed on 07.01.2021

Higgins, A. (2018) *The Future of Neighbourhood Policing.* The Police Foundation. Available at: http://www.police-foundation.org.uk/2017/wp-content/uploads/ 2010/10/TPFJ6112-Neighbourhood-Policing-Report-WEB_2.pdf, Accessed on 12.02.2020.

HISTORY OF MET WOMEN POLICE OFFICERS. Available at: https://www.oldpoli cecellsmuseum.org.uk/content/history/women_police_officers/history_of_met_ women_police_officers, Accessed on 06.02.2020.

Initial Police Learning. Available at: https://www.college.police.uk/What-we-do/L earning/Curriculum/Initial-learning/Pages/Initial-learning.aspx, Accessed on 09.06.2020.

Kofler, A. (2011) Frauen und Männer in der Polizei 2011. Es gibt noch viel zu tun... *SIAK-Journal – Zeitschrift für Polizeiwissenschaft und polizeiliche Praxis* (4), 51-59, Available at: http://www.bmi.gv.at/cms/BMI_SIAK/4/2/1/2011/ausgabe_4/ files/Kofler_4_2011.pdf, Accessed on 10.12.2015.

Lercher, C. (2019) *Einkommensbericht 2019 gemäß § 6a Bundes-Gleichbehandlungsgesetz*, Available at: https://www.oeffentlicherdienst.gv.at/Einkommensbericht_20 19.pdf?76a4tp, Accessed on 02.06.2020.

LGBT Police Network UK. "As it's International Non binary People's Day" *Facebook*. Available at: https://www.facebook.com/lgbtpoliceuk/posts/339098332424 7904, Accessed on 15.07.2020.

LGBT+ network for North Yorkshire Police, Available at: https://twitter.com/NYP_LG BT, Accessed on 24.06.2020.

Loick, D. *"But who protects us from you? Zur kritischen Theorie der Polizei"* (Near final draft, erschienen in jour-fixe-initiative Berlin (Hg.): Souveränitäten. Von Staatsmenschen und Staatsmaschinen, Münster 2010: Unrast) Available at: https://ww w.academia.edu/11408377/But_who_protects_us_from_you_Zur_kritischen_Th eorie_der_Polizei, Accessed on 06.05.2020.

MacPherson, William (1999) *The Stephen Lawrence Inquiry*. Report of an Inquiry., Available at: https://assets.publishing.service.gov.uk/government/uploads/system /uploads/attachment_data/file/277111/4262.pdf, Accessed on: 27.01.2020.

Maxwell, K. (2020) 'I was a boy who wanted nothing so much as to join the police' https://www.theguardian.com/books/2020/may/03/i-was-a-boy-who-wanted-noth ing-so-much-as-to-join-the-police, Accessed on 04.05.2020

Meyer, S. and Mestrović, M. (2017) *Herr Inspektor, bitte!*, Available at: https://www. dasbiber.at/content/herr-inspektor-bitte, Accessed on 29.06.2020.

"Neue Polizisten: Das Niveau sinkt ab". https://kurier.at/chronik/oesterreich/neue -polizisten-das-niveau-sinkt-ab/400113092, Accessed on 03.02.2020.

Neyroud, P. (2013) *Review of Police Leadership and Training*, available at: https://ww w.gov.uk/government/uploads/system/uploads/attachment_data/file/118227/rep ort.pdf, Accessed on 09.06.2016.

North Wales Police 2020/022 *Maternity & Paternity Leave*. Available at: https://ww w.north-wales.police.uk/media/657447/2020-022-maternity-paternity-leave.pdf, Accessed on 19.05.2020.

Police chiefs admit failures on diversity 21 years after pledge. Available at: https://www. theguardian.com/uk-news/2020/jan/27/police-chiefs-admit-failures-on-diversity-2 1-years-after-pledge?CMP=Share_iOSApp_Other, Accessed on 27.01.2020.

"Police fitness tests failed 1,863 times in 12 months". Available at: https://www.bbc. co.uk/news/uk-36851755, Accessed on 03.02.2020.

Police:Now, *What we do*. Available at: https://www.policenow.org.uk/about-us/, Accessed on 23.01.2020.

Police use of firearms statistics England and Wales: April 2018 to March 2019 Available at: https://assets.publishing.service.gov.uk/government/uploads/system/uploads/ attachment_data/file/820556/police-use-firearms-statistics-england-and-wales-apri l-2018-to-march-2019-hosb1319.pdf, Accessed on 07.09.2020.

Police Workforce, England and Wales, 31 March 2017 (2017). [London]: Home Office. Available at: https://assets.publishing.service.gov.uk/government/upload s/system/uploads/attachment_data/file/630471/hosb1017-police-workforce.pdf, Accessed on 14.07.2020.

Police Workforce, England and Wales, 31 March 2019 second edition. [London] Home Office. Available at: https://assets.publishing.service.gov.uk/government/uploads /system/uploads/attachment_data/file/831726/police-workforce-mar19-hosb1119. pdf, Accessed on 14.07.2020.

Police workforce, England and Wales, as at 31 March 2020, [London]: Home Office. Available at: https://assets.publishing.service.gov.uk/government/uploads /system/uploads/attachment_data/file/905169/police-workforce-mar20-hosb2020. pdf, Accessed on 04.01.2020.

Policy. Equality. What the government's doing about equality. Available at: https://ww w.gov.uk/government/policies/equality, Accessed on 19.04.2017.

Polizei – Ablauf des Auswahlverfahrens, Available at: http://www.polizeikarriere.gv .at/ablauf_des_auswahlverfahrens.html, Accessed on 05.01.2021.

Polizei – Einstellungsvoraussetzungen prüfen, Available at: http://www.polizeikarrie-re.gv.at/einstellungsvoraussetzung_pruefen.html, Accessed on 05.01.2021.

Polizei aktuell, *"Schaffung eines Karenzpools"* (S. 6) Available at: https://www.poli zeigewerkschaft-fsg.at/assets/paktuell/Polizei_aktuell_Ausgabe_160-19.pdf, Accessed on 14.05.2020.

"Polizisten müssen zum Fitness-Check", Available at: https://wien.orf.at/v2/news/st ories/2836772/, Accessed on: 20.01.2020.

Scherschneva-Koller, E. (2012) *"Eine lohnende Erfahrung"*, Available at: https://w ww.bmi.gv.at/magazinfiles/2012/09_10/files/cobra_frau.pdf, Accessed on 28.01.2020.

Second European Union Minorities and Discrimination Survey. Being Black in the EU (2018) Available at: https://fra.europa.eu/sites/default/files/fra_uploads/fra-2018 -being-black-in-the-eu_en.pdf, Accessed on 27.01.2020.

Sex discrimination | Acas advice and guidance, Available at: http://www.acas.org.uk/i ndex.aspx?articleid=1814, Accessed on 22.09.2017.

Stonewall Riots, Available at: https://www.history.com/topics/gay-rights/the-stonewa ll-riots, Accessed on: 24.06.2020.

The Equality Strategy – Building a Fairer Britain, Available at: https://assets.publishin g.service.gov.uk/government/uploads/system/uploads/attachment_data/file/8529 9/equality-strategy.pdf, Accessed on 05.01.2021.

The National LGBT+ Police Network, Available at: https://lgbt.police.uk/, Accessed on 24.06.2020.

UK Police Assessment Centre: What It Involves and How To Prepare, Available at: https://www.how2become.com/blog/uk-police-assessment/, Accessed on 05.01.2021.

Verhältnismäßiges Einschreiten Die Bundespolizei verfügt über eine Reihe von Dienstwaf-fen. Available at: https://www.bmi.gv.at/magazinfiles/2009/01_02/files/dienstwaf fen.pdf, accessed on 07.09.2020.

Warren, R. (2020) Former officer claims racism forced her out of Met police, Available at: https://www.theguardian.com/uk-news/2020/jun/24/bame-ex-officer-claims-racis m-forced-her-out-met-police, Accessed on 24.06.2020

References

What qualification levels mean, Available at: https://www.gov.uk/what-different-q ualification-levels-mean/compare-different-qualification-levels, Accessed on 05.01.2021

What is evidence-based policing? Available at: https://whatworks.college.police.uk/Ab out/Pages/What-is-EBP.aspx, Accessed on 09.07.2020.

Women in Policing History, BAWP, Available at: https://www.bawp.org/women-poli cing-history, Accessed on 04.01.2021.

Legal Sources

138a-d. Gutachten: Sexuelle Belästigung (April 2014), Available at: https://www.bmgf .gv.at/cms/home/attachments/4/4/1/CH1600/CMS1468233793862/bgbk_senat_ i_ga_138d_27120.pdf, https://www.bmgf.gv.at/cms/home/attachments/4/4/1/C H1600/CMS1468233793862/bgbk_senat_i_ga_138c_27119.pdf, https://www.b mgf.gv.at/cms/home/attachments/4/4/1/CH1600/CMS1468233793862/bgbk_se nat_i_ga_138b_27118.pdf, https://www.bmgf.gv.at/cms/home/attachments/4/4/ 1/CH1600/CMS1468233793862/bgbk_senat_i_ga_138a_27117.pdf, Accessed on 22.09.2017.

142. Gutachten: Belästigung / Beruflicher Aufstieg – Geschlecht (November 2014), Available at: https://www.bmgf.gv.at/cms/home/attachments/4/4/1/CH1600/CMS146 8233793862/bgbk_senat_i_ga_142.pdf, Accessed on 23.09.2017.

145. Gutachten: Belästigung Geschlecht (Dezember 2014), Available at: https://ww w.bmgf.gv.at/cms/home/attachments/4/4/1/CH1600/CMS1468233793862/bgbk_ senat_i_ga_145.pdf, Accessed on 23.09.2017.

164. Gutachten: Beruflicher Aufstieg – Geschlecht, Alter (August 2015), Available at: https://www.bmgf.gv.at/cms/home/attachments/8/3/2/CH1600/CMS1468232479 311/bgbk_senat_i_ga_164.pdf, Accessed on 23.09.2017.

172. Gutachten: Beruflicher Aufstieg, Verletzung des Frauenförderungsgebotes – Geschlecht (Jänner 2016), Available at: https://www.bmgf.gv.at/cms/home/attach ments/9/4/2/CH1600/CMS1468232028618/bgbk_senat_i_ga_172.pdf, Accessed on 23.09.2017.

BGBl. II Nr. 65/201 – *65. Verordnung des Bundesministers für Inneres betreffend den Frauenförderungsplan des Bundesministeriums für Inneres (Frauenförderungsplan – BMI).* Available at: https://www.ris.bka.gv.at/Dokumente/BgblAuth/BGBLA_20 17_II_65/BGBLA_2017_II_65.pdf, Accessed on 22.09.2017.

BGBl. II Nr. 346/2019 – *Änderung der Verordnung betreffend den Frauenförderungsplan des Bundesministeriums für Inneres.* Available at: https://www.ris.bka.gv.at/Doku mente/BgblAuth/BGBLA_2019_II_346/BGBLA_2019_II_346.html, Accessed on 06.04.2021.

Bundesgesetz über den Zivildienst (Zivildienstgesetz 1986 – ZDG)StF: BGBl. Nr. 679/1986 idF BGBl. I Nr. 107/2018. Available at: https://www.ris.bk a.gv.at/GeltendeFassung.wxe?Abfrage=Bundesnormen&Gesetzesnummer=10005 603, Accessed on 20.01.2020.

Bundes-Gleichbehandlungsgesetz (2017) Available at: https://www.ris.bka.gv.at/Gelten deFassung.wxe?Abfrage=Bundesnormen&Gesetzesnummer=10008858, Accessed on 23.04.2017.

Employment Rights Act 1996, Available at: https://www.legislation.gov.uk/ukpga/19 96/18/contents, Accessed on: 06.04.2021.

Equality Act 2010 c 15, Available at: http://www.legislation.gov.uk/ukpga/2010/15/c ontents, Accessed on 20.05.2020.

Mutterschutzgesetz 1979 – MSchG BGBl. Nr. 221/1979.

Police Reform Act 2002 c.30. Available at: www.legislation.gov.uk/ukpga/2002/30/c ontents, Accessed on 06.04.2021.

Regierungsvorlage Bundesgesetz über die Organisation der Sicherheitsverwaltung und die Ausübung der Sicherheitspolizei (Sicherheitspolizeigesetz – SPG), NR: GP 18 RV 148.

Sex Disqualification (Removal) Act 1919. Available at: https://www.legislation.gov. uk/ukpga/Geo5/9-10/71/section/1, Accessed on 06.04.2021.

Strafprozeßordnung 1975. Available at: https://www.ris.bka.gv.at/Dokumente/Bunde snormen/NOR40217874/NOR40217874.html, Accessed on: 07.04.2020.

Literature

Adensamer, A. and Sagmeister, M. (2016). Die Ausweitung von Polizeibefugnissen und deren politische Dimensionen. *Juridikum Zeitschrift Für Kritik | Recht | Gesellschaft*, 2016(4), 516-526.

Angrosino, M. and Rosenberg, J. (2011). Observations on observation: Continuities and challenges. In: N. Denzin & Y. Lincoln (eds), *The Sage handbook of qualitative research* (4th ed.,). Thousand Oaks, CA: Sage. 467–478.

Bayley, D. H. (2001). *Policing hate: What can be done?* Policing & Society, 12(2), 83–91

Baylis, M. and Matczak, A. (2019). Tracking the evolution of police training and education in Poland: Linear developments and exciting prospects. *Police Practice and Research*, 20(3), 273-287.

Bazley, T.D., Lersch, K.M. and Mieczkowski, T. (2007) Officer force versus suspect resistance: A gendered analysis of patrol officers in an urban police department, *Journal of Criminal Justice*, 35 (2), 183-192. doi:10.1016/j.jcrimjus.2007.01.005.

Behr, R. (2003) Polizeikultur als institutioneller Konflikt des Gewaltmonopols. In: Lange HJ. (eds) *Die Polizei der Gesellschaft. Studien zur Inneren Sicherheit*, vol 4. VS Verlag für Sozialwissenschaften, Wiesbaden.

Behr, R. (2008) *Cop Culture – Der Alltag des Gewaltmonopols. Männlichkeit, Handlungsmuster und Kultur in der Polizei*, VS Verlag für Sozialwissenschaften, 2.Auflage.

Behr, R. (2016) Diversität und Polizei: Eine polizeiwissenschaftliche Perspektive. In: Genkova P., Ringeisen T. (eds) *Handbuch Diversity Kompetenz: Perspektiven und Anwendungsfelder.* Springer NachschlageWissen. Springer, Wiesbaden.

Behr, R. (2017). Maskulinität in der Polizei: Was Cop Culture mit Männlichkeit zu tun hat: Ein Essay. *Juridikum. Zeitschrift Für Kritik | Recht | Gesellschaft,* 2017(4), 541-551.

Behr, R. (2019) *"Die Polizei muss ... an Robustheit deutlich zulegen": Zur Renaissance aggressiver Maskulinität in der Polizei,* In: Loick, D. (ed) *Kritik der Polizei.* Campus Verlag GmbH.

Ben-Galim, D., Campbell, M. and Lewis, J. (2007). Equality and diversity: A new approach to gender equality policy in the UK. *International Journal of Law in Context,* 3(1), 19-33.

Blum, S. Dobrotić, I., Koslowski, A. Macht, A., Moss. P. (2018). *14th International Review of Leave Policies and Related Research 2018.* DOI: 10.13140/ RG.2.2.18149.45284.

Brand, R. and Matranga, M. (1993). *The Relevance of Basic Law Enforcement Training in Nevada: Does the Curriculum Prepare Recruits for Police Work?,* ProQuest Dissertations and Theses.

Bratich, J. (2018) Observation in a Surveilled World. In: Denzin, N., & Lincoln, Y. (eds) *The SAGE handbook of qualitative research* (Fifth ed.). Los Angeles London New Delhi Singapore Washington DC Melbourne: SAGE. page 911-945.

Brinkmann, S. (2013). *Qualitative interviewing* (Series in understanding qualitative research). Oxford: Oxford Univ. Press.

Brown, J. (1998). Comparing Charges: The Experience of Discrimination and Harassment among Women Police Officers Serving in Australia, the British Isles and the United States of America. *International Journal of Police Science & Management,* 1(3), 227–240.

Brown, J. (2000a) Occupational culture as a factor in the stress experiences of police officers. In: Leishman, F.; Loveday, B.; Savage, S. P. (ed) *Core issues in policing.* 2nd ed. Harlow, England, New York: Longman.

Brown, J. (2000b) *Discriminatory Experiences of Women Police. A Comparison of Officers Serving in England and Wales, Scotland, Northern Ireland and the Republic of Ireland,* International Journal of the Sociology of Law, 28 (2), 91-111. doi:http:// dx.doi.org/10.1006/ijsl.2000.0119.

Brown, J. (2018). Do Graduate Police Officers Make a Difference to Policing? Results of an Integrative Literature Review. *Policing: A Journal of Policy and Practice,* 11/15/2018.

Brown, J., Fleming, J., Silvestri, M., Linton, K., and Gouseti, I. (2019). *Implications of police occupational culture in discriminatory experiences of senior women in police forces in England and Wales.* Policing and Society, 29(2), 121-136.

Brown, J., and Gillick, M. (1998). Differing Perspectives on a Police Force's Equal Opportunities Grievance Procedure: Viewpoints of Police Managers and Front-Line Personnel. *International Journal of Police Science & Management,* 1(2), 122-132.

Brown, J., Gouseti, I., and Fife-Schaw, C. (2018). Sexual harassment experienced by police staff serving in England, Wales and Scotland: A descriptive exploration of incidence, antecedents and harm. *Police Journal (Chichester)*, 91(4), 356-374.

Brown, J. and Heidensohn F. (2000) *Gender and policing: comparative perspectives*. Basingstoke: Basingstoke: Macmillan.

Brown, J., and King, J. (1998). Gender differences in police officers attitudes towards rape; Results of an exploratory study. *Psychology, Crime & Law*, 4(4), 265-279.

Brown, J., and Sargent, S. (1995). Policewomen and firearms in the British police service. *Police Studies*, 18(2), 1-16.

Brown, J., and Silvestri, M., (2020). A police service in transformation: Implications for women police officers. *Police Practice & Research*, 21(5), 459-475.

Brown, J., and Woolfenden, S. (2011). Implications of the Changing Gender Ratio amongst Warranted Police Officers. *Policing: A Journal of Policy and Practice*, 5(4), 356-364.

Bryman, A. (2008) *Social research methods* (3rd ed.). Oxford: Oxford University Press.

Burgess, R. G. (1982) Elements of Sampling in Field Research. In: Burgess, R.G. (ed) *Field Research: A Sourcebook and Field Manual*. London: George Allen&Unwin.

Burke, M. (1994) Homosexuality as deviance: The case of the gay police officer. *The British Journal of Criminology*, 34(2), 192-203.

Butler, J. (1997) *The Psychic Life of Power. Theories in Subjection*. Stanford University Press Stanford, California.

Carbado, D., Crenshaw, K., Mays, V. and Tomlinson, B. (2013) INTERSECTIONALITY Mapping the Movements of a Theory. *Du Bois Review: Social Science Research on Race*. Volume 10, Issue 2, 303-312.

Charlesworth, S. and Whittenbury, K. (2007) 'Part-time and Part-committed'?: The Challenges of Part-time Work in Policing. *Journal of Industrial Relations*, 49(1), 31-47.

Charmaz, K. (2014) *Constructing grounded theory* (2.nd ed., Introducing qualitative methods). London: SAGE Publ.

Cockburn, C. (1991) *In the Way of Women. Men's Resistance to Sex Equality in Organizations*, London.

Cockcroft, T. (2020) *Police Occupational Culture*, Policy Press, Bristol.

Collins, P. H. (2000) *Black feminist thought: Knowledge, consciousness, and the politics of empowerment* (Rev. 10th anniversary ed.). New York: Routledge.

Colvin, R. (2017) Female Police Officers and Their Experiences: The Metropolitan Police of Buenos Aires Context. *Women & Criminal Justice*, 27(4), 219-234.

Connell, R. W. and Messerschmidt, J.W. (2005) Hegemonic masculinity: rethinking the concept. *Gender and society*, 19(6), 829-859.

Connell, R. W. (2013) Embodying Serious Power. Managerial Masculinities in the Security Sector. In: Hearn, J., Blagojević, M., Harrison, K. (eds) *Rethinking Transnational Men: Beyond, Between and Within Nations*. Routledge. 1. Edition.

Cordes, M. (2010) "Gleichstellungspolitiken: Von der Frauenförderung zum Gender Mainstreaming", In: Becker, R.; Kortendiek, B. (eds) *Handbuch Frauen- und Geschlechterforschung: Theorie, Methoden, Empirie*, Wiesbaden: VS, Verlag für Sozialwissenschaften. 3., extended and rev. Ed. 2010, S. 924 – 932.

Cordner, G. and Cordner, A. (2011) Stuck on a Plateau?: Obstacles to Recruitment, Selection, and Retention of Women Police. *Police Quarterly*, 14(3), 207–226. https://doi.org/10.1177/1098611111413990.

Crank, J. P. (1998) *Understanding Police Culture*. Second ed. [Cincinnati, OH]: Anderson Pub., 2004. Web.

Crenshaw, K. (1991) Mapping the margins: Intersectionality, identity politics, and violence against women of color. (Women of Color at the Center: Selections from the Third National Conference on Women of Color and the Law). *Stanford Law Review*, 43(6), 1241.

Davies, M. (2016) To What Extent Can We Trust Police Research? - Examining Trends in Research 'on', 'with', 'by' and 'for' the Police. *Nordisk Politiforskning*, 3(02), 154-164.

Dedeoglu, S. (2012) Equality, Protection or Discrimination: Gender Equality Policies in Turkey. *Social Politics*, 19(2), 269-290.

De Haas, S. and Timmerman, G. (2010) Sexual harassment in the context of double male dominance., *European Journal of Work and Organizational Psychology*, 19(6), 717-734.

De Haas, S., Timmerman, G., Höing, M. and Tetrick, L. E. (2009) Sexual Harassment and Health Among Male and Female Police Officers. *Journal of Occupational Health Psychology*, 14(4), 390-401.

Dick, P. (2006) The psychological contract and the transition from full to part-time police work. *Journal of Organizational Behavior*, 27(1), 37-58.

Dixon, D. (1997) *Law in Policing: Legal Regulation and Police Practices*. Oxford: Clarendon Press.

Dowler, K. and Arai, B. (2008) Stress, Gender and Policing: The Impact of Perceived Gender Discrimination on Symptoms of Stress. *International Journal of Police Science and Management* 10(2):123-135.

Dworkin, R. (1977) *Taking Rights Seriously*. 16. Print. ed. Cambridge, Mass.: Harvard U Pr., 1997.

Edwards, C. Y. and Robinson, O. (1999) Managing part-timers in the police service: A study of inflexibility. *Human Resource Management Journal*, 9(4), 5-18.

Edwards, C. Y. and Robinson, O. (2001) "Better" part-time jobs?: A study of part-time working in nursing and the police. *Employee Relations*, 23(5), 438-454.

Edwards, R. and Holland, J. (2013) *What is Qualitative Interviewing?* London: Bloomsbury Publishing.

Ellis, L. K. (2016) *Policemoms: Perceptions of Motherhood and Policy in Ohio Police Organizations*, Walden University, Ann Arbor. ProQuest.

Ermer, V. B. (1978) Recruitment of female police officers in New York City. *Journal of Criminal Justice*, 6, 233– 246.

Ertan, S. (2016) How to Study Gender Equality Policy Cross-Nationally? Aggregate or Disaggregate Gender Equality Policy Indices? *Social Indicators Research*, 125(1), 47-76.

Fassin, D. (2013). *Enforcing order: An ethnography of urban policing*. Cambridge [u.a.]: Politiy Press.

Fejes, A. and Haake, U. (2013) Caring and Daring Discourses at Work: Doing Gender Through Occupational Choices in Elderly Care and Police Work. *Vocations and Learning*, 6(2), 281-295.

Fenn, L., Marks, J., Christoforides, K. and Coupar, F. (2019) Applying Research beyond the Ivory Tower: Reflections from Police Now. *Policing: A Journal of Policy and Practice*, 01/23/2019.

Fielding, N. (1988) *Joining forces: police training, socialization and occupational competence*. London: London: Routledge.

Fischer-Kowalski, M. and Steinert, H. (1982) *Polizei und Öffentlichkeit: Endbericht; eine Untersuchung der Wiener Sicherheitswache und ihres Verhältnisses zur Bevölkerung 1972* (Institut für Höhere Studien, Wien: Sonderpublikationen). Wien: Inst. für Höhere Studien.

Flood, M., and Pease, B. (2006) Undoing Men's Privilege and Advancing Gender Equality in Public Sector Institutions, *Policy and Society*, 24(4), 2005.

Foley, P., Guarneri, C. and Kelly, M. (2008) Reasons for Choosing a Police Career: Changes over Two Decades. *International Journal of Police Science & Management*, 10(1), 2-8.

Frankenberg, R. (1995) *White women, race matters: The social construction of whiteness* (5. print.; 7. print. ed.). Minneapolis, Minn.: Univ. of Minnesota Press.

Franklin, C.A. (2007) Male Peer Support and the Police Culture, *Women & Criminal Justice*, 16:3, 1-25, DOI: 10.1300/J012v16n03_01.

Frederiksen, A. (2008) Gender differences in job separation rates and employment stability: New evidence from employer-employee data, *Labour Economics*, Volume 15, Issue 5, 2008, Pages 915-937, ISSN 0927-5371, https://doi.org/10.1016/j.labeco.2007.07.010.

Gass, S. and Mackey, A. (2000). *Stimulated recall methodology in second language research* (Second language acquisition research). Mahwah, NJ: Erlbaum.

Haarr, R. and Morash, M. (2013) The Effect of Rank on Police Women Coping With Discrimination and Harassment., *Police Quarterly*, 16(4), 395-419.

Hanak, G. and Hofinger, V., (2005) Dokumentation und Kommentierung polizeirelevanter Forschung in Österreich 1945-2004. In: *SIAK-Journal – Zeitschrift für Polizeiwissenschaft und polizeiliche Praxis* 4, 32–41, Online: http://dx.doi.org/10.7396/2005_4_D.

Hanak, G. and Hofinger, V. (2008) Polizeirelevante Forschung in Österreich. 2004-2007. In: *SIAK Journal – Zeitschrift für Polizeiwissenschaft und polizeiliche Praxis* 4, 10–18, Online: http://dx.doi.org/10.7396/2008_4_B.

Hassell, D., Archbold, A. and Stichman, J. (2011) Comparing the workplace experiences of male and female police officers: Examining workplace problems, stress, jobs satisfaction and consideration of career change. *International Journal of Police Science & Management*, 13(1), 37–53.

Heidensohn, F. (2005) Women in control? In: Newburn, T. (ed) *Policing: key readings*. Cullompton: Willan.

Heidensohn, F. and Silvestri, M. (2012) Gender and Crime. In: Maguire, M., Morgan, R. and Reiner, R. (eds) *The Oxford Handbook of Criminology.*, pp 336-369 5th ed. Oxford: Oxford University Press.

Herrnkind, M. (1999) "Der Polizei": Geschichte und Gegenwart der Männerdomäne im Spiegel der Wissenschaft, In: *Unbequem*, Juni, 11-19.

Hoffman, P.B. and Hickey, E.R. (2005) Use of force by female police officers, *Journal of Criminal Justice*, 33 (2), 145-151. doi:10.1016/j.jcrimjus.2004.12.006.

Holdaway, S. and Parker, S. (1998) Policing women police – Uniform patrol, promotion and representation in the CID. *British Journal Of Criminology*, 38(1), 40–60.

Holliday, A. (2016) *Doing and Writing Qualitative Research* (3rd ed.) Los Angeles. London. New Delhi. Singapore. Washington DC. Melbourne. SAGE Publications Ltd.

Holzleithner, E. (2002) *Recht, Macht, Geschlecht: Legal Gender Studies; eine Einführung*. Wien: WUV-Univ.-Verl.

Holzleithner, E. (2015) Legal Gender Studies: Grundkonstellationen und Herausforderungen. *Juridikum Zeitschrift Für Kritik / Recht / Gesellschaft*, 2015(4), 471-481.

Holzleithner, E. (2016) Gerechtigkeit und Geschlechterrollen. *Rechtsphilosophie*, 2(2), 133-151.

Holzleithner, E. (2017) Gender Equality and Physical Requirements, in: *European Equality Law Review* 2017/1, 13-22.

Holzleithner, E. (2019) Geschlecht als Anerkennungsverhältnis. Perspektiven einer Öffnung der rechtlichen Kategorie im Lichte gleicher Freiheit, In: Baer, S.; Lepsius, O.; Schönberger, C.; Waldhoff, C.; Walter, C. (eds) *Jahrbuch des öffentlichen Rechts der Gegenwart*. Neue Folge/Band 67, 457-485

Horn, R. (1997) "Not 'one of the Boys': Women Researching the Police." *Journal of Gender Studies*. 6.3 (1997): 297-308. Web.

Houdmont, J. (2013) UK police custody officers' psychosocial hazard exposures and burnout. *Policing: An International Journal of Police Strategies and Management*, 36, 620-635.

Huang, Q. and Sverke, M. (2007) Women's occupational career patterns over 27 years: Relations to family of origin, life careers, and wellness. *Journal of Vocational Behavior*, 70(2), 369-397.

Innes, M. (2003) *Understanding social control. Deviance, crime and social order* (Crime and justice). Open University Press.

Jacobs, P. (1987) How female police officers cope with a traditionally male position. *Sociology and Social Research*, 72, 4–6.

Jensen, H., Larsen, J. and Thomsen, T. (2018) The impact of shift work on intensive care nurses' lives outside work: A cross-sectional study. *Journal of Clinical Nursing*, 27(3-4), E703-E709.

Jordan, J. (2002) Will any woman do? Police, gender and rape victims. *Policing: An International Journal of Police Strategies & Management*, 25(2), 319-344.

Jordan, W., Fridell, L., Faggiani, D. and Kubu, B. (2009) Attracting females and racial/ethnic minorities to law enforcement. *Journal Of Criminal Justice*, 37(4), 333-341.

Lester, D. (1983) Why do people become police officers: A study of reasons and their predictions of success. *Journal of Police Science and Administration*, 11, 170–174.

Lichtenberg, I. D. and Smith, A. (2001) How dangerous are routine police–citizen traffic stops?: A research note, *Journal of Criminal Justice*, Volume 29, Issue 5, 2001, Pages 419-428, ISSN 0047-2352, https://doi.org/10.1016/S0047-2352 (01)00106-4.

Loftus, B. (2008) Dominant Culture Interrupted: Recognition, Resentment and the Politics of Change in an English Police Force, *British Journal of Criminology*, 48 (6), 756-777. doi:10.1093/bjc/azn065.

Lombardo, E. (2003) EU gender policy: Trapped in the 'Wollstonecraft dilemma'? *European Journal of Women's Studies*, 10(2), 159-180.

Lorde, A. (1984) *Sister Outsider: Essays and Speeches*. Feminist Series. Freedom, CA: Crossing Press.

Lonsway, K., Paynich, R. and Hall, J. (2013) Sexual Harassment in Law Enforcement., *Police Quarterly*, 16(2), 177-210.

Lueger, M. (2010) *Interpretative Sozialforschung: Die Methoden.* Facultas Verlags- und Buchhandles AG: Wien Österreich.

MacKinnon, C. (1987) *Feminism Unmodified: Discourses on Life and Law*. Cambridge, MA: Harvard University Press.

Martin, S. and Jurik, N. (2007) *Doing justice, doing gender: Women in legal and criminal justice occupations* (2nd ed., Women in the criminal justice system). Thousand Oaks, Calif: Sage Publications.

McCarthy, D. J. (2013) Gendering 'Soft' Policing: Female Cops, Multi-agency Working and the Fragilities of Police Culture/s. *Policing and Society*, 23 (2), 261-278.

McKenzie, I. (2000) Policing force: rules, hierarchies and consequences. In: Leishman, F.; Loveday, B.; Savage, S. P. (eds) *Core issues in policing*. 2nd ed. Harlow, England, New York: Longman.

Meagher, S. and Yentes, N. (1986) Choosing a career in policing: A comparison of male and female perceptions. *Journal of Police Science and Administration*, 14(4), 320– 327.

Mensching, A. (2008) *Gelebte Hierarchien. Mikropolitische Arrangements und organisationskulturelle Praktiken am Beispiel der Polizei.* VS Verlag für Sozialwissenschaften: Wiesbaden.

Miller, S., Forest, K. and Jurik, N. (2003) Diversity in Blue: Lesbian and Gay Police Officers in a Masculine Occupation. *Men and Masculinities*, 5(4), 355-385.

Morash, M., Kwak D. and Haarr, R. (2006a) Gender differences in the predictors of police stress, *Policing*, vol. 29, no. 3, 541-563.

Morash, M., Kwak D. and Haarr, R. (2006b) Multilevel Influences on Police Stress, *Journal of Contemporary Criminal Justice*, vol. 22, no. 1, 26-43.

Müller, U. (2007) Body and Culture in German Police. In: Lenz, I.; Ullrich, C.; Fersch, B. (eds) *Gender Orders Unbound? Globalisation, Restructuring and Reciprocity*. Barbara Budrich Publishers, Opladen & Farmington Hills 2007. 327-344.

Nguyen, A. (2008) Patriarchy, Power, and Female Masculinity. *Journal of Homosexuality*, 55(4), 665-683.

Notz, G. (2010) Arbeit, Politik und Ökonomie, In: Becker, R., Hortendiek, B (eds), Handbuch Frauen- und Geschlechterforschung. Theorie, Methoden, Empirie (3., erweiterte und durchgesehene Auflage, Vol. Bd. 35). Wiesbaden: VS Verlag für Sozialwissenschaften, 480-488.

O'Connor Shelley, T., Schaefer, M., Tobin-Gurley, M. and Tobin-Gurley, J. (2011) Gendered institutions and gender roles: understanding the experience of women in policing, *Criminal Justice Studies*, 24:4, 351-367, DOI: 10.1080/1478601X.2011.625698.

Oliva, J. and Compton, M. (2010) What do police officers value in the classroom? *Policing: An International Journal of Police Strategies & Management*, 33(2), 321-338.

Pagon, M. and Lobnikar, B. (2000) Reasons for Joining and Beliefs about the Police and Police Work among Slovenian Female Police Rookies. *International Journal of Police Science & Management*, 2(3), 252–266. https://doi.org/10.1177/14613557 0000200306.

Panter, H. (2018) 'We're the ugly child of the LGBT world': Trans police occupational experiences within police culture. In *Transgender Cops: The Intersection of Gender and Sexuality Expectations in Police Cultures* (1st ed., Vol. 1, 145-169). Routledge.

Pateman, C. (1989) *The Disorder of Women*. Cambridge: Polity Press.

Paterson, C. (2011) Adding value? A review of the international literature on the role of higher education in police training and education, *Police Practice and Research*, 12:4, 286-297, DOI: 10.1080/15614263.2011.563969

Prokos, A. and Padavic, I. (2002) 'There Oughtta Be a Law against Bitches': Masculinity Lessons in Police Academy Training. *Gender, Work and Organization*, vol. 9, no. 4, 439-459.

Rabe-Hemp, C. (2008a) Female officers and the ethic of care: Does officer gender impact police behaviors? *Journal of Criminal Justice*, 36(5), 426-434.

Rabe-Hemp, C. (2008b) Survival in an "all boys club": policewomen and their fight for acceptance, *Policing: An International Journal of Police Strategies & Management*, Vol. 31 Iss 2 251 – 270.

Raganella, A. and White, M. (2004) Race, gender, and motivation for becoming a police officer: Implications for building a representative police department. *Journal of Criminal Justice*, 32(6), 501–513.

Reiner, R. (2000) *The Politics of the Police* (3rd edn). Oxford: Oxford University Press.

Reiner, R. (2016) Opinion. Is Police Culture Cultural? In: *Policing*, paw046. DOI: 10.1093/police/paw046.

Ridgeway, G., Lim, N., Gifford, B., Koper, C., Matthies, C., Hajiamiri, S. and Huynh, A. (2008) *Strategies for improving officer recruitment in the San Diego Police Department.* Santa Monica, CA: Rand.

Riegraf, B. (2005) "Frauenbereiche" und "Männerbereiche". In: Ahrens, J.-R.; Apelt, M.; Bender, C. (eds) *Frauen im Militär. Empirische Befunde und Perspektiven zur Integration von Frauen in die Streitkräfte.* VS Verlag für Sozialwissenschaften, Wiesbaden. 1. Auflage. 134-155.

Riggins, E.S. (2015) *Career Goals for Joining Law Enforcement and Subsequent Career Stress*, Walden University.

Rogers, D. (2004) *Recruitment and Retention of Minorities and Women in Law Enforcement*, ProQuest Dissertations and Theses.

Saini, A. (2017) *Inferior. How Science Got Women Wrong-and the New Research That's Rewriting the Story.* Harper Collins Publ. UK.

Sbraga, T. P. and O'Donohue, W. (2000) Sexual harassment., *Annual Review of Sex Research*, 11, 258–285.

Scharff, C. (2011) Disarticulating feminism: Individualization, neoliberalism and the othering of 'Muslim women'. *European Journal of Women's Studies*, 18(2), 119-134.

Schulze, C. (2010) Institutionalized masculinity in US police departments: how maternity leave policies (or lack thereof) affect women in policing, *Criminal Justice Studies*, 23:2, 177-193, DOI: 10.1080/1478601X.2010.485485.

Silvestri, M. (2003) *Women in Charge: Policing, Gender and Leadership.* Cullompton, Devon: Willan Publishing.

Silvestri, M. (2017) Police Culture and Gender: Revisiting the 'Cult of Masculinity'. *Policing: A Journal of Policy and Practice* 11.3 (2017): 289-300. Web.

Silvestri, M., Tong, S. and Brown, J. (2013) Gender and Police Leadership: Time for a Paradigm Shift? *International Journal of Police Science & Management*, 15(1), 61-73.

Skolnick, J. (1966) *Justice without Trial.* New York: Wiley.

Smart, C. (1995) *Law, crime and sexuality: essays in feminism.* London: London: Sage.

Spasić, D. (2011) Police Culture And Gender Identity. *Western Balkans Security Observer – English Edition*, (19), 25-35.

Spasić, D., Djurić, S. and Mršević, Z. (2015) Survival in an "all boys club": Policewomen in Serbia. Women's Studies International Forum, 48(C), 57-70.

Steinert, H. (1997) Schwache Patriarchen – gewalttätige Krieger, In: Kersten, J., Steinert, H. (eds) *Starke Typen: Iron Mike, Dirty Harry, Crocodile Dundee und der Alltag von Männlichkeit* 1. Ed., Baden-Baden: Nomos-Verl.-Ges.

Stölting, E. (2009) Geleitwort zur Soziologie der Polizei. In: Grutzpalk, J.; Bruhn, A.; Fatianova, J; Harnisch, F.; Mochan, C.; Schülzke, B.; Zischke, T. (eds) *Beiträge zu einer vergleichenden Soziologie der Polizei.* Universitätsverlag Potsdam 2009. 7-12.

Strauss, A. L. (1991) *Grundlagen qualitativer Sozialforschung. Datenanalyse und Theoriebildung in der empirischen soziologischen Forschung.* München: Fink.

Teubner, U. (2010) Beruf: Vom Frauenberuf zur Geschlechterkonstruktion im Berufssystem, In: Becker, R., Hortendiek, B (ed), *Handbuch Frauen- und Geschlechterforschung. Theorie, Methoden, Empirie* (3., erweiterte und durchgesehene Auflage, Vol. Bd. 35). Wiesbaden: VS Verlag für Sozialwissenschaften, 499-506.

Thürmer-Rohr, C. (2010) Mittäterschaft von Frauen: Die Komplizenschaft mit der Unterdrückung. In: Becker, R., Hortendiek, B (eds), *Handbuch Frauen- und Geschlechterforschung. Theorie, Methoden, Empirie* (3., erweiterte und durchgesehene Auflage, Vol. Bd. 35). Wiesbaden: VS Verlag für Sozialwissenschaften, 88-93.

Urquhart, C. (2013) *Grounded theory for qualitative research: A practical guide.* Los Angeles, Calif.; London: SAGE.

Van der Lippe, T., Graumans, A. and Sevenhuijsen, S. (2004) Gender policies and the position of women in the police force in European countries. *Journal of European Social Policy*, 14(4), 391-405.

Venditti, V. (2018) Exponential territorialization. Reduce, refuse or reuse? An exploration of the territories of inclusive legal norms and gender binary. In: Agha, P. (ed) *Law, Politics and the Gender Binary* (1st ed.). Boca Raton, FL: Routledge, an imprint of Taylor and Francis. 21-32.

Verro, M.A. (2009) *Psychosocial motivation of career choice for contemporary law enforcement officers*, Walden University.

Walklate, S. (2000) Equal opportunities and the future of policing. In: Leishman F., Loveday, B., Savage, S.P. (eds) *Core issues in policing.* Pearson Education Limited. Second Edition 2000. 232-248.

Weinberger, B. (1995) *The Best Police in the World: An Oral History of British Policing* Aldershot: Scolar Press.

Weiss, V. (2009) *Die österreichischen Gewaltschutzgesetze.* Ein Überblick, *SIAK Journal – Zeitschrift für Polizeiwissenschaft und polizeiliche Praxis* (3), 49-54, Online: http://dx.doi.org/10.7396/2009_3_G.

Werdes, B. (2003) Frauen in der Polizei – Einbruch in eine Männerdomäne. In: Lange, H.J. (ed) *Die Polizei in der Gesellschaft; Zur Soziologie der Inneren Sicherheit.* Springer Fachmedien Wiesbaden. 195-211.

West, C; Zimmerman, D.H. (1987) *Doing Gender.* Gender and Society, Vol. 1, No. 2. (Jun., 1987), 125-151.

Wilson, J. M. (2012) Articulating the dynamic police staffing challenge: An examination of supply and demand, *Policing: An International Journal*, Vol. 35 No. 2, 327-355. https://doi-org.uaccess.univie.ac.at/10.1108/13639511211230084

Wilson, J. Q. (1968) *Varieties of Police Behavior: The management of law and order in eight communities.* Cambridge, MA: Harvard University Press.

Workman-Stark, A. L. (2017) Understanding Police Culture. In: Workman-Stark, A. L. *Inclusive Policing from the Inside Out. Advanced Sciences and Technologies for Security Applications.* Springer, Cham. 19-36.

Yesberg, J.A., Bradford, B. and Dawson, P. (2020) An experimental study of responses to armed police in Great Britain. *J Exp Criminol* 17, 1–13 (2021). https://doi.org/10.1007/s11292-019-09408-8.